SELLING DIGITAL MUSIC, FORMATTING CULTURE

Selling Digital Music, Formatting Culture

JEREMY WADE MORRIS

UNIVERSITY OF CALIFORNIA PRESS

University of California Press, one of the most distinguished university presses in the United States, enriches lives around the world by advancing scholarship in the humanities, social sciences, and natural sciences. Its activities are supported by the UC Press Foundation and by philanthropic contributions from individuals and institutions. For more information, visit www.ucpress.edu.

University of California Press
Oakland, California

Library of Congress Cataloging-in-Publication Data

Morris, Jeremy Wade, 1976– author.
  Selling digital music, formatting culture / Jeremy Wade Morris.
    pages cm
  Includes bibliographical references and index.
  ISBN 978-0-520-28793-8 (cloth : alk. paper)
  ISBN 978-0-520-28794-5 (pbk. : alk. paper)
  ISBN 978-0-520-96293-4 (ebook)
  1. Music trade—Technological innovations.   2. Music and the Internet.   3. Digital jukebox software—Case studies.   I. Title.
  ML3790.M618   2015
  381'.4578—dc23

                                               2015016443

Manufactured in the United States of America

24 23 22 21 20 19 18 17 16 15
10 9 8 7 6 5 4 3 2 1

In keeping with a commitment to support environmentally responsible and sustainable printing practices, UC Press has printed this book on Natures Natural, a fiber that contains 30% post-consumer waste and meets the minimum requirements of ANSI/NISO Z39.48–1992 (R 1997) (*Permanence of Paper*).

For Leanne, the song in my head and heart

Contents

List of Figures ix

Acknowledgments xi

Introduction: The Digital Music Commodity 1

1 Music as a Digital File 30

2 Making Technology Behave 66

3 This Business of Napster 94

4 Click to Buy: Music in Digital Stores 131

5 Music in the Cloud 166

Conclusion: Exceptional Objects 192

Notes 215

Works Cited 223

Index 253

List of Figures

1. Digital music time line   xvi
2. Winamp main window (version 2.0)   51
3. Winamp equalizer and playlist window (version 2.0)   52
4. Winamp visualizer (version 2.0)   55
5. Winamp skin   57
6. Winamp integrated browser (version 2.10)   63
7. Music without metadata   69
8. Napster main search window (version 2.06)   114
9. Napster transfer window (version 2.07)   115
10. Napster Chat and Hot List features (version 2.0)   117
11. iTunes media player (version 1.1)   147
12. The iTunes Music Store (version 4.1)   148
13. "Buy Song" and quick links (version 8.0)   150

Acknowledgments

This book is about music in a transitional state. Here is my unavoidably incomplete attempt to thank the people who've added much music to my life and witnessed the numerous transitions that have taken place since the crazy idea to leave a stable job for graduate school first landed in my head almost ten years ago.

My first set of thanks belongs to Jonathan Sterne, whose dedicated mentorship and careful guidance seems to know no bounds. I finished my PhD during what I can only assume was one of the most challenging years of his life (note: not entirely my dissertation's fault), yet he barely missed a beat; his attention to my work and my career was unparalleled, and I am forever grateful. I assumed once I had completed my PhD that I'd stop asking him questions or seeking his advice. I could not have been more wrong, and thankfully, he could not be more kind and consistently willing to make time for my emails, calls, and visits. His contributions to this book, and to my development as a scholar, will echo for years.

I also owe thanks to my other committee members, mentors, and professors at McGill. Darin Barney's commitment to, and compassion toward, my research and general well-being still surprises and inspires me. The courses I took, or comments I received from him, as well as from Will Straw, Becky Lentz, Derek Nystrom, Carrie Rentschler, Marc Raboy, and Jenny Burman, were formative, and I can safely say there's a line of argument or reference from conversations I've had with each of those people herein. Along with Catherine Middleton, whose support helped guide me through my MA program, these professors are the most recent in a long line of teachers I've had in my life (stretching back to Mr. Myles) who have profoundly shaped how this brain of mine works, on the odd occasions when it does.

To the classmates and colleagues who helped this project along during its earliest scribblings at McGill and Ryerson, I am grateful for all the conversations and ideas. Whether through student associations, the vaguely named but unendingly insightful *Sound and Stuff* reading group, or the awkwardly awesome departmental softball and hockey teams, I am happy to have worked with Greg Taylor, Erin MacLeod, Mike Baker, Laurel Wypkema, Tara Rodgers, Jeremy Shtern, Tim Hecker, Lilian Radovac, Andrew Gibson, tobias c. van Veen, Caroline Habluetzel, Neal Thomas, Hélène Laurin, Anuradha Gobin, Jessica Santone, Paulina Mickiewicz, Rafico Ruiz, Samantha Burton, Constance Dilley, Leslie Wilson, Rob Burkett, Peter Ryan, and others. Outside the classroom I would also like to acknowledge the not-so-broken social scene of friends I had and continue to have in Toronto and Montreal who were sources of much support and distraction throughout my graduate experience (especially anyone who ever attended a New Math show or "worked" with me at Midnight Poutine).

The grad school idea seemed a little less crazy when it landed me a job in the Communication Arts department at the University of Wisconsin-Madison. I'm now fortunate to be surrounded by a great community of colleagues who support, challenge, and entertain me. I thank (but won't list) all the faculty and graduate students here but feel especially lucky to work just a few doors away from Jonathan Gray, Lori Kido Lopez, Derek Johnson, Jason Kido Lopez, Eric Hoyt, and Michele Hilmes. They are as smart as they are kind, and I have benefited greatly from my interactions with each of them. I am also indebted to Jeff Smith, who serves as my faculty mentor, and to my tireless research assistants: Andrew Bottomley, Nora Patterson, Evan Elkins, and Sarah Murray, who deserves special mention for her heroic final read-through effort in the dwindling hours before this book's deadline.

Beyond my department there are far too many scholars to thank for their feedback on various versions of this work. I am grateful to audiences at conferences held by the Canadian Communication Association, the International Association for the Study of Popular Music, the Society for Cinema and Media Studies, and the International Communication Association. I am especially thankful for my discussions about music, sound, and all kinds of other topics with Patrick Burkart, Peter Schaefer, Tamara Shepherd, Brian Fauteux, Craig Eley, Fenwick McKelvey, Molly Wright Steenson, Paul Aitken, David Hesmondhalgh, and Tarleton Gillespie. If it was not clear from the multiple panels I've coordinated with Devon Powers and Eric Harvey, they are two people who write and think like I wish I could.

While music is increasingly transitioning from a physical object to a digital file, this digital thing is finally becoming an object. The diligent, hard-working, and patient people at the University of California Press are to thank for that. To Mary Francis, for believing in this project and for the attention you paid to the book in its early stages. To my copy editor, Joe Abbott, for what can only be considered eagle eyes. I am sorry for the extra hours stolen from you by my flippant use of EndNote. To Kate Hoffman, Aimee Goggins, Bradley Depew, Zuha Khan, the book's reviewers, Pilar Wyman for indexing, and others behind the scenes at UC Press who helped guide this first-time author on the winding path to publication.

This project was helped along by various influxes of research funding from the Social Sciences and Humanities Research Council (SSHRC), Les fonds de recherche sur la société et la culture (FQRSC), and the UW-Madison's Graduate School. But it would not have been possible without the constant and unwavering support from my closest family and friends. As a father who is everyday humbled by the act of parenting, I can only look with awe at my own parents, John and Claire Morris, for the inspiring examples they set for living full, generous, and meaningful lives. Dad, thanks for instilling an intellectual curiosity in me and for always making me look it up in the dictionary. Mom, if I've inherited even a fraction of your optimism and strength (especially in the last few years), I'll count myself fortunate. I should also thank my younger brother, Regan, whom I tormented for many of his childhood years and continued to torment as an adult when I asked him to read early drafts of my dissertation. I make playlists for him and his wonderful family—Elizabeth, Thomas, and Henry—every year as ongoing penance. I am also grateful to Suzanne Labarge for her boundless generosity, Monica Labarge, Jake Brower, Emily Labarge, and the rest of the Labarge/Morris clan for their continued encouragement through this project, and to the 377 Earl and Banff/Ptarmigan crews for their friendships. While most people joke about having to spend time with their in-laws, I can't think of a better way to pass my summers and holidays than with Peter and Carol Williams. I appreciate the trust you've put in me and the respective contributions you've made to this project (ideas, discourse, copyedits, and more). Thanks also to each and every one of the four Ps and the extended family at Black Lake (especially the Everetts, whose steady wi-fi and pleasant porch made a number of these chapters possible).

To my monkeys, Lucas, Rachel, and Justine: you are a constant source of joy and surprise. You probably care very little about the difference between music on CDs and music as a digital file, so long as you can have a dance party in our kitchen. I look forward to dancing with you for years to come.

Finally, and most importantly and sentimentally, I owe this entire project and so much more to my favorite person in the world, Leanne Morris. You've made this whole crazy idea, and several others we've had, seem possible. Thank you for believing in me, encouraging me, and for taking multiple leaps of faith with me, from those first awkward dance steps to our journey to the Midwest. Your brain, your smile, your friendship, and your trust in me remind me that I can always do more, that I can always be better. A perfect partner and an amazing mother to our kids, you've made the hard times less hard and the good times even better. Whatever format music ends up in, I want to keep listening to it with you: the moon stuck in my sky, the calm to my commotion.

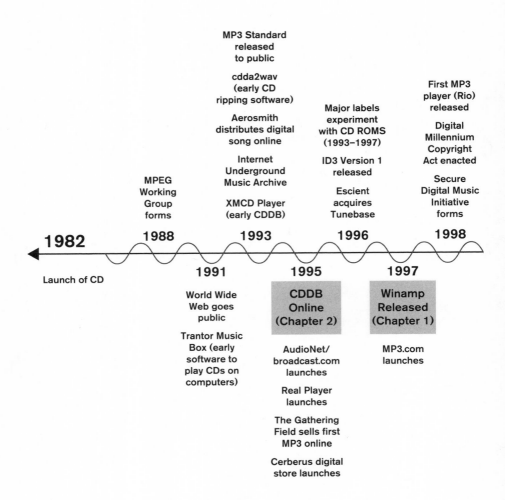

Figure 1. Digital music time line. This time line represents some of the major developments in the digitization of the music commodity covered in this book. The events in gray boxes are the cases that I explore in depth.

Labels launch PressPlay store

CDDB renamed Gracenote

Roxio buys Napster assets

Pandora Radio launches

2000   **2002**   **2005**   **2012**

1999   **2001**   **2003**   **2008**

Napster Released (Chapter 3)

Napster shuts down

iTunes Music Store Launch (Chapter 4)

Music in the Cloud (Chapter 5)

SHOUTcast launches

iTunes software launches (Jan.)

MySpace launches

Sony buys Gracenote

SoundJam launches (becomes iTunes)

iPod introduced (Oct.)

Best Buy acquires Napster

MyPlay.com (early cloud service)

Labels launch MusicNet

Spotify Music launches

Project Madison (online distribution system by IBM)

Introduction

The Digital Music Commodity

Every day, it seems, a new headline surfaces about the troubled fate and state of recorded popular music. Today, it's news that the influential hip-hop collective Wu-Tang Clan will make and sell just one copy of its upcoming album: *The Wu—Once upon a Time in Shaolin*. In an era in which music circulates ubiquitously via digital copies and streams, the single-copy stunt means to provoke a wider discussion on the current value of music, especially "nowadays when it's been devalued and diminished to almost the point that it has to be given away for free" (RZA, qtd. in Greenburg 2014). The perception of a decline and devaluation in music is tied almost entirely to the technologies through which it circulates. Where listeners once bought music on CDs from music retailers, they increasingly find it cheaply as a digital file from online retailers, acquire it freely from file-sharing networks, or stream it plentifully from a host of emerging streaming audio services. Where listeners once bought and paid for full albums, increasingly they own and consume bits and fragments of music for which they have never paid and for which they may never pay, music that has been disaggregated into individual singles or reaggregated into playlists or other musical groupings. Whereas the compact disc was once the dominant format for personal music consumption, there are now a series of hardware technologies, software interfaces, and computer applications that make digital files playable, sortable, and savable. Although the migration away from CDs is far from complete, music's new digital formats are quickly becoming the primary ones for the circulation and consumption of music. If the Wu-Tang Clan's single-copy concept is an attempt to question what value listeners, producers, and distributors make and take from music in light of its digitization, this book is mine.

Selling Digital Music is about the digitization of popular recorded music during the last thirty years and what this process can tell us about digital objects, the value of cultural goods, and the conflicted assemblage of technologies, users, and industries that contributed to the uses and meanings of music's new formats. It has been more than two decades since the first digital music files began circulating widely in online music archives and sounding out through new software media players, and we have yet to fully internalize the cultural and aesthetic consequences of these shifts for how we make, market, and use music. The move from a collection of digital files on compact discs to music as individual digital files on computers, the Internet, and various digital devices has significant repercussions for the nature of the music commodity and the ways the commodity form affects people's relationships and encounters with music in their everyday lives. The digitization of the music commodity is a story of media convergence that connects industrial production, popular culture, technology, and commerce. It is a narrative that concerns the aesthetics of music and computers, the labor of producers and everyday users, and the ways listeners make and take value from digital objects. It is a powerful illustration of how shifts in technology and social life are written in—and can be read from—music and other cultural commodities. Above all it is a story of how the commodity form changes through digitization and why this matters for the music and media we love.

This book focuses on the shifts taking place in the value and role of popular music in everyday life. It does so by tracing the emergence of what I call the *digital music commodity:* a particular combination of data and sound that exists as an entity in and of itself for sale or acquisition in online outlets via computers or other digital portable devices. While the compact disc, launched in 1982, may have been music consumers' first widespread introduction to music in its digital form and set off discussions about the benefits and drawbacks of digital sound and playback capabilities, the term *digital music commodity* is meant to mark an important distinction between the two formats. The music on CDs is, of course, digital, as was the music on some of the early digital audiotape products in the 1970s. But the CD commodity as a whole was only musically digital. CDs come with very nondigital packaging—discs and jewel cases that require physical retail stores, manufacturing plants, distribution trucks, and store shelves. CDs, in other words, rely on the same industrial infrastructure that many music commodities that came before them did. Digital music files of recorded popular music on computers, in contrast, are data without that same kind of packaging. They are ones and zeroes, bits and bytes that, together with the right software and hardware, play music. This process entails both an aesthetic change to the commodity form and a sonic change to the music format. It also requires a reconfiguration of the industrial models and mechanisms used to make, market, and move music commodities in a way that, say, the shift from cassette tapes to CDs did not. To sell CDs is to sell digital music but not to sell a digital music commodity. I use the term *digital music commodity* not because it is the first time music has been digital but because the digitization of music as a cultural product only fully comes into form during and after the 1990s.

Conceived in this way, the digital music commodity is both a thing and a moment. It is, on its surface, an audio file: an MP3, a WAV file, an AAC; it is a digital file format designed to encode, transmit, produce, and reproduce sonic material. The digital music commodity has a form and a function that is distinct though related to previous versions of the music commodity. Like CDs, tapes, and vinyl records, it plays audio in specific ways and with specific sonic artifacts that are tied to its format. Like other new media, it incorporates qualities of older formats (certain models of listening and forms of playback) and embodies new potentials (modularity, customizability, transmissibility). The digital music commodity is an object in its own right, though it is made visible, audible, and tangible through various software interfaces, media players, metadata, and hardware devices.

The term *digital music commodity,* however, goes beyond its objectness. It is also a specific moment in the music commodity's history when most of the materials that give music its commercial, aesthetic, technical, and functional form manifest themselves largely thanks to computers, the Internet, or other digital technologies. Traditional industrial infrastructures are reconfiguring themselves around the distribution, circulation, and presentation of digital music in online retail outlets, file-sharing services, and other emerging services. This moment has provoked changes to the policies and regulations for managing sound recordings, to the business models for selling music and compensating artists, and to the ways musicians and listeners make and use music in their lives.

As both thing and moment, digital music is a special kind of commodity. It draws on previous conventions of the music commodity while offering new materials, uses, and experiences. It is an industrial product, but one that is heavily shaped by the labor and actions of users. It is a fragmented commodity, one that recombines through the multiple interfaces that exist to play, use, sort, and sometimes buy it. As with other commodities, the uses and meanings surrounding digital music reflect our cultural secrets back to us. Any commodity is a marker of time and history, a "petrified historical event" where the abstract and the concrete coalesce (Taussig 1993). Commodities reveal something, culturally, about what people value, what they circulate, and what they've forgotten. Like other commodities, the digital music commodity is a sign and a symbol; it has its own "economy of meaning and practices of expenditure in which an object, be it a commodity or a fetish, spills over its referent and suffuses its component parts with an ineffable radiance" (Taussig 1993, 233). The digital music commodity has these things to tell us and more. Within its data and code lie insights about music as a cultural form and lessons for all kinds of commodities that are currently undergoing digitization.

Selling Digital Music plays with the word *sell* to explore what the digital music commodity has to tell us. First, the book is concerned with the technologies, processes, people, and practices that made digital files of recorded popular music sellable objects in the commercial sense. Like CDs before them, digital files needed to be presented in ways that made them understandable to users and sellable as digital goods. On computers and mobile devices music underwent a re-tuning of its interface: new features like metadata, codecs, visualizers, and other sonic and visual features—collectively called the interface—combined to give music a "new" kind of packaging. On computers, the Internet, and digital portable devices the popular music commodity in its CD format was temporarily de-tuned, stripped of key attributes (album art, physical packaging, a particular quality of audio data, etc.) before being re-tuned by the efforts of software designers, rogue digital start-ups, entrenched industry players, and everyday hobbyists and users. In other words the digital music commodity looks, sounds, and works the way it does because of the hardware, software, and internal attributes that "package" digital music, as well as the social and cultural conditions that fueled their creation. This assemblage of technologies and the people that create and use them mediates how music is organized, presented, heard, and discovered in digital environments. It makes music sortable by metadata, visible through graphical user interfaces, audible through different codecs, and accessible through various online databases and services. But the digital music commodity also takes its particular shape because of different and competing economic and industrial visions for music and the Internet. This book is concerned with the conditions that existed in which the music commodity's re-tuning took place. Even though a substantial amount of digital music is never actually purchased in the traditional sense, the way digital music looks, sounds, and works is intimately bound up in its status as a commodity. Digital music files, as commodities, condense and embody insights about our relationships with music, media, and the circulation of cultural goods.

Second, and more important, this book is concerned with a broader understanding of the word *sell:* how did a disparate assemblage of companies, musicians, users, and technologists go about selling *the idea* of music as a digital file and its attendant technologies and cultural practices? Playing music on computers, sharing files over the Internet, or buying songs online were never natural and inevitable developments. It took the combined efforts of music companies, tech outfits, start-up entrepreneurs, and the labor and contributions of users and hobbyists to create a digital music format that would be as useful as the formats of recorded music that came before it. All the hardware, software, and other tools that emerged to play and present digital music were thus simultaneously selling themselves as technologies and selling digital music files as new, useful, and improved formats for the circulation and experience of music. This book is a record of this sales pitch, a transcript documenting the shared fate of music and computing during the last two decades and what this union has meant for both.

Selling Digital Music stems from my uneasiness about how heavily weighted public discussion around digital music has been toward piracy and economics. Driven largely by the major record labels and the major industry associations, the campaign against "piracy" has created a heated rhetorical ground around digital music. Those not fretting about how to curb unauthorized copying or how to make digital files more secure through digital rights management technologies are focusing on how to "monetize" digital music files and services. But piracy and the availability of "free" music is only one factor driving the current shift in the music industries. There are bigger changes taking place with the form and function of cultural commodities in the current moment. A narrow focus on the legality of file sharing or the quest for new business models means that many interesting questions about the digitization of music remain unanswered.

This book aims to shift the discussion away from the language of piracy, devaluation, economic crises, and intellectual property toward a conversation about the process of cultural commodification. *Selling Digital Music* combines insights from the fields of new media studies, popular music studies, and communication studies to piece together how a dispersed network of institutions and individuals contributed to the conditions in which the digital music commodity could emerge. Recognizing that the moment of newness for a technology or medium is a key moment of negotiation over its eventual meanings,[1] I trace the industrial and cultural struggles that took place over the specific materials that gave digital music its form, function, and sound (the software, hardware, metadata, interfaces, etc.) during the 1990s and early 2000s. Appreciating that any experience of recorded music is bound up in, but never reducible to, its form as a commodity, I look at the ways listeners used digital music to re-tune music's commodity form, sometimes in conjunction with, other times in opposition to, the industrial and ideological drives under-pinning music's digitization. While there have been several notable cultural (T.J. Anderson 2014; Burkart and McCourt 2006; Katz 2004; Suhr 2012), legal (Fisher 2004; Lessig 2004; McLeod 2005; Vaidhyanathan 2003), and journal-istic (Alderman 2001; Haring 2000; Knopper 2009; Kot 2009) accounts of music's digitization, my most direct models are Jonathan Sterne's *MP3: The Meaning of a Format* (2012) for his attention to the materials of music files and Ted Striphas's *The Late Age of Print* (2009) for his belief that the com-modity form opens up new questions about the value and materiality of digital objects, the convergence of culture and computing, and the ongoing histories of cultural practices like reading or, in my case, listening. Digital goods call into question how scholars have typically understood commodi-ties,[2] and the case of music highlights how the digitized commodity form is reconfiguring the circulation and experience of cultural goods. Despite fears over how digitization might destroy the value of the music commodity and the ability of labels, artists, and other participants in the music industries to profit from music, digitization has decidedly not ended the role of recorded music as a commodity. Rather than dematerializing and devaluing music or disrupting business models, digitization creates a new set of materials through which the commodity form is manifest and through which value accrues. Music's new commodity form, for better or for worse, has trans-formed digital music files into conflicted, networked, information-rich, trace-able, and manipulable cybernetic commodities.

Music has been digital for several decades now, but *Selling Digital Music* argues that the story of the digital music commodity is much more recent and much less told. Teasing out the differences between the commodity aspects of the CD and those of digital files points us to the intersections of materiality, aesthetics, labor, and value in an era of digital goods—goods that, because of their digital nature, seem to turn us away from precisely these issues. Music is a case study for a much wider set of media digitiza-tions taking place across the cultural industries and provides theoretical insights into the changing nature of cultural commodities, as well as meth-odological tools for how to study digital goods. It is a metonym for digital culture and what's at stake when media are increasingly presented, sold, stored, and consumed as digital objects.

UNDERSTANDING THE DIGITAL MUSIC COMMODITY

How do you sell music digitally? This was the question Prince was wres-tling with in 1998, as he prepared to release his epic four-disc album *Crystal*

Ball. As could be expected from the Artist Formerly Known as a Symbol, who was also a vocal critic of major record labels, Prince saw *Crystal Ball* as an opportunity to use new technologies to skirt the traditional constraints of record production and distribution (Kot 2009). Prince built a website for fans to visit and preorder the album. Once enough preorders came in—one hundred thousand, to be exact—Prince would produce and distribute the album, complete with packaging that folded into a 3D, transparent crystal ball (Strauss 1997). Excitedly and idiosyncratically, Prince announced the initiative on his website: "Dig if u will this picture: the first release by a major artist solely on the Internet. . . . Call 1–800-Newfunk now 2 order. This is how a record company should work" (Strauss 1997; Prince 1997). Despite his optimism, Prince's digital foray backfired. Fans who preordered *Crystal Ball* had to wait more than eight months for enough orders to accumulate (Reiss and Nelson 1998). Adding insult to long delays, copies of the album started appearing in mass retailers like Best Buy, Blockbuster, and MusicLand very shortly after mailing of the preordered album began, leaving disgruntled fans wondering why they had raced to order early (Glaister 1998).

Crystal Ball was a conflicted mix of new and old ways of producing and distributing music. Prince's high-tech release strategy relied as much on phones, the postal service, and retail stores as it did on the Internet. It was "solely on the Internet" but only if you "call 1–800-Newfunk 2 order." *Crystal Ball* was just that: an attempt to gaze into the future of music but one that was a little fuzzy. Prince sold CDs digitally, but he didn't truly sell a digital music commodity. *Crystal Ball* shows that in 1998 music that sold "solely on the Internet" was still bumping up against technologies, infrastructures, and cultural practices associated with earlier forms of the music commodity.

Prince's experiment—neither the first nor the last attempt to use computers and the Internet to sell music—stands in for a whole series of false starts, honest attempts, and misguided stumbles that characterize the convergence of music commodities and computing. While music has always depended on the technologies of its production, distribution, and playback, the level of this dependence has increased dramatically. Music's circulation is now thoroughly intertwined with computing technologies, and this has led to a series of innovations, interfaces, and ideas for music that reorient the role of music in everyday life. For some artists and fans this has been an occasion to question the codes and conventions that have traditionally governed the circulation of music. For others, such as industry executives, record labels, and technology companies, music's new digital formats have enabled greater control over the flow of music through new possibilities for surveillance, advertising, versioning, and technological interference.

Crystal Ball also serves as a reminder that the commodity form still matters in the digital realm, however contradictory that may seem. Although digitization often implies dematerialization, the pull of music's commodity form is very much present in the digital realm. It manifests itself in smaller, less obvious, materials, like the metadata fields users employ to sort their music or the visualization plugins that accompany media players. Just as the packaging and materials accompanying CDs, records, and tapes shaped the experience of music in those formats, the interfaces and materials of the digital music commodity govern its circulation and consumption. As much as *Crystal Ball* looked forward to a day when artists could deliver music directly to consumers via the Internet and computers, it was still bound by the very nondigital aspects of the CD commodity (duplication costs, shipping troubles, etc.). Similarly, the digital music commodity's possibilities are inextricably tied to its material attributes.

This book focuses on the decades that bookend Prince's *Crystal Ball*, roughly from 1987 to 2007 (see fig. 1 for a time line). It centers on case studies of five key technologies—media player software (Winamp), metadata (The CD Database), file sharing (Napster), online retail (the iTunes Store), and cloud music services—that have defined, and continue to define, music's move from CDs to digital files. It looks at how each of these individual moments shaped the development of the digital music commodity and the roles that technologies, entrepreneurs, users, and hobbyists played in the process. It traces the ways in which music's commercially packaged form (largely in the form of CDs) migrated to digital and then online spaces and considers the impact of this process on the shape of the digital music commodity.

It may seem quaint to talk about a music "commodity" in an era where billions of files are swapped instead of sold. Digital music, however, offers a unique opportunity to reenvision traditional conceptions of the commodity. Like all commodities, the digital music commodity turns us toward questions of labor and economic exchange. How are these things produced, priced, and sold? But music's digital-commodity form also asks us to consider issues of ownership, cultural value, and aesthetics, particularly as they relate to objects that are digital rather than tactile, abundant and infinitely reproducible rather than scarce and available in limited runs. Because of its mobility, abundance, and origins in multiple industries, the digital music commodity hovers among multiple states. It waffles between good and service, owned and rented, legitimate and illegitimate, and material and immaterial. It implicates its users in its own production in ways that differ from traditional goods. It is a digital object that gathers value as it circulates, though its circulation often occurs far from the traditional realms of money and value. It is a consumable commodity, and its digital nature integrates that consumption into more and more aspects of everyday life.

What Does It Mean to Call Music a Commodity?

Karl Marx described the commodity as an object outside of us, as anything that through its attributes satisfies human wants. Commodities are products of human labor transforming raw materials into something useful, giving them "use value" (Marx 1978, 303). As useful things begin circulating through society, they gather an exchange value. Their worth becomes detached from their use and becomes embedded in their relations to other things (Marx 1978, 304). A table is useful because you can eat on it, but it is also valuable since it can be exchanged for another object of worth, like a chair (or money). Marx, however, was also attuned to the commodity's more mystical qualities. When we equate and exchange commodities like tables and chairs, we equate and abstract the labor that went into creating them (Marx 1978, 305). Marx called the result of this abstraction "commodity fetishism." Instead of seeing commodities for what they are—a combination of matter and human labor—we ascribe mysterious qualities to them, and they become substitutes for the social relations that lie behind their production (Marx 1978, 319). Although *commodity fetishism,* like *false consciousness,* now seems a dated term, when scores of consumers and journalists welcome new tech products like Apple's iPhone as the Jesus phone (Brown 2007; Kedrosky 2007), it is hard to deny that material and human resources continue to be regularly detached from the value of products.

Since Marx, value has remained a central concept, especially as the industrialization of cultural production has intensified the role of commodities in everyday life (see, e.g., Adorno 2001; Baudrillard 1981; Benjamin 1969; Debord 1995; Gunster 2004; Haug 1987; Lukács 1971). As exchange value overtook use value, commodification challenged the creative force of cultural goods by reducing them to mere products or advertisements for further acts of consumption. But scholars also addressed commodities as social objects in their own right and located value in the process of exchange itself. Hardly an inert economic object, the commodity is, as Arjun Appadurai notes, a moment in the broader social life of things: "the social life of any thing [can] be defined as the situation in which its exchangeability (past, present, or future) for some other thing is its socially relevant *fungibility of a commodity*

feature" (Appadurai 1986, 13). Commodities are artifacts in a particular situation, the commodity situation, and the conditions of their exchange determine their value (Appadurai 1986, 13–16; Kopytoff 1986, 68).

How Do These Conceptions of the Commodity Apply to Music?

Music represents a particular kind of commodity. Because of the artistic, social, economic, and personal roles it serves, music is often called a cultural commodity. (Lacher and Mizerski 1994; Miege 1979; Straw 2002). This is not to suggest that other industrial commodities like soap, cereal, or shoes are not also, in many ways, cultural but rather to recognize that objectified versions of music, film, books, and other such media deserve specialized terminology given the role they play in structuring identity, expression, and communication. The value of cultural commodities is marked by their fragility: their use value is hard to pin down (e.g., what pleasures do we get from music? how do we describe them? what needs do they fulfill?). Cultural commodities are also characterized by a kind of chronic economic overproduction in which the amount produced vastly exceeds the number that achieve financial success (Straw 2002, 149–51). Their fetish value comes from the objects themselves (e.g., albums, books, or movies) but also from the technologies used to play them back (the record player, the television, etc.) and the system of texts and commodities that circulate peripherally (advertising, reviews, the star system, etc.) to give cultural commodities their meanings. Furthermore, in the case of music, consumers typically sample the product before they purchase it, and while cultural commodities are rarely designed for repeated purchase, they frequently experience repeated consumption, making them more like "non-narrative cultural 'texts'—such as decorative objects or easel paintings" than like traditional goods (Lacher and Mizerski 1994, 367; Straw 2002, 155).

How Did Music Become a Commodity?

It is tempting to associate music's commodity status with the advent of recording, but even during the times of minstrels in the Middle Ages, music could be considered a commodity (Attali 1985, 47). The advent of sheet music and modern recording technology simply changed the process of commodification and the end commodities that resulted (performance for hire vs. sheet music for further performances, etc.). Over the course of the twentieth century the mechanical reproduction of the performance became the central mode of music consumption. Recorded music took on a life of its own that could be "possessed as a thing" (Adorno 1990, 58). Adorno and

Attali were highly critical of the objectification of music into a commercial product, but even contemporary scholars who take a more lenient view of commercial recorded music recognize the centrality of understanding music within its commodity context and its status as an industrial cultural good (T. J. Anderson 2014; Frith 1996; Gracyk 1996; Negus 1992; Wikström 2009).

Music's commodity status is inherently tied to the technologies through which it is reproduced and consumed. From musical instruments to studio engineering equipment to CDs, MP3s, and, now, the Internet, a diverse assemblage of technologies influence the sound, look, and movement of music in its various guises (i.e., as raw sound or as packaged good). Many of these technologies are commodities in and of themselves, and as Timothy Taylor notes, "the commodity status of each depends on the other: music could not exist as a commodity without the technologies involved with its making and transmission; nor would those technologies serve much purpose without the music they purvey" (2007, 283).

The recorded music commodity, then, is both sound and artifact. It is the music, the disc or file that contains the music, the CD player that plays it back, and the software needed to accomplish communication across these disparate elements. The interplay of sound and its artifacts is "vitally important in shaping the possible meanings of the commodity" (Wallach 2003, 51). There are, of course, physiological, neurological, and psychological reactions to music and sound that should be recognized (Levitin 2006), but these effects/affects depend on how and where we experience music and the format of the music itself: how it looks, sounds, feels, plays, and moves. Our experience of music, and the value we place on it, is highly dependent on its commodity character. Music is not, as Taylor reminds us, "a commodity all the time, or always in the same way" (2007, 282). A brand-new record released by an indie band capitalizing on the resurgence of vinyl versus a discarded mix tape in a garage sale bin versus a song streamed freely (with ads) on Spotify are all different manifestations of music as commodity. Dissecting the historical, cultural, and social circumstances behind various moments of commodification in music's long history helps us understand why and how music means, whatever it means, at both an individual and social level.

What's New about the Digital Music Commodity?

The digital music commodity marks an evolution of the commodity form. As such, it opens up questions about the "digitalness" of the cultural commodity, as well as about the "commodityness" of digital objects. Although some of the characteristics of the digital music commodity apply to other commodities, the digital music commodity amplifies five key features:

1. A transectorial commodity that is the result of planned and unplanned convergence between the music and computing industries

2. A highly mobile and fluid commodity that largely expresses itself through software interfaces and hardware devices and gathers value through its exchange

3. A rematerialized commodity that was stripped of much of its materiality and embedded with new micromaterials to give it shape and value

4. A cybernetic commodity that is highly dependent on informational paratexts like metadata for its functional, economic, and aesthetic duties

5. A conflicted commodity that is shaped by competing demands of industries and users, one whose value is determined as much by its ubiquity and usefulness as by its price, and one that promises to disrupt traditional ways of making, and distributing music even as it closes off those very possibilities

Part of the fear over the devaluation of music stems from the fact that the digital music commodity came out of *transectorial* developments in which it was not initially clear that digital music was or even should be a commodity. Rather than a preplanned industry-sanctioned format change, like the move to compact discs in the 1980s, music on computers was more of a by-product of convergences in multimedia computing in the 1980s and 1990s. As software programmers started designing new tools and purposes for computers, music was put to use in a variety of novel ways, some of which were in line with the desires of the major players in the music industries, some of which were not. The digitization of music was driven as much by computing technology as it was by new models for music distribution; sound and recorded music were fodder for software programs and hardware development. Music files on the computer, at least initially, seemed to be just another function that computers provided rather than a potential new market.

Digital music is also a highly *fluid, mobile,* and *social* commodity that shifts in exchange value. As with previous formats, the digital music commodity takes on different economic and cultural value depending on who is exchanging it and on the context in which that exchange takes place. Think, for example, of the value of a hockey trading card at an auction versus a garage sale, or the value of the same card for a nonhockey fan. Digital music's ability to circulate, however, far surpasses that of previous formats, making music's mobile and social potentials ever more pronounced. The value that gets created during exchange and circulation is not only valuable for users, but it also constitutes music's *cybernetic* potential: it is a commodity that creates data through its use, and the results of the data can be used for means of surveillance, market research, and other sorts of value-generating activities, sometimes at the expense of users.

These two registers of value also contribute to making digital music a *conflicted* commodity. The nature of the digital music commodity and its associated technologies implicates users in its own reproduction and circulation more so than previous formats. Users are co-creators of a kind of user-generated commodity; they create value for their own experiences of digital music and act as sources of value for others. While previous recorded music formats facilitated sharing and user-driven production (e.g., piano rolls, tapes, CDs), the digital music commodity depends heavily on the intentional and unintentional labor of its users. It owes as much of its shape to the technologists, entrepreneurs, and users who embedded it with certain information, functionality, and aesthetics as it does to the companies in charge of marketing and distributing it.

In this way much of the labor that goes into the production of the digital music commodity is masked, be it the hidden labor that goes into the production of the devices we use to consume digital music or the labor that users themselves put into the digital music commodity and its interfaces. This is not to say that labor, and the social relations behind that labor, are no longer central to the value of the music commodity. Rather, the labor that goes into digital cultural goods is so highly distributed and dispersed among artists, producers, sound engineers, marketers, record labels, distributors, and other industry entities that traditional Marxist labor theories of value are difficult to apply in any direct sense. In other words the politics of cultural labor extend far beyond any one particular music commodity and encompass an entire relationship among artists, users, music, and the industries that produce it.

Finally, digitization alters music's materiality. Most disconcertingly for those involved in producing and selling recorded music, digital formats strip recorded music of much of its context and content, lacking as it does the packaging, materiality, and "thingness" that contributed to the commodity character (Styvén 2007, 57–60). Put simply, digital music lacks some of the things that previously made music a sellable thing. The CD's

Digital Music as or NFT recorded?
early NFT? as digital commodity d.g.

packaging, contents, artwork, and liner notes provide use and exchange value and fix the music commodity in a desirable objectified form. Digital files, at first glance and certainly in their earliest iterations, lack many of these value-generating attributes. Without something to hold, consumers undertake a different value equation (Styvén 2007). Furthermore, even though there is clearly human and machine labor that goes into the production of a digital music commodity (the writing, recording, and formatting of a song; the hosting of a file on a music store's servers), the costs of its reproduction are significantly reduced. Whereas rivalrous goods like a table or a CD gain their value from their singularity—if I own and am using it, you cannot—nonrivalrous goods like digital files seem to eschew this logic with their infinite reproducibility. Music as a digital file, some argue, "lacks potential emotive contexts" and is "emotionally less valuable" than a physical artifact (McCourt 2005, 250). Instead of finding value in the aura of an artifact "fluidity, rather than integrity, is the defining characteristic of digital technology" (McCourt 2005, 249–51). Dematerialization through digitization robs the music experience of some of its defining attributes.

While dematerialization seems to be at the heart of the devaluation and "death of music" arguments, the link between music's materiality and its value seems like a relic from of an era that locates the aura of an object in the physical expression of the artifact (rather than in the interplay between the content and its materials).[3] Even if digital music brings with it different conditions of value, the digital music commodity is not as intangible as it is sometimes presented (McCourt 2005; Rothenbuhler and Peters 1997). Digital files still take up space and computing resources: folders filled with MP3s or other formats eat up hard drive space, and the software interfaces occupy limited screen real estate. Mice need clicking, servers and hard disks need filling, and credit card statements need paying. Users may not be flipping through album covers or poring over album liners, but they are still touching, looking, and sorting. Digital objects, in other words, often "enter into very intimate relationships with physical artifacts" (Kirschenbaum 2002, 20). Information is not immaterial or dematerialized. It is always embodied or expressed materially (Wark 2006, 173). Rather than a dematerialization, digital music is a *rematerialized* commodity, one whose materials bring new sources of value for listeners, companies, and music itself.

This brings us to thornier issues about what makes a digital object "digital." Although I have no intention of turning this into an ontological exploration of the digital—already thoroughly examined in Evens (2005) and Sterne (2006a)—I do want to discuss digitality enough to provide context for the differences the digital music commodity brings to the table compared to previous formats. As Aden Evens suggests, what digital things have in common is "their *form*, a string of 0s and 1s" (2005, 65; emphasis in original). Treating something as digital means turning it into a collection of binary digits. Sound and music, in other words, leave the world of pitch, tone, and frequency and become a list of numbers meant to represent pitch, tone, frequency, and so on. Because all media that go through digitization follow this same process—the transition of phenomena into information— Evens argues the digital is "indifferent to content and material, [and] the digital renders everything it touches in the pure abstract form of form" (2005, 75–76). The digital, in this light, becomes a means of representing and ordering content, regardless of the original character of that content.

Music was first made widely digital through the compact disc. Users not only saw the benefits of digital music in their ability to skip, rewind, and play CDs with greater precision than they could in previous formats but also heard the benefits in the sound reproduction. Digital recording processes relied on digital sampling of sound waves at discrete points in time rather than the continuous mechanical impressions provided by analog recording equipment, so the CD's possibilities for a broader dynamic range, a higher signal-to-noise ratio, better channel separation, and other features all resulted in a sound that was "clearer, sharper, and more exactly representative of the original performance" (Kaptanis 1983). Although not all listeners were necessarily as enamored with clearer, sharper sound—many audiophiles still preferred vinyl for its "warmer" sounds and "trueness" to the original recording (Davis 2007)—digital sound on CDs seemed to promise, as one writer noted, "the most perfect alternative yet devised to putting a symphony orchestra in your living room" (Mitchell 1987).

But this initial moment in music's digitization was not its full realization as a digital object. The CD may have changed the ways listeners experienced recordings for better or worse depending on taste, but as a commodity the CD still relied for the most part on the same infrastructure that had supported cassette tapes and vinyl records. The conversion of phenomena into information, in other words, only applied to the sound itself. This is the reason for marking the digital music commodity—the shift from music on CDs to music as a stand-alone digital file—as a distinct moment in the history of the music commodity. The expression of music as collections of 0s and 1s was a sonic precursor to the more complete digitization of the music commodity itself, the result of which has set off a much larger series of industrial, social, and cultural reconfigurations with respect to music's production, circulation, and consumption.

Numerical representation brings a number of novel capabilities to media objects. As binary digits, media becomes more modular; separate entities like pixels, characters, and scripts, can be combined and recombined in countless ways to produce new and different objects (Manovich 2001, 27–48). This modular, numerical nature of digital objects also means that digital media can be automated (i.e., produced and circulated without explicit human intervention) and variable (i.e., made available in many different iterations and versions). Ultimately, this leads to what Lev Manovich calls transcoding, where digital media still appear as recognizable cultural objects (pictures, songs, videos), but these media now follow "the established conventions of the computer's organization of data" (2001, 45). A digital photo, for example, is a visible whole that creates meaning through representation or semiotics, but it can also be parsed into the color values of its pixels, the metadata embedded in its file structure, and other attributes that make it more similar to other digitized objects than to other traditional photographs (Manovich 2001, 45). The digital music commodity, by the same logic, is a discrete sonic entity, but it is also significantly dependent on its format, file type, file compression, and the various interfaces through which it is made visible and audible. The transcoded music commodity, in other words, takes on new capabilities as a result of being numerical, modular, automated, and variable. This book is an exploration of what digitization brings not just to the sound of music but also to the process of selling a sonic commodity.

RE-TUNING MUSIC'S INTERFACE

The music commodity's material attributes are central to understanding its transition to digital formats. Just as the CD and cassettes had novel material and sonic differences from the music commodities that preceded them, so, too, does digital music bring with it a series of new sounds, materials, and experiences. As data, the digital music commodity sheds its previous material signifiers and sonic artifacts (album artwork, stretched cassette tape, the hiss of an analog record), but this leaves room for other signs, materials, and artifacts to take their place. Through various technologies, software, and interfaces designed to play, distribute, and consume digital music files, recorded music as a digital file was gradually redressed with features, attributes, and sonic qualities that reworked its commodity form.

In other words music on computers experiences a *re-tuning* of its interface. As music migrated from previous formats to computers, it was detuned: after years of use the traditional packaging that contributed to the

CD or cassette's commodity character no longer seemed to hold its tune. High-quality CD sounds were compressed, and excess sonic data were thrown away. Highly crafted artwork, album graphics, and liner notes were reduced to thumbnail images and metadata. But while this temporary de-tuning produced some strange sounds (and strange technologies and strange attempts at commodifying digital music), the music commodity's re-tuning made new features visible and made novel attributes audible. As music and computing collided, the music commodity was re-tuned and transcoded, made to look and sound similar but different from what it had looked and sounded like before. The music commodity's re-tuned interface was more modular, variable, and malleable but also more contingent on the technologies of its playback and presentation. Just as the relatively minor tweaks to an instrument's sound during tuning produce major changes in the sound of the instrument and the way that instrument interacts with other instruments and musicians around it, the changes to the music commodity's interface have affected how users view, hear, and interact with the music commodity and its associated technologies. Music's re-tuning has made it playable in new ways and left it conditional on a network of hardware and software that alters its materiality and affects how users are able to access and experience music.

The crucial role of software and hardware interfaces has been of interest in the fields of software studies (Cramer and Fuller 2008), game studies (Rhody 2005), and in new media research more generally (Bolter and Grusin 1999; Chun 2011; Galloway 2012; S. Johnson 1997; Manovich 2001), but these insights have yet to be applied to the music commodity in a sustained fashion. Journalistic accounts of music's digitization are often attuned to the individual technologies but neglect the specific features and functions of the interface in favor of delivering a broader industrial history (Knopper 2009; Kot 2009). There is also work on interfaces in the fields of human-computer interaction and user experience design, though it focuses largely on detailing the technical and cognitive aspects of how people make use of computational devices and their interfaces and on designing interfaces that improve the performance, efficiency, and utility of computing experiences (Carroll 2002; Lazar et al. 2010; Preece et al. 1994; Rogers et al. 2011). While highly useful from a design point of view, this heavy emphasis on the cognitive, technical, and ergonomic aspects of interfaces sometimes forecloses larger questions about the cultural and historical nature of interfaces.

At their most basic, interfaces are manifestations of how *"software appears to users"* (Manovich 2013, 29; emphasis in original). They are key sites at which remediation—the process by which new media extend previous media by incorporating and refashioning some of their codes and conventions (Bolter and Grusin 1999)—takes place. Whereas remediation is largely taken as a visual process, though, the idea of re-tuning is meant to call attention to the way interfaces sound or affect the experience of sound. Today's interfaces, after all, are not strictly visual affairs; they are multimedia interfaces that engage visual senses and sonic, haptic, and sometimes other senses as well (Manovich 2013, 29). The alerts, beeps, and buzzes of our software and hardware matter as much as what we see on our screens. Media interfaces, in other words, shape how users see, hear, feel, and experience the functions of any given piece of software and the cultural content that passes through it. Interfaces also reveal the assumptions and models about users and their needs. The cultural contexts in which software programs have developed are encoded at the very level of the interface (Manovich 2013, 29). Software studies (e.g., Berry 2011; Chun 2004; Fuller 2008; Kitchin and Dodge 2011; Manovich 2001, 2013; Montfort and Bogost 2009) has a rich vocabulary for understanding interfaces as both highly representational and logistical. Interfaces represent code to users and act as the code through which users experience other representations.

As such, analyses of popular music can no longer afford to take the work of interfaces for granted. Music, after all, has a rich visual culture history— from sheet music, to album packaging, to music videos—and the interfaces of digital music can be placed within this larger evolution of music's visual representations. The interface is such an integral and integrated component of digital objects that it is easy to overlook its importance. The interface is what allows us to interact with digital objects as commodities. It is the point where user and commodity meet. When users look at and listen to computers, portable MP3 players, cell phones, and other devices, they see and hear through the interface. It stands between their technologies and the cultural goods (music, movies, information, etc.) they access through those devices. Conversely, the interface is the commodity's window outward. It presents and mediates the music commodity (and other digital objects). Digital music faces outward, toward the user, through the interface. Music's features, sounds, and appearances depend on what takes place at the level of the interface, where users and their machines interact. The idea of a re-tuned interface acknowledges the importance of the interface as a site for these changes, as well as the work that was needed to recalibrate and ready digital files for their moments as commodities.

The interface is where the various materials of digital music come together. These materials are what Jonathan Gray (2010) and Will Straw (2009) refer to as "paratexts," and they are crucial to our encounters with the music commodity. Paratexts are the extratextual elements of a text that prepare audiences for its reception. Not just limited to packaging, paratexts include movie trailers, advertisements, promo campaigns, and other discourses surrounding cultural products (Gray 2010). Paratexts add meaning to texts; they are both part of the text and about it. The digitization of music has directly altered the way users interact with the music commodity's most immediate paratexts. In their place new information and attributes arise to give the digital music commodity its unique specificity as a format for the consumption and circulation of music.

Through digitization music's paratexts become much less obvious and much more embedded into the commodity itself. Digitization represents a turn toward what some have called the "micromaterials" of music: the informational and infinitesimally small layers of materials that make up digital culture (see, e.g., the discussion of Sherburne 2003 in Sterne 2006b, 831–32). If music's most immediate paratexts were once the album cover, the jewel case, the labels and graphics on the CDs or tapes, the paratextual materials that now shape music's use and exchange values are getting smaller and smaller. The digital music file is made up of metadata that affect how it appears, how it can be used, and how it can be sorted and stored on a user's various devices. It is made up of software code that is largely visible through other interfaces and devices. It is made up of compression algorithms that determine how much or how little of the original sound file is audible and how easily it can be circulated over digital networks.

Despite being micro and operating at a level ignored by most users, digital music's micromaterials are deeply embedded in the way the music commodity looks, sounds, and gets put to use. Even though many of the materials of digital music commodities are "born digital" and may be less visible than those of previous music commodities, they still exert an influence over the expression and representation of music.[4] Just as music on plastic or vinyl required certain materials for distribution, dissemination, and playback, so, too, do the micromaterials and paratexts of digital music affect how it looks, feels, gathers, and circulates in our culture. Rather than suggesting that digital music represents a complete dematerialization, or, conversely, that it shares the same materiality as physical objects, I propose that music as software is, to borrow from David Berry, "differently material, tenuously material, almost less materially material" (2012, n.p.). These differently material micromaterials may be much smaller and less tangible paratexts than what listeners had with CDs or albums, but music's new paratexts have concrete effects and traces and create their own kinds of value.

The tendency to treat digital files as immaterial is partly why the micro-materials central to digital music's commodity form have received so little attention (metadata, interfaces, etc.). But despite the apparent lack of physical weight or dimensions of digital goods, the fetish qualities and exchange values of music still hold tremendous weight. This should not be surprising. The wonder and mystique of the commodity fetish is precisely that it is not located in the object itself. It is something created around the object through the unseen labor that goes into it. Still, the apparent lack of value and worth of something as micromaterial as a digital file makes these relations difficult to analyze. This is why the work of digital music's "packaging" and paratexts is so crucial, and why much of this book is devoted to analyzing how this micromateriality emerged. As with other commodities (Willis 1991), packaging sets the context through which users interact with the digital music commodity. It is as much a contributor to the value of the digital music commodity as its price or the conditions of its production.

This is particularly important for the digital music commodity. Millions of digital music files move across hundreds of networks every hour. Some of this movement is part of the regular, sanctioned market economy where files are bought or streamed in online outlets and revenues are divided among the various rights-holders. Much of it is not. Some estimates suggest that 95 percent of all digital music is downloaded without payment (IFPI 2013a; Wikström 2009, 151). Digital music is widely circulated in alternative "gift economies," through peer-to-peer file sharing, and via other forms of exchange. Musicians, labels, and tech companies are toying with a series of experiments in "free" (T.J. Anderson 2014). In many of these spaces it is users who are responsible for embedding the digital music commodity with information, features, and functions that make it more usable, organizable, and desirable. The result is that digital music "partakes of both commodity form and something else" and occupies "an ambiguous position that is both inside and outside market economies" (Sterne 2012, 384, 400). Frequently, users who have not paid directly for files they download still feel and act as if they "own" them (Burkart 2008; Sterne 2012, 385; McCourt 2005).[5] This sense of ownership, I argue, is partly due to the pull of the commodity form. Price is only one of many characteristics of a commodity's value; it is not its distinguishing feature. The interfaces, metadata, and micromaterials that make up digital music contribute to its objectness and to users' sense of propriety over it, even in the absence of a clear moment of purchase. In other words we need not have paid for a good in order for it to be, or to act like, a commodity. Even in its freest of forms, digital music can be packaged, treated, and made to act like a commodity.

Music's re-tuning is a direct result of the convergence of music and computing technologies. While there has long been cross-pollination between the music industry and developers of new technologies (e.g., Edison cylinders, Berliner records, Philips and the audiotape, Sony/Philips and the CD), the migration to digital music is unique in how tightly it has woven music and computing. This "transectorial innovation" (Jenkins 2006; Théberge 1997) fuses once-distinct sectors, creates converged products, and spurs organizational changes within the industries themselves. The computing industry is now one of the key developers of new means of finding, playing, storing, and experiencing music, while the recorded music industry owns swaths of content that make computers and other high-tech products more desirable. Sectors that once exerted influence over the promotion and sales of the CD commodity—record labels, physical retail outlets like Tower Records, radio, music television stations, etc.—now find themselves in competition with ringtone makers, computer hardware and software producers, Internet service providers, social media, and a host of other new businesses suddenly interested in the business of music, each with its own divergent visions for what the digital music commodity should look like and how it should work. Transectorial innovation has made music and computing interdependent and conflicted bedfellows.

The re-tuning of music's interface is also highly tied to recent developments that extend music's mobility and portability. Although much of the work on mobile devices and mobile listening has focused on how users "manage" their experience of the space around them (Bull 2005, 344–46; Bull 2007; Thibaud 2003) or as a "technology of the self" to navigate their everyday lives and activities (DeNora 2000), newer research on mobile music has looked beyond the idea that mobile music is a concept that is limited to portable music players to consider the new spaces through which the music commodity travels and the larger network of infrastructure and systems that support it (see Beer 2010; Gopinath 2013; Gopinath and Stanyek 2014b). As music's mobility increases, and its interfaces continue to multiply through the various apps, devices, and services that emerge to cater to this market, so, too, does its ubiquity (Kassabian 2013). New micromaterials and paratexts arise with each new technological development. The re-tuning of music's interface, in other words, is far from finished.

While this book makes no claims to predict the future form music may take, it aims to provide the conceptual tools for understanding how this particular re-tuning has shaped music and, by extension, its listeners during the last two decades. It documents how digitization has altered music's most immediate paratexts and the impact this has had for our encounters with music as a commodity. The cultural interfaces that structure our relationship with digital music help make the idea of digital music understandable to those involved in its circulation and use. They remediate music by reminding users of familiar practices while introducing them to newer ones (Bolter and Grusin 1999; Gitelman 2006; Manovich 2001). They help explain how we got to where we are going. Their features, evolution, and what they make possible or unthinkable raise questions about how music appears to consumers, how companies replicate and circulate the material attributes of digital products, and what value consumers ascribe to products that largely exist as digital data on servers and hard drives.

MOMENTS IN MUSIC'S DIGITIZATION

Selling Digital Music uses software and close readings of various audio technologies as a way into both technical (i.e., what do these new technologies do?) and cultural (i.e., what can users do with these new technologies?) questions. It charts a middle ground between legal/political economic analyses of media digitization (Andrejevic 2007; Burkart and McCourt 2006; Gillespie 2007; Lessig 2004) and more user-centric research on the media and the cultural industries (Baym 2010; DeNora 2000; Jenkins 2006). The book is based on five key moments that called into question the music commodity's shape while at the same time helping to re-tune it:

1. The popularization of software media players and the case of Winamp (1997–2001)

2. The rise of metadata and the case of the CD Database and ID3 tags (1996–2003)

3. The advent of file sharing and the case of Napster (1998–2002)

4. The growth of online music retailing and the case of the iTunes Music Store (2003–2006)

5. Cloud computing and the transition to music in the "cloud" (2007–2012)

Although there is no shortage of digital technologies and moments to explore, I chose these particular cases for the telling configurations of aesthetics, technologies, users, and artists they reveal. These cases tell a chronological story—a narrative, as visualized in the time line at the beginning of this chapter, that spans digital music developments from the late 1980s to the first decade of the new millennium. They also tell a thematic story that, like a version update for a piece of software, iterates based on the arguments and technical developments that preceded it. Understanding metadata and file sharing, for example, requires a lengthier history of music media players, just as the latter requires understanding the push toward computers as multimedia devices. In some cases the selection of cases was a quantitative argument: Napster, Winamp, and the iTunes Store all gathered numbers of users that far surpassed their competition. Other cases relied on a more qualitative assessment. ID3 tags and the Compact Disc Database (CDDB) are less measurable, but they are part of the fabric of the everyday transactions and circulation that occurs with digital music files. All these cases and technologies, I argue, were deeply embedded in the emerging infrastructure for digital music.

The "documents" that make up the primary materials for analysis include a mix of trade articles, popular press, and academic research about the technologies in question, software version logs (the documents that accompany each new version of a piece of software and list the changes from version to version), company press releases and other internal documents, older versions of the software in question run on older computers to which I had access, and an extensive archive of screenshots from sites like the Internet Archive's "Wayback Machine"—a search engine that provides snapshots of websites over time. As a research tool, the Wayback Machine (and the Internet Archive more generally) is not without its quirks (Murphy et al. 2007). Screenshots of websites are often incomplete or unavailable, some of the archive's data are inaccurate, past data can be modified from the present, and many websites are not tracked by its search robots (Garfinkel and Cox 2009). Still, the fractal glimpses and echoes of the interfaces and websites the archive does provide are some of the only records of how companies presented and marketed themselves and their new technologies online.

Chapter 1 looks at the rise of media "jukebox" players on computers and argues that the interfaces through which users encounter music matter more than we give them credit for. Embedded in the interface are assumptions about how a particular media object should and can be represented and about people's relationships with technology more generally. Using the case of Winamp, I look at how software media players initiated the retuning of music's interface. A thoroughly transectorial effort, Winamp was the direct result of a push toward multimedia-capable devices in the late 1980s and early 1990s. As part of the "multimedia revolution," music was bound up in a drive to realize the goal of making computers truly devices for personal expression and liberation. Winamp relied on this rhetoric to sell its software and to sell digital music more generally. Using a critical interpretative reading of Winamp's interface, an analysis of comments on user forums, version logs, Internet Archive snapshots of the Winamp.com website, and older versions of the software and some of its related plugins,[6] I argue that Winamp reveals itself as a cultural interface that put music in context on computers and made music as a digital file recognizable and user-friendly. In doing so, it also marked the beginning stages of the commodification of music as a digital file. Winamp, as a company and as a piece of software, may have hoped to liberate music from the confines of its commodity status, but it also presented a coherent vision not only for how music playback could function on computers but also for how music could be a sellable thing.

The second chapter addresses the importance of the informational layer of the digital music commodity and, relatedly, the role users play in the commodification process by contributing to and shaping that information. Specifically, it looks at the rise of metadata for music—the information about the information on CDs and digital files—through the cases of the CDDB and ID3 tags. Like elements of Winamp's interface, metadata were micromaterials designed to fill music's emptied material markers. Metadata, however, work more directly on the functionality of digital files, making them visible and organizable in new ways. They embed digital music with information for handling and understanding music outside the context of its traditional paratexts and give it added forms of value for users and institutions. As part of a broader historical discussion about the role information has played historically in shaping how consumers use, experience, and think about the music commodity, metadata provide the information backbone of the digital music industry and raise issues of privacy, surveillance, and the role of digital databases. However, since both the CDDB and ID3 tags started as side projects of hobbyists and involved countless user-generated contributions from scores of enthusiastic Internet users, metadata also complicate how we understand commodification and the labor involved in the production of cultural goods. Metadata implicate users in the commodity creation process and focus our attention on what might be called user-generated commodities.

The re-tuning of the digital music commodity continued, paradoxically, with the advent of the peer-to-peer file-sharing service Napster. Chapter 3 argues that even technologies that seem designed to destroy the commodity status of digital goods contribute to their further commodification. Even though the "free" nature of many file-sharing services seems to negate the very idea that digital music could be a commodity, Napster's software and website interfaces brought together a community of users bound by an interest in circulation and connection in ways that helped further digital music's commodification. Chapter 3 reexamines the Napster case over the period from 1998 to 2002 and argues that despite all its disruptive potential, Napster was also a business that sought to develop and eventually commodify an audience. Through this commodity community—and its practices of sharing, connecting, circulating, and discussing music—Napster provided evidence that a market for digital music commodities was not only possible but already extant. Napster, the company, planned and cultivated a unified group of users that provided benefits not just for Napster but also for a host of companies that sought to mine value from the activity taking place on the file-sharing service's networks.[7] The usefulness of the metadata Napster's users were generating, as with the CDDB or ID3 tags, speaks to the importance of user labor in creating the digital music commodity and remains foundational for practices and techniques of online audience measurement that persist today. Although the record labels frequently blame Napster for sparking the current crisis in recorded music, Napster users contributed to the shape of the digital music commodity even as they willingly traded digital copies of recorded music commodities in ways unsanctioned by many music industries. Even technologies and user practices that seem to explicitly contradict the logic of commodification contribute to the shape of the digital music commodity.

After the arrival of file sharing, music as a digital file seemed as if it might not ever be sellable again. Chapter 4 looks at the history of online music retail outlets and perhaps the most convincing argument that the price function of the music commodity had not completely disappeared with digitization: the iTunes Music Store. As part of music's re-tuning, Apple's software and hardware combined the act of playing music with the act of shopping for and buying it. Taking cues from Napster and the CDDB, the iTunes Store brought traditional practices of seeking, sorting, and selling music into dialogue with new ones (fragmentation of the music commodity, user-generated content, etc.) in an attempt to reinject value that had seeped out of the music commodity. Rather than simply trying to sell music as a digital file, Apple sought to commodify a digital music lifestyle wherein the entire experience of finding, accessing, and using music was subject to commodification. The history of online retail, and Apple's role in it, speaks to how the network of technologies required to support digital commodities provides those in the business of selling media and entertainment with troubling forms of control over the commodities and devices we use to play, access, and enjoy culture.

Yet, just as Apple established its dominance in the digital retail market, the music commodity appeared to be on the brink of another shift, moving even further away from its previous iterations. This transition makes digital commodities even more vulnerable and places greater boundaries between users and their cultural commodities. The final chapter looks at the push toward cloud-based music services—services that offer to host, stream, store, and manage users' music collections for them over the Internet—and suggests this move represents a new relationship between users and their music, one where the sounds and songs of our social lives are increasingly contingent on the control and technology of music service providers. Part metaphor, part vision for the future of music, the cloud analogy conceals as much as it reveals. The cloud is a diffuse and indeterminate space where music acts not just as a commodity but also as the background noise for a series of networked interactions and digital initiatives. Music becomes a complement to other digital activities, and the rights of users and musicians are overlooked in the process. In the cloud, music is subsumed in a complex technical relationship that shapes the meanings and histories users make from their music collections.

Together, these five cases and the practices they have enabled have helped re-tune music's interface and have sparked the development of digital music as a commodity. Although they follow a roughly chronological narrative, each chapter looks both backward and forward, with threads from each case overlapping and interweaving throughout. The cases follow the bridges between old software interfaces and new behaviors. They mine dead links, obscure press releases, and obsolete technologies to make arguments about how programs worked, how they made music appear and sound, and how they guided users through the initial experiences of playing music on the computer. Rather than read developers, users, artists, or executives from a traditional ethnography or from interviews, these cases try to read them *through* the interfaces of the software and through the ways in which the features of the technologies position them (Bolter and Grusin 1999; Gitelman 2006; Manovich 2001). This methodology has its limits; beyond user comments in forums or other documented press reactions to the technologies, this book attempts to make no broader claim about how users ultimately experienced digital music. As with any kind of cultural good, this type of universalizing statement is ultimately impossible to achieve, given the subjective nature of media experiences like music. But the traces left behind in the technologies themselves, and in their assumptions about how users could and should use them, provide an equally rich avenue for the analysis of technical and cultural associations governing listeners' relationships with music.

The focus on the United States, and on California in particular, is also a limitation. Digital music is a highly global commodity. Although California is a particularly important locus for the development of many of the technologies key to a digital music commodity, there are other countries, regions, and spaces where music's commodity status may not be as fully entrenched or where there exist wholly different ideas about exchange, consumption, and the circulation of music. In many countries, for example, mobile phones are much more prevalent than computers as a means for going online, and the online experience is often conditioned by slower speeds, antiquated technologies, government regulations, or spotty connections. Experiences of digital music files are subject to the specific geographic, technical, and socioeconomic conditions that frame the technologies that accompany and mediate it. There are also varying levels of formal and informal economies in place around music in various global centers and peripheries, an infrastructure that contributes to both market and antimarket practices (Lobato 2012). Joe Karaganis's research report on piracy in emerging economies, for example, speaks to the ways piracy and commodification are always intertwined, the former often a response to the lack of a proper market for the latter (Karaganis 2011). Where possible, I have incorporated insights on digital music use from other regions, though admittedly the focus is on the markets in which the digital music commodity and its associated technologies first developed.

There are other key moments, as the time line suggests, that have been important to digital music's evolution: the advent of RealPlayer and streaming audio, the formation of the Secure Digital Music Initiative (SDMI), legislation like the Digital Millennium Copyright Act (DMCA), and the rise of music-focused social networks like Myspace. However, my insistence on finding technologies that were both highly embedded into the emerging infrastructure for digital music at the moment of its newness and that displayed a visible effect of the digital commodity's form helped determine which cases to include and exclude. File sharing, for example, did not begin with Napster, but Napster was the first to present music and connect users in a way that significantly altered the future of the distribution of digital music. The Pirate Bay and other non-US file-sharing sites now have traffic that dwarfs Napster's original numbers, but my interest here is in what Napster's interface brought to digital music that still persists today. Similarly, the CDDB and ID3 tags are the de facto standards for organizing a significant portion of digital music interactions, and they most clearly display the value and labor that users put into digital music. Although Myspace is probably the most problematic omission from this project, I examine it in conjunction with other similar services in the final chapter on cloud computing (and recommend the already existing book-length project on social media and music by Suhr 2012). Finally, legislation like the DMCA has without argument affected what is and is not possible with digital music, but since so much of the music commodity's key features continued to develop in spite of regulatory developments, the DMCA's place in my final analysis is more as part of the historical context than as a stand-alone case study.

The interfaces and technologies of digital music represent distinct material and aesthetic mediations of music that contribute to the commodification of music in its digital form. Rather than a top-down process imposed by industry onto unsuspecting consumers, the commodification of music as a digital file reveals itself as an ongoing cultural process as dependent on users as it is on industries and institutions. User labor is implicated in the production, reproduction, and circulation of the digital music commodity, though the forms this labor takes are not obvious. The commodification process is further complicated by the fact that many of the changes in digital music took place outside of the realms of traditional manufacturing, production, and marketing. The digital music commodity is surrounded by a massive legal, technical, and cultural gray area, and many of the technologies above emerged under the radar of, or at least in blind acknowledgment of, the rules and rule-makers. The stories here underscore the amount of innovation that takes place in that hazy space where cultural and technological practices have yet to stabilize or get circumscribed by law, regulation, or the normalization of corporate and economic activity.

This is more than just an issue for music. As I argue in my conclusion, at stake more broadly are questions about how we encounter commodities in our culture and what meaning those commodities have when they assume a digital form. The migration to digital files and online distribution occasions a rethinking of how culture circulates in current moments and through contemporary spaces. Books, movies, and a number of other cultural goods are currently in the midst of their own digital shifts, posing their own social, aesthetic, economic, and political challenges. Manufacturers of these other products are watching the shifting terrain of popular music with anxiety. On account of its relatively small file size, its ubiquity, and its low bandwidth requirements, music was one of the first electronic commodities (other than text documents and still images) to make its way online and to populate file-sharing networks. Music was ahead of its peers in providing a consistent (or at least recognizable) experience between its digital and nondigital forms. Music also felt the impact of digitization most intensely and immediately thanks to file sharing. The case of the recorded music industry may be particularly acute, but it signals larger changes across all cultural industries. Music is prophetic, not just theoretically (Attali 1985, 4) but more immediately: what we learn from music's migration to digital formats holds lessons for cultural commodities of all kinds.

While music has been digital for several decades now, we have only just begun buying it as a *digital* commodity and *buying into* digital consumerism as a means of handling and storing musical experiences. With an increasing amount of goods and services moving into digital forms, the history of the development of the digital music commodity provides philosophical insights into the changing nature of commodities and digital goods. It is too early to tell if the Internet, file sharing, and the digital commodity will permanently disrupt the economics or power structure of the media industries. The dramatic shift in the form and character of the music commodity has certainly shaken the foundations of traditional modes of creation, distribution, and consumption; for every glimmer of an alternative industrial structure for the music industries, there are equal reminders that complete disruption is unlikely or at least overrated. Models for the retail of digital goods seem strikingly similar to their analog precedents, and digitization has provided numerous opportunities for new forms of control and power (surveillance, data mining, advertising) that limit rather than enhance the rights of users and musicians.

The digital music commodity, however, does promise to turn our attention back toward the value and meaning of the music commodity and other objects that circulate in our social lives. A host of musicians, labels, entrepreneurs, and everyday users are engaging in experiments that put into question the conventions about how to present, use, or sell a particular digital song, album, or playback technology. These experiments force a reconsideration of the role of music in the contemporary moment and the worth we ascribe to digital goods. While the rise of the digital music commodity is clearly a technological story, the migration of music on CDs to music as digital files is not simply about making sure an old commodity is compatible with new technologies; it is a cultural process of adaptation that leaves us not just with new formats and devices but also with new ways storing, sorting, finding, buying, and experiencing music. In a world where millions of digital songs are produced each year, each one is a statement about the contours of the digital music commodity. Each one is evidence that selling the idea of digital music is no small or inevitable task, and that the reformatting of culture is still under way.

1 Music as a Digital File

OLD-TIMERS

I came along around [Winamp version] 2.03 when MP3 didn't mean anything. It was a time when if we wanted a copy of a song, we would rip WAV straight from the CD-ROM. And then a friend of mine introduced MP3 and Winamp to me and I downloaded it. I loved it ever since.

—Jstalilwyrd 2001

I've been using Winamp since v1.00 hit the scene. I think it was around May 1997. My first MP3s were encoded with L3ENC at 56 kbps, and I was proud. I turned on Creative WaveStudio and click[ed] Record, then I played the song I wanted to "rip."

—Nexxus 2001

I remember the original fraunhoffer l3enc. I remember waiting 1/2 hour to encode an MP3. I remember not being able to play a 128 kbps MP3 because my computer wasn't fast enough (I miss my 486). Those were good times.

—OneJ1Way 2001

ive used winamp since around 1.x i dont really remember. damn that was a long time ago [. . .] im only 15, but i feel so old.

—s1138 2001

Winamp was one of the first widely used programs for playing digital recorded music files on computers. The comments above come from the user forums on the Winamp website in a discussion thread from 2001 called "Old Timers," where users who remembered the "early days" of digital music could share their experiences. Put aside for a moment the specific technologies they mention (L3ENC, WAV files, CreativeWave Studio, etc.).

You may be more or less familiar with them, and for now that matters little. Consider instead the *moment* these users are describing: their first memories of recorded music on the computer. At first glance their conversation hardly seems like a very musical discussion, concerned as it is with encoding software and processor speeds. Underneath this high-tech talk, however, these "old-timers" are also bonding over fond memories of early digital audio and expressing the technical and aesthetic pleasures that came with playing music on their computers. One user even half-jokingly admits to getting "tearfully nostalgic" reading through the thread (Dellis 2001).

The user discussion above offers a snapshot of a particular moment in time: a moment when sound, technology, and interface combined in a novel way to create powerful and valuable new experiences of music. This discussion thread thus provides a fitting outline for the two main themes of this chapter. First, their discussion underscores the significant convergence that has taken place in the music and computing industries; a union that has defined the production, circulation, and consumption of recorded music for the better part of the last two decades and one that continues to have implications for how users access and experience music. The fusion of music and computing has made music a "transectorial" commodity, one that is pulled by the competing demands of various industries, actors, and devices. This has long been the case for music, but the last twenty years have intensified music's transectorial status. The resulting changes have been rapid and profound; the "old-timers" above, waxing nostalgic about what sounds like a distant past, are mostly teenagers talking about technologies that at the time of their discussion were barely five years old. The history of digital music on computers was in its opening chapters, yet here was a group of users trying to ensure that the memory of digital music's beginnings did not fade away.

Second, the Winamp users' collective stroll down memory lane speaks to the important role various pieces of software, hardware, and cultural practices played in readying music for its life in digital contexts. The affective relationship these users had with Winamp and other early computer audio technologies that mediated their initial experiences with music on the computer suggests this was more than just new gear for accessing music. The in-depth details about encoding files or the demands digital audio placed on their systems reinforce the devotion these users had for making music playable in a new environment. Their attachment to the work they carried out and to the technologies they used in the process are emblematic of a wider value relationship that was beginning to form between users and music in its digital form, as aesthetic object and as commodity.

Following these two general threads, this chapter begins by briefly reviewing some of the developments in the late 1980s and early 1990s that shepherded popular recorded music on to the computer. Winamp could not have existed without (at least) a decade-long effort on the part of computer manufacturers to create a multimedia machine that could handle the demands of digital audio. It represents the culmination of years of transectorial innovation (Théberge 1997, 58) and is a primary example of the kind of technical and cultural challenges that arise as industries and products converge. Winamp's status as a poster technology for an "MP3 generation" set on disrupting the music industry, despite its creators' ambiguous relationship with early efforts to create a market for the sale and distribution of digital music, is not just the result of technological convergence but is part of a much longer tradition of seeing computers as devices for personal transformation.

The second half of the chapter builds on this transectorial history by considering how the movement of music onto computers called into question the status and the character of the music commodity. Stripped of the physical packaging that accompanied CDs, tapes, or records, music as a digital file was initially an unmanageable commodity that was open to a virtual repackaging, a re-tuning of its interface. Winamp was a cultural interface that presented and represented sound. It filtered how users thought about, interacted with, and experienced music. Through material metaphors, it borrowed from past designs, devices, and conventions of music playback in order to transition users to newer practices (Bolter and Grusin 1999). In doing so, the media player set the context in which a digital music commodity could exist. Winamp and the migration of music onto computers represented a transitory moment that called into question the status of the recorded music product while simultaneously presenting digital music as a viable commodity. Winamp contributed to a new environment, beyond the confines of physical packaging, within which users could play, store, hear, and see music as a commodity.

SYSTEM REQUIREMENTS

Winamp launched in 1997 as one of the first and most popular full-featured MP3 and audio software players. It provided a unique and influential visual and sonic interface for users adopting new sets of practices and technologies associated with digital music. The program still exists today, as a property of the online radio network called Radionomy, though it was owned for many years by multinational media company AOL. Winamp is now one of many media players through which users can play digital music (e.g., Windows Media Player, iTunes, Spotify, etc.) though its early prominence and its unique mix of features set the standard for the design of many of today's best-known media players. Moreover, the program's interface and the practices it encouraged and discouraged contributed to one of the first coherent visions of digital music as a commodity. It repackaged music for the computer, embedding it with new paratextual materials.

Winamp's development from hobby project to an offshoot of a multimedia tech giant underscores the difficulties that arise during moments of transectorial innovation. Paul Théberge, in his study of the rise of microprocessors in the music instrument industry, refers to this mixing of diverse sectors as transectorial innovation; it is meant to signify the increasing interrelationship among once distinct industries (Piatier 1987/88; Théberge 1997). This process is more commonly referred to as convergence, though studies of convergence tend to focus on the ways the media products themselves converge. Transectorial innovation focuses on the organizational changes within the industries themselves as "each sector has become more and more dependent for its own development on all others" (Piatier 1987/88, 209). As computing and music entwine, they depend on each other not just for technologies and content but also for people, ideas, and practices (Théberge 1997, 63). Transectorial innovation is not just a technical process then; it manifests itself in all facets of production, distribution, and consumption. For digital music transectorial innovation has meant that the computing industry is now one of the key developers of new means of finding, playing, storing, and experiencing music, while the recorded music industry owns swaths of content that make computers and other high-tech products more desirable.

Transectorial networks complicate the typical view of industries as distinct entities. As convenient as shorthand descriptions like "music industry" or "computer industry" may be, they are misleading representations of the push and pull of the various groups and ideas that make up such networks (Williamson and Cloonan 2007). The "music industry," for example, is often treated synonymously with the "recording industry," when in reality there are publishers, retailers, advertisers, concert promoters, radio broadcasters, critics, journalists, and a host of tangential services that contribute to the circulation and production of music (Williamson and Cloonan 2007, 305). Given the recent amount of transectorial innovation, descriptions of the contemporary music landscape would be inadequate without including computer companies, Internet service providers, online retailers, cell phone content providers, social networks, and an increasingly important army of consumers, bloggers, podcasters, and other new media users who take part in the business of music. The music industries, in other words, extend far beyond simply recorded music to include an increasing array of technology companies with competing or at least divergent interests.

Despite the number of businesses now involved in the business of music, much of the music industries' activities are still dominated by the three main multinational companies that control approximately 70 to 80 percent of all global recorded music sales: Warner Music, Sony Music Entertainment, and Universal Music Group. These companies are "loosely integrated" and "tightly diversified" with the wider entertainment industries (Burkart and McCourt 2006, 29). Together, they own a vast amount of copyrights and other intellectual properties, and they exert significant political influence in matters of technology and intellectual property policy through industry associations and lobby groups such as the Recording Industry Association of America (RIAA) and the International Federation of the Phonographic Institute (IFPI). Historically, the dominant players in the music industries have shifted in light of new technologies of production and changing social relations. Music publishing houses gave way to record companies, which then gave way to transnational entertainment corporations (Garofalo 1999). But for the last quarter of the twentieth century the trend moved toward a smaller number of corporations that exerted a kind of oligarchic control over the flow of recorded music (Burkart 2005; Burkart 2009). This is not to minimize the impact digitization has had on the major recording labels but rather to situate the current shifts within the larger history of recorded music. Once worth approximately US$45 billion in 1997 (Hodgson 2007), recorded music has seen its value cut to less than a third of that (IFPI 2013b). Although Winamp did not draw the same kind of music industry ire that Napster would a few years later, it was nevertheless seen as an enabling technology in the movement toward music as a digital file outside the confines of the compact disc (Atwood 1997; Behar 1999; Greenfeld et al. 1999).

Winamp's emergence in 1997, then, comes at an important historical moment, one in which the political economy of the music industries was in the process of shifting as a result of transectorial innovations. But the roots of Winamp's capabilities come from a longer history of transectorial innovations in multimedia computing in the 1980s and 1990s that made a program like Winamp, and the many that would follow it, possible.

While we take sound on computers—and the ability to play CDs in them—for granted today, these capabilities are relatively recent and were not immediately obvious in the 1980s and early 1990s. The computer was not initially a device designed for the playback of popular recorded music.

The last two decades of the twentieth century, then, brought not just changes to music but also to the capabilities of both music and computers. Transectorial innovation helped translate a whole series of technologies and practices onto the computer in order to make playback of recorded music possible.

Take, for example, a piece of software called Music Box from a company named Trantor. Released in 1991 for $59, the software enabled users to play audio CDs in the CD-ROM drives of computers. Initially, CD-ROM drives played CD-ROM discs that held video games, encyclopedias, and other large database programs; they were not originally capable of reading audio CDs, with the exception of a few "audio-enabled" or "Option A" drives (Grunin 1991; Manes 1989). Music Box let users play CDs and allowed them to "choose a desired track, randomly shuffle tracks, repeat an entire disk, search forward and backward, pause a track" and more (Grunin 1991). The program also told users how much time was left in a track and on the disc. Music Box, in other words, turned the CD-ROM drive and the computer into a stereo-like device for music playback. Familiar features from CD players—like pause, search, and shuffle—were novel enough at the time to warrant special mention in Grunin's software review, an indication of how impractical the computer had previously been as a playback device.

The very existence of Trantor's program and others like it speaks to how foreign the concept of using computers for music playback was, even in the early 1990s. Sound on personal computers was an afterthought, and using the device for general music consumption was clearly a side interest for developers, at least initially (Petzold 1991). The first personal computers were marketed as office tools, as calculating machines to enhance productivity at work, and the earliest successful programs were spreadsheet applications like VisiCalc (Friedman 2005, 102–21). As personal computers started appearing in homes, consumers usually placed them in the study and treated them as extensions of the workplace with limited usefulness in other realms (Venkatesh 1996; Venkatesh and Vitalari 1987). The machines and their software were not initially designed or perceived as entertainment devices, and their audio capabilities were limited during the rise of the "personal" computers in the 1970s and 1980s (Friedman 2005; Venkatesh 1996, 48).

This is not to say computers had no entertainment purposes or sonic capabilities. Many electronic music composers had been experimenting for decades with computer music (Manning 2004), and early mainframe computers of the 1960s and 1970s were capable of, and in some cases designed specifically for, processing sound. Gaming had also been a focus of early computer development at universities, and the 1980s saw a rise in platforms that called for more capable graphic and sonic hardware and software (Dyer-Witheford and de Peuter 2005). Again, the innovations were highly transectorial: companies like Apple, Amiga, and Atari developed more elaborate soundcards for games, protocols like the Musical Instrument Digital Interface (MIDI) standard emerged in the 1980s to connect computers to instruments, and music instruments themselves became more highly computerized with the addition of processors and microchips to synthesizers (Dyer-Witheford and de Peuter 2005; Théberge 1997, 83–90; MacUser 1989)

Though these developments helped boost the computer's basic sound capabilities, the introduction of CD-ROM discs and drives proved to be Trojan horses for getting recorded music onto the computer. Originally conceived for reference, gaming, and storage purposes—many CD-ROMs were bigger than hard drives at the time—CD-ROMs also introduced users to the possibility of playing CDs on something other than a CD player. At the functional level they made CDs playable on computers. More metaphorically, they helped recontextualize music on a new device and laid the groundwork for the existence of a digital music commodity as a distinct, saleable file.

CD-ROM drives also brought verbs like *ripping* and *burning* to the music experience to signal the ability to extract data from or store data on discs (though this was more of a lexical innovation than a functional one since making a mix tape from a CD is just a less efficient version of the same process). Initially, the computer's ripping and burning capabilities were limited. When Sony and Yamaha introduced a CD burner for desktop computers in 1989, priced at a stunning $30,000, it is hard to imagine consumers were lining up for the devices (Feeley and Stefanac 1995). Although the cost would drop to a few hundred dollars a decade later (Somogyi 1998), burning music was still primarily for experienced users. A 1996 "How To" guide for burning CDs coaches users through a six-step process that involves preparing the data, partitioning the hard drive, connecting peripheral cables, and turning off all other computer applications (Breen 1996). Ripping music was equally challenging since there was no easy way to extract data from CD-ROM to a usable format on the computer. Innovative users, like those quoted at the start of this chapter, could plug a microphone into the input on their computer and digitize by recording the analog output, though this primitive ripping resulted in a noticeable decrease in audio quality (Gruberman and McQuillin 1991). Programs like cdda2wav and XingSound—which launched in 1993—were among the first to offer users the ability to rip audio, though their playback functions did not even include a "pause" button (Amorim 2007; Ness 1993). As advanced as XingSound's encoding and compression features seemed, the $100 software only let users open, play, and repeat a file (Ness 1993).

Like Trantor's Music Box, these awkward examples of ripping, burning, and playback reinforced how ill-prepared the computer was for handling the music commodity or, at least, for handling music in ways with which consumers were familiar. There was no obvious or simple connection between how music existed in CD format and how music should exist on computers. CD-ROM drives opened the door for music on the computer, though they were still not musical devices. Digitization, compression, and decoding were separate practices that each required dedicated software and hardware. Getting digital music onto the computer also required sufficient hard drive space on which to store and archive the imported content. Although a few dozen megabytes of data seems miniscule now, it was a sizable demand at the time. Computers could not readily play music collections or convert them into digital formats. As a result there are handfuls of halfway technologies like Trantor and XingSound that exist as relics of transectorial innovation in process. Computers became musical as programmers and users started conceiving of them as machines for music.

Early technologies like XingSound and Trantor were largely under the radar of record label executives. They were almost exclusively discussed and reviewed in computer magazines like *PC Magazine, Macworld,* and *CD-ROM Professional,* and they were absent from *Billboard* and *Rolling Stone.* Most record label executives had little to no knowledge of these, and those who did were often brought in as technology consultants to the labels. As Jim Griffin of Geffen Records—one of those tech consultants turned music execs—noted: "You have to remember that entertainment companies didn't even have computers on the average person's desk in 1993, 1994, 1995, or 1996. It's very, very hard to understand the future unless you participate in it" (qtd. in Haring 2000, 41). Though this started to change as tech companies started showing labels the possibilities for their artists that could be mined with CD-ROMs, interviews with label executives at the time suggest there was still widespread resistance to or ignorance of the transectorial fusions taking place (Alderman 2001; Haring 2000).

CD-ROM drives were one of the central technologies of the "multimedia revolution" of the late 1980s and early 1990s, a movement that brought a number of changes to the computer's audio and video capabilities (Friedman 2005; Venkatesh 1996, 121). Multimedia—more a cluster of technologies, applications, and hardware developments than a singular technology per se—was a "catchall phrase for the convergence of media technologies with computing" (Angell and Heslop 1993). Hardly a unified movement, the arrival of multimedia was a disorganized transectorial collision that lurched forward in fits and starts and was fueled as much by hype as by actual innovation. Even so, the vigor with which companies of all kinds embraced and pursued multimedia made it more than a benign technical description of convergence. Multimedia splashed in on a wave of promises. Articles in news and tech magazines proclaimed: "Multimedia is Here, and it's Amazing" (E. I. Schwartz 1991); and books like *Multimedia Madness* and *The Desktop Multimedia Bible* gave consumers tips on how to navigate this new media-rich landscape (Angell and Heslop 1993). As one technology researcher noted, it was "almost impossible to pick up a computer magazine these days without encountering something on 'multimedia'" (Saffo 1989). And usually that "something" was about the changes multimedia would bring: "Just a decade after it revolutionized the computer industry and the businesses of most of its customers, the personal computer is set to do it again. Before, it simply crunched numbers and processed words, throwing in the occasional bar chart or digitized sketch for decoration. Now, . . . the PC may become a 'multimedia' tool that—once again—could change the way people work, learn, and play" (Shao et al., 1989). In other words multimedia was a particular vision of what the computer could and should be. It was a way of imagining the role computers should play in our lives. In the same way that Moore's law is more of a collective goal than a scientific law (Friedman 2005, 88, Sterne 2007, 20; Auletta 2009, 52), the multimedia revolution was a disparate effort on the part of manufactures, software developers, and tech journalists to expand the market for personal computers.

Multimedia, ultimately, was another step in the technical and cultural reimagining of computing that took place throughout the 1960s, 1970s, and 1980s.[1] After their introduction as cold war technologies of bureaucracy and rationalization, the perception of computers slowly transitioned from abstract mainframe machines to "personal" devices during the second half of the twentieth century (Ceruzzi 1998; Friedman 2005; Turner 2006). Central to this shift, at least in Fred Turner's argument (2005), were the countercultural values and ideals of groups like the New Communalists, who believed fervently (if conflictingly) in the power of nature, the radical possibilities of technology, and new kinds of economic and affective commodity exchange. The New Communalist ethos of autonomous personal and collective expression through technology, Turner argues, mapped onto the social construction of early computer technologies and positioned subsequent Internet-based communities as technologies for individual and collective transformation (Turner 2005, 493). Multimedia, then, wasn't simply an isolated innovation meant to enhance the computer's technical capabilities. Rather it was part of a much longer process of domestication and personalization that sought to position computers as objects for aesthetic self-fashioning and as "small-scale technologies . . . for the transformation of consciousness and community" (Turner 2005, 489).

By the mid 1990s, users were increasingly ready for music on computers, even if computers themselves were not necessarily completely equipped for music. Early online music sites like the Internet Underground Music Archive (IUMA), launched in 1993, along with other music-based newsgroups and BBSs emerged, connecting music enthusiasts who were converting and uploading bootleg versions of concerts, creating fan sites for their favorite artists and posting MIDI files, long before most mainstream users had the computing skills or abilities to fully make use of these (Alderman 2001, 12–14; Haring 2000, 36–38). Hard-drive storage space, soundcard hardware, bandwidth, and the speed/stability of average Internet connections were still far too limited to make the transfer and use of audio files a regular practice for many, but this did not stop some users from establishing early networks of exchange based around music (sharing lyrics, files, or just discourse about music). Like other early online virtual communities (Rheingold 1994; Turkle 1995; Turner 2006; Wellman 1999), these user communities were often the earliest adopters of new technologies and were active members on the discussion forums for many new audio software products.

The development of music on computers also benefited from transectorial innovations in compression and digitization. Compression, broadly put, decreases the size of a digital file by removing excess or unneeded data, making it quicker to upload, download, or send and easier to store in larger quantities.[2] While a number of companies spent the early and mid-1990s creating new music formats intentionally designed to make sound more suitable for computers and the web, other formats emerged from developments taking place in sectors such as radio, film, and television (Sterne 2012). The MP3 format (a.k.a. MPEG-1 or 2 Audio Layer 3), for example, was the result of a transectorial consortium of radio and television broadcasters and the film industries known as the Motion Picture Experts Group. Although it's now hard to think of MP3 beyond its role as a music format, the Fraunhofer Institute—the German engineering company that began working on the MP3 format in 1987—was originally trying to design a format for compressing, transmitting, and storing the large amounts of digital video and audio data that develop during the production of broadcast content (Dowd 2006, 219; Katz 2004, 160; Sterne 2012).

Although the MP3 is widely considered the de facto standard for digital music files, there were a host of other compression and transmission formats in competition for that title in the mid-1990s. In 1995 a company called Progressive Networks (RealNetworks) introduced Real Audio, a technology that relied on a "streaming" process that broke audio files down into smaller parts and then reassembled them on the user's machine (Haring 2000, 65–66; Rothenberg 1999). Whereas downloading songs with an average residential modem then took users up to fourteen hours to access a three-minute song, streaming allowed users to listen to a file in real time (though anyone who used to stream over a slow connection knows the qualifier "real" came with a grain of salt). Other companies introduced formats of their own, like Liquid Audio, a2b, Windows Media Audio, and Advanced Audio Coding. Some of these were developed by prominent players (Microsoft, AT&T, Sony, Dolby, etc.); others came from start-ups looking to fill a new niche in the music industries (e.g., Liquid Audio), and still others, like the predecessors of what would become Ogg Vorbis were open-source community-based efforts (Haring 2000, 64–68; Xiph 2009).

Digital music's competing formats offered slightly different features and functionality. Like formats more generally, they represented a set of rules that merged technology and cultural expectations, ultimately affecting the way media content was mediated. As Sterne argues, format "denotes a whole range of decisions that affect the look, feel, experience and workings of a medium. It also names a set of rules according to which a technology can operate" (2012, 7). Usually, these codes or rules are not particularly visible—the MP3's compression algorithm, for example, is based on a century's worth of research on human hearing and perception—so they often seem like they're part of the essence of the object. Formats are part of the wider protocols that govern technology (Galloway 2004; Gitelman 2006). Protocols, like formats, encompass both the specific technical details of how technology and media work, as well as the conventions of how people use new devices, how they access them, and a whole series of economic and social infrastructure elements (Gitelman 2006). Taking the phone as an example, Lisa Gitelman considers the social protocols that surround the device: the convention of answering with "Hello," the economics of billing and rate plans, the type of access (home phones, public pay phones, etc.), the type of call (conference calls, long-distance calls, etc.), and other aspects of phone use (2006, 7). Since these protocols affect the uses and ends to which media and technologies can be put, they are, at their core, about control. They are a way to ensure certain outcomes or at least limit the possible number of uses to which a device or technology can be put.

Protocols are especially effective in an age driven by digital technology, where they are often embedded in the software. For Alexander Galloway these protocols play out in code: "Code is a set of procedures, actions, and practices, designed in particular ways to achieve particular ends in particular contexts. Code = Praxis" (Galloway 2004, xii). Format decisions, then, are as technical as they are social; they affect how files work but also the kinds of uses and meanings that develop around certain technologies and media. Music as code meant that the experience of music as a digital file would be a different one from digital music on CDs. Although each format (Real, MP3, Liquid, etc.) had distinct technical attributes and features (higher versus lower audio fidelity, better versus worse security, etc.), the real differences between the files were in their protocols: what users could and could not do with the files and the software that accompanied them. Some formats, like Liquid Audio, were proprietary and came with restrictions on how they could be used or played (see chapter 4 for further discussion). Others, like Ogg, were available for use by anyone. The MP3 was a hybrid of the two models. Although users could get and play MP3s on a variety of players and devices without any kind of payment, developers of MP3 playback software had to pay royalties to the format's "proprietary" creators, after a certain level of commercial activity (Borland 2000; Hansen and Van Buskirk 2007a; Sterne 2012; Xiph 2009). Open or proprietary, the protocols of each format offered their own version of the digital music experience. The differences between streaming and downloading, or the rest of digital music's various formats, were each expressions of what digital music should and could be.

I dwell on this microhistory of multimedia, formats, and protocols to underscore how Winamp emerged from a particular moment in both the music and computing industries. Far from a preplanned industry-sanctioned format change, like the move to compact discs, recorded music on computers was a messy by-product of transectorial innovation in the 1980s and 1990s. Winamp arrived at a time when the hype around multimedia was starting to congeal in audio and video technologies that made personal computers more personal. Through their growing capacity to play, share, and distribute music, personal computers were being marketed as devices that could, through multimedia, unlock creative and expressive potentials (Streeter 2010). Despite the promises of these marketing campaigns though, and the possibilities hinted at by CD-ROM drives, soundcards, and ripping/burning software and hardware, digital music playback was still hindered by the complexity and variety of these transectorial technologies. Music's availability on the computer was by no means haphazard, but it was also not a cohesive or coherent shift driven by one industrial sector at the expense of another. Rather, the recorded music commodity made its way onto the computer because of disparate innovations in CD-ROM technology and other hardware/software, the growth of online communities like the IUMA and other hobbyist services and devices, and a host of music- and technology-based businesses with an interest in developing new formats of accessibility for music. It was only thanks to this series of interrelated but incohesive transectorial developments that users were able to enjoy audio on their computers. The parameters for the commodity form for music's new digital format were still very much in question.

BUILDING WINAMP

Credit for Winamp generally belongs to Justin Frankel, a self-schooled computer whiz who designed Winamp as a means to play MP3s and other digital files he was finding online (Greenfeld et al. 1999; Kushner 2004).[3] He released the first version of Winamp in April 1997 as freeware. As the program's user base increased, Frankel and others developing the software solicited donations from interested users, which brought in enough revenue to pay for the bandwidth and hosting fees for Winamp's heavily trafficked website and for a used car for Frankel (Bronson 1998; Haring 2000, 99). Known more formally as "shareware," this release strategy is relatively common for upstart software programs. Sometimes the software's functionality is limited unless users donate, but in the early stages of Winamp, the $10 contribution was just that, a contribution, since the free version of the program was fully functional.

Winamp's rapid growth also brought more traditional revenue sources like advertising, ranging from partnerships with music sites such as Artist Direct; high-tech entities like IBM, Compaq, Hotmail, and ZDNet; and more traditional companies like Toyota and Eddie Bauer (Alderman 2001, 56; Winamp 1998). The business model of giving the primary product away for free in an attempt to gain awareness and an audience for advertisers was very much in keeping with other tech start-ups during the dot-com boom (Ankerson 2010), and it allowed Frankel to incorporate a company called Nullsoft—a nerdy jab at the dominance of software giant Microsoft. After a year and a half online Winamp.com was bringing in $8,000 a month in advertising and the software had more than fifteen million users (Greenfeld et al. 1999; Kushner 2004). Although the ultimate business plan for the company was still relatively unclear, the program's early success pointed to the potential market that might exist around digital music. More important, given that the program was one of the earliest available software media players, as more users started playing music on computers, Winamp's features and functionalities established conventions for how music was made visible and audible on computers.

Despite Nullsoft's reliance on commercial tactics like advertising, the company still saw itself and its software as an underdog and anti-industrial in nature. Part of the reason for this image was because of Winamp's affiliation with MP3 files. Nullsoft marketed the software as *the* player for MP3 files. The format leaked from Fraunhofer to wider web users in the mid-1990s and quickly drew criticism from record labels and the RIAA because it offered little means for tracking copyright infringement. Although some labels were curious about the possibilities of digital music and worked with the likes of IUMA or Liquid Audio on digital strategies to promote lesser-known artists, the majority drew the line when it came to MP3s (Alderman 2001, 15, 40; Haring 2000, 40). Labels and the RIAA ordered sites hosting MP3s to shut down and waged a public relations campaign against the format and any company supporting it (Alderman 2001, 30; Haring 2000, 41). The popularity of MP3s and the perceived threat the format posed to traditional distribution and consumption channels for popular music meant that, as *Billboard* writer Brett Atwood (1997) noted, "The music industry should be afraid—*very* afraid." As such, most of the major record labels looked skeptically on technologies like Winamp that depended on the widespread availability of MP3s (Behar 1999; Greenfeld et al. 1999).

Nullsoft turned this anti-industrial image into one of its key messages to users. From the irreverent news updates on the Winamp website to the program's quirky slogan—"Winamp, it really whips the llama's ass"—the company actively positioned itself as a subversive upstart that hoped to upend music consumption. The company used the open nature of MP3 files to position its player as a source for limitless listening. It also stressed how use of Winamp could turn everyday users into producers through features such as SHOUTcast—a cross-platform streaming technology that allowed for the recording and broadcasting of MP3 audio streams. Foreshadowing features that would emerge half a decade later in the form of podcasting, social playlisting, and other forms of user-generated content, SHOUTcast foregrounded the ease with which anyone could become a broadcaster or radio DJ, share songs and build an audience, as well as increase the diversity of audio options available on the Internet (Frankel et al. 1999, 239). It was rhetoric that was repeated by users of the technology. As one prominent early SHOUTcaster noted: "You want an example of my nightmare . . . ? Turn on your FM radio and spin around the dial. Welcome to my hell. You want an example of my heart's desire? Tune in to SHOUTcast streams, turn on to creativity and individualism and drop out of the bland regulated waves that pass for most broadcasts" (Frankel et al. 1999, 284).

Winamp's anti-industrial marketing stance is most explicit in the three-hundred-plus-page book *MP3 Power! With Winamp* (Frankel et al. 1999). Ostensibly a how-to guide for using Winamp and other digital music technologies, the book pits millions of technology users and music lovers against a slow and out-of-touch music industry: "Call it an audio or musical renaissance of sorts, we will see a revival of artistic progress and achievement. The power to join this renaissance is right here" (Frankel et al. 1999, 15). From the book's cover—lightning bolts striking through previous generations of audio technology like an old radio, a tabletop jukebox, and a gramophone—to its lengthy descriptions of different digital music services for the computer, the authors argue that digital music is not just a format but a movement: "In fact, what was once the moniker and file extension of just another file format has grown to a technology used by millions of people and is on the verge of revolutionizing the entire music and audio industry. . . . MP3 is a format, but to think of it as strictly just a format is truly missing the point of what it has actually become" (Frankel et al. 1999, 31). The book's charged graphics and language were a call-to-arms to use Winamp and join the MP3 revolution. Users of Winamp or MP3s were not just exploring the possibilities of a new musical format; they were leading-edge adopters taking a stand against the unequal distribution of power in the recorded music industry.

This revolutionary rhetoric is not entirely surprising. Like the hype that accompanied the drive toward multimedia more generally, *MP3 Power!* suggests that through Winamp users could hold the balance of power over the corporations that had traditionally controlled the flow of recorded music. While entrepreneurs often seek out means of infusing particular objects or practices with radical disruptive capabilities in order to bolster their appeal (T. Frank 1997; Heath 2005; Klein 2000), this logic is also where the transectorial ideas and values surrounding the personal computer map onto the industrial and popular discourse around the music commodity. This anticommercial and disruptive discourse was particularly common during the high-tech boom of the 1990s and dates back to historical discourses about computing, personal liberation, and social transformation through technology (Barbrook 1996; Streeter 2010; Turner 2006). It is part of what Thomas Streeter refers to as the "romantic framing of computer use," a framing from decades of marketing and cultural discourses that have marked the computer as "playful, expressive, even rebellious" and have created a kind of "rebel-hero identity" not just for software and tech industry workers but also for users (Streeter 2010, 68). Despite revolutionary claims, the charged language surrounding Winamp was entirely consistent with more general discourse about the personal computer over several decades.

Winamp's rhetoric is problematically misleading though. While Winamp was a disruptive technology on some level, Nullsoft's anti-industrial messaging diverted attention away from the ways in which Winamp, through its interface, was simultaneously sketching out the contours for a sellable digital music commodity and selling the idea of the computer as the future device for music playback. Winamp's anti-industrial image first came into question in June 1999, when Internet media giant AOL purchased the start-up for $100 million as part of a $400 million deal involving other online music entities (Kushner 2004; Tedesco 1999). Even though Shawn Fanning had just released Napster that same month, digital music on computers, at the time, was still primarily a fringe activity. AOL saw the Nullsoft acquisition as an opportunity to bring digital music to mainstream users and to bring some industrial legitimacy to these new technologies for media consumption (Kushner 2004; Tedesco 1999).

Many Winamp enthusiasts who were drawn to the anti-industrial aspects of the software and digital music were unhappy about the AOL sale and equated it with selling out (Kushner 2004), but Nullsoft's relationship with its new mass media owners was marked by tension. Working styles at the start-up clashed with AOL's overly corporate approach (Alderman 2001, 146–47). Take, for example, the March 2000 launch of Gnutella, a Napsteresque application Nullsoft designed and released. Gnutella was a program/protocol that let users share files through a largely decentralized system of peers (similar to Napster, though without relying on a central server to house and index files). Gnutella seemed both a competitive response to Napster and a public relations retort to critics of the AOL acquisition; when Frankel and his colleague uploaded the program, they included a note saying, "Justin and Tom work for Nullsoft, makers of Winamp and SHOUTcast. See? AOL CAN bring you good things!" (Kushner 2004). AOL was pulled in opposing directions. On the one hand the company was aggressively acquiring new technologies and software programmers to develop its online presence. On the other hand it was also looking to expand its ties to the content industries, making deals with major record labels and considering a proposed merger with Time Warner. To be fit to merge, AOL had to present itself as a good corporate citizen, one that respected the content and copyrights of its potential partner(s). Ultimately, AOL distanced itself from Gnutella, claiming it was an "unauthorized freelance project" on Nullsoft's part. A day after Gnutella was uploaded, AOL shut down the site (Kushner 2004; C. Jones 2000).[4]

The troubled relationship between Nullsoft and AOL is not just a story of different working styles. It speaks to the difficulties that arise when companies with interests in multiple industries collide. Winamp was not necessarily the first program to allow music playback on the computer, but its popularity and the ways in which it promoted the use of digital music made it a threatening piece of software for record labels and even for its mass media owners, AOL. Had Nullsoft been working on an isolated program that was limited to a specific practice or industry, little fuss would have been made. Instead, as part of AOL, the programs Nullsoft developed affected the field of computing, as well as the entertainment and cultural industries. Frankel and his colleagues had envisioned digital music as an alternative form of music consumption and Winamp as a small player in a wider attack against the traditional music industries. These ideas were sometimes in step with, and other times at odds with, the goals of its corporate owners. Perhaps unsurprisingly, then, by 2004 almost all of the Winamp team's original members had left (Kushner 2004).

Winamp's rapid growth owes a debt to the fact that it operated in a kind of industrial and economic liminal space: *between* sectors in a marketplace where legal and commercial boundaries had yet to form. Nullsoft was allowed, perhaps even encouraged, to work on projects like Gnutella because the conventions of this new market and product were still being worked out. Winamp was an exemplary case of transectorial innovation and of the wider economic and technical developments taking place during the dotcom boom and bust. But while Nullsoft may have presented itself, through Winamp and Gnutella, as an industrial threat and a reimagination of the way users consume and experience music, it was also looking to create and capitalize on digital music's emerging market. Although this somewhat contradictory image is evident from the above sketch of Winamp's evolution from hobby project to AOL property, it is even clearer from an analysis of the original software's interface and key features. Winamp's look and feel seemed like a radical reconfiguration of music consumption practices. On closer examination, though, Winamp's design provided a new kind of packaging for music in its digital form, making it a unique and distinct experience that opened up the possibility for the commodification of music as a digital file.

RE-TUNING THE INTERFACE

The transectorial movement of music onto computers called into question music's sonic and visual materials. Over the last century, recorded music has taken on several different forms (records, tapes, CDs, etc.), and each one has presented challenges for the various actors seeking to profit from it (Garofalo 1999; Eisenberg 2005). Despite the widely different designs, interfaces, and abilities of these technologies, the recorded music commodity has maintained several enduring characteristics. The media, usually fragile, is typically wrapped in some kind of packaging that is at once protective and descriptive. It bears functional features like the spine or barcode that help consumers order their collections or retailers track their sales. But the music commodity is much more than this. It includes paratexts—like images, artwork, liner notes, song names, lyrics, production details, etc.— that play a role in shaping how users find, sort, and receive value from the music (Gray 2010; Straw 2009, 86). The packaging, in other words, is not simply a neutral container for the end product. It is the stuff that gives the music commodity its exchange value and provides the materials and symbols through which listeners make sense of the sounds and songs within.

On computers, digital music files transcode music from a defined product in a relatively contained format to one among many other data documents that populate a user's computer. This leaves digital files of recordings drifting in a transitory state: not fully commodities yet not wholly detached from the broader forces, materials, and symbols that make popular music a commodity in the first place. To be sure, this digital drift began in the mid-1990s as mixed CDs and the general circulation of CDs (in cars, portable CD players, etc.) separated discs from their packaging (Straw 2009, 85). We might even consider as far back as the jukebox and the way it presented single songs as detached from the album recording. The difference with digital files, however, is that they migrated not only away from their packaging but toward the computer, toward a new environment through which to see, hear, use, and understand the product. Mixed CDs may have come with a user's handcrafted packaging, and jukebox songs may have encouraged single-song consumption, but neither offered the wholly different combination of packaging and consumption that digital files represent. The jukebox, for example, still relied on foregrounding the song name, the artists name, and the packaging from the album from which the song came. The micromaterials that eventually made up digital music's packaging, however, were much more embedded and integral, affecting both the presentation and use of the song files in question. As Taylor rightfully asserts, recorded music is not always a commodity, or not always consistently the same form of commodity; instead, it undergoes "constant periods of commodification and decommodification" (2007, 282). The ripping of music from CDs and their subsequent expression through software like Winamp meant that temporarily and partially, the aesthetic and economic aspects of the commodity form were in flux, from both industrial and consumer points of view. What should digital music look and sound like? How should it function? What should users be able to do with music on computers? The answers to many of these questions were, for a time, mutable and not necessarily given.

In this light the advent of Winamp can be read as an attempt to fill in some of the gaps between music's previous commodity form and its future shape created by digitization. In the simplest terms Winamp is a computing solution. The problem was a desire to play MP3s and other digital music files on personal computers. The program, however, also addressed a cultural issue: to play music on a new device in a way that was as usable and understandable as it had been on previous playback devices. Winamp was neither the first software media player of its kind nor even the most capable (Fraunhofer's WinPlay3 in 1995 or a versatile program called MuseArc probably deserve those honors). But Winamp was perhaps the first to understand, or at least internalize, the cultural dimensions of technological innovation and incorporate them into the design process. In doing so, Winamp's interface familiarized users with music playback on computers.

A journalist interviewing Frankel explains the motives behind Winamp's look: "[Frankel] wanted to build [a software player] that would look as familiar as a home stereo, with the sound quality jacked up with effects like 3-D surround sound and reverb. He also wanted a playlist feature that allowed you to sort MP3 tracks or play them randomly like a jukebox" (Greenfeld et al. 1999). The result was software that resembled a cross between a car radio and a CD player (Frankel et al. 1999, 48). It had the functionality of a CD player and the look and style of a high-end stereo's front panel. In many ways Winamp's transectorial roots became visible through its interface; the design hinted at conventions from computing, recording technology, and stereo playback devices.

Like media more generally, interfaces are hardly neutral conveyors of messages. They are designed with specific goals in mind, with certain affordances and prescriptions. Manovich notes that "the interface shapes how the computer user conceives of the computer itself. It also determines how users think of any media object accessed via a computer. Stripping different media of their original distinctions, the interface imposes its own logic on them" (Manovich 2001, 65). Decisions at the level of the interface promote or encourage some behaviors or modes of interaction and make others "unthinkable" (Manovich 2001, 64). Manovich notes that while interfaces have traditionally been associated with the Graphical User

Interface (GUI), media interfaces increasingly include sonic and tactile feedback that incorporate other senses (Manovich 2013, 29). Hardly just a visual affair, media interfaces are multisensory meeting points between humans, computers, and cultural content. They condition users' relationships with the computer and with the media objects with which they interact on the computer; they are a sociocultural mode of representing and experiencing information. This is not to suggest the design of an interface determines an object's use but that an object's features and attributes come embedded with expectations about use, and these expectations reveal something about the object, the people who made it, and those who use it (Latour 1988, 306).

Winamp's interface included basic controls like play, pause, skip tracks, and the like, but it was how the software presented these features aesthetically that made Winamp novel. Just as Bolter and Grusin argue that what's new about new media is the way they refashion or remediate older media (Bolter and Grusin 1999), Winamp took ideas from previous audio playback devices and other genres of software and reconfigured them into a digital music player. Its main reference points were standard CD or tape players, car stereo panels, and hi-fi stereo systems, but it combined these features with the modular aspects of digital software to create novel audio experiences.

Put more theoretically, Winamp is a collection of skeuomorphs: "a design feature that is no longer functional in itself but that refers back to a feature that was functional at an earlier time" (Hayles 1999, 17). Originally a term from archaeology and architecture, *skeuomorph* points us to the design leftovers that persist through various iterations of objects, programs, and devices. For example, plastic tables that have a wood-grain pattern on their surface, the copper color of zinc pennies, or the recorded "click" you hear when the "shutter" on a digital camera takes a picture are all skeuomorphic in nature. Skeuomorphs extend the concept of remediation by helping explain the appearance of the old within the new. They are particularly prevalent in software, since designers regularly borrow cues and signals from the noncomputer applications they are trying to emulate. Though graphical representations of trash cans or the "files" and "folders" that resemble those in our office drawers don't necessarily originate with application software, these icons are certainly an integral part of the graphical user interfaces of everyday computing. The presence of these features on our "desktops" no longer attests to their original functions, yet the ideas they represent remain embedded in the design.

Skeuomorphs are more than just a design concept, though; they are templates for thought and experience: "Skeuomorphs are material metaphors.

They are informational attributes of artifacts which help us find a path through unfamiliar territory. They help us map the new onto an existing cognitive structure, and in so doing, give us a starting point from which we may evolve additional alternative solutions. They provide us with 'a path' instead of 'no path' at all" (Gessler 1998, 230). Skeuomorphs, then, are crucial for innovation. The incorporation and remediation of past appearances and design ideas smooth the process of adoption and makes new technologies feel more familiar. Skeuomorphs borrow from the past to make the future possible in the present. New interfaces and technologies are always a careful balance between the new and the known. As N. Katherine Hayles suggests, new innovations put in play "a psychodynamic that finds the new more acceptable when it recalls the old that it is in the process of displacing and finds the traditional more comfortable when it is presented in a context that reminds us we can escape from it into the new" (Hayles 1999, 17). Skeuomorphs are vestiges that represent the material weight of the past on the present (and the future).

Winamp's early design remediates previous audiovisual conventions and presents them in new ways to provide a novel music-listening experience. The very idea of playing music on the computer was still so new that Winamp's design had to account for the fact that, for many users, Winamp was their first experience with digital music. Winamp mimicked practices users knew in order to make the process of adapting to new behaviors less daunting. It included enough associations to older media devices (CD players, videocassette players, etc.) to feel familiar while also introducing enough new features (visualizations, customizable playlists, skins, etc., which I describe below) to make it a distinct musical experience. Winamp also used the modular quality of the digital platform to give users added control and customization options over how the player appeared and how the music sounded. As a program that introduced millions of users to music on the computer, Winamp had the twin task of acclimatizing users to a new technology for music consumption and, more broadly, teaching them to treat computers as multimedia devices that could be part of a home sound system. Nullsoft had to promote Winamp, the program, but it also had to sell users on the idea of digital music as a possible new format for music consumption.

Winamp's main window (see fig. 2) was a small console that contained the essential song data and the playback controls (Frankel et al. 1999, 48). Users could add songs to the "playlist" window, which allowed for reconfigurable lists of songs to be played back in sequence or "shuffled" into a random order. This allowed for new kinds of musical organization—

Figure 2. Winamp main window (version 2.0). Winamp's main playback window, featuring transport controls (play, pause, stop, etc.), volume, file details, and the spectrum analyzer (the bars underneath the time code).

playlists for certain moods (e.g., relaxing music), times of day (e.g., dinner tunes), occasions (e.g., party mix), or more personal/eccentric choices (e.g., songs my dog likes). Playlists could range from a few songs to thousands, providing hours or days of continuous music. Winamp was not the first media player to make use of this feature, nor was this practice simply the result of a shift to digital music software (Drew 2005; Razlagova 2013). Digital playlists draw from practices established by radio DJs as early as the 1930s and 1940s (Razlagova 2013, 64–65). Radio playlists, though they varied from station to station and DJ to DJ, presented a multiplicity of connections that could be made across individual songs, either for artistic, commercial, or other goals. Although the role of the radio, and radio DJs by extension, is in the midst of its own set of shifts brought on by digital technologies and automated playlists, the radio playlist remains a powerful frame for users' understanding of music discovery and continues to inform much of the way users make sense of current digital music playback software (Razlagova 2013, 65).

I discuss playlists and their similarity to pre-Winamp practices such as mixed tapes and CDs further in chapter 4, but it is important to highlight here that what distinguishes Winamp from these earlier forms was that it was one of the first players to put the potential of playlists on display by making them a central part of the program's interface. Winamp's playlist window transferred the ability to design a radio-like playlist to the user and made the mixed-disc-making process visible and immediate. Winamp was one of the first players to realize that the disaggregation of music from its album actually opened the music commodity up for new forms of aggregation.

Figure 3. Winamp equalizer and playlist window (version 2.0). Winamp's equalizer controls contributed to the stereo-like feel of the interface. The playlist window allowed users to cue tracks up for future listening.

Winamp's main window also housed the Spectrum Analyzer: a series of bars that rise and fall based on the frequencies of the song that is playing and an equalizer (EQ) feature (Frankel et al. 1999, 49). Similar in concept to some of the high-end stereo systems or portable audio devices available at the time, the EQ window let users affect and customize the sound by moving volume sliders (see fig. 3). The spectrum analyzer and the EQ sliders placed Winamp in a long line of high fidelity technologies that came with their own class, gender, and taste assumptions. Keir Keightley's excellent analysis of the rise of high-fidelity audio culture in the 1950s and 1960s notes how hi-fi technologies like stereos, receivers, and amplifiers were often positioned as highbrow and masculine, especially compared to lowbrow feminine technologies like the television or radio (Keightley 2003). The marketing and social discourses around hi-fi technologies seemed to encourage active manipulation and fine tuning while television and radio were seen as merely passive technologies for consumption. Despite the significant investment required for hi-fi gear, hi-fi was made to seem less commercial, more intellectual, and mostly removed from commodification (Keightley 2003, 241). Hi-fi also offered an opportunity for men to carve out a uniquely male leisure space within the home, often at odds with the domestic space as it had previously existed—an "apartness" within the "togetherness" of the home (Keightley 2003, 247).

Winamp's user forums offer some evidence that the hi-fi features of the program appealed to male users' desires to manipulate and affect the sound in a more active way than simply consuming it. Several threads on the

Winamp forums are dedicated to debates about sound quality and tips around how to enhance sound quality through various plugins:

> My fave DSP plug-in is Audiostocker. Dee and Enhancer are popular also (do a search on the plug-ins page), but I find they distort the sound too much for me. . . . Winamp is pretty basic with the initial download, and certainly needs some tweaking when you first get it, but it allows for so much more variety than other players because there are so many plug-ins, etc. It allows you to get the sound that is right for your ears and your hardware. There is a forum for plug-ins you may want to browse for info. There is no one "right" configuration. Stick around and learn a few things about the player and I think you'll really like it. (Sandman2012, 2002)

Users also debated the virtues of CD quality sound versus digital audio files and generated countless threads about the best quality soundcards (e.g., Soundblaster live platinum 5.1, X-Gamer 5.1, Diamond MX-300), speakers (Altec-Lansing, JBL, Bose, Boston, etc.), headphones (Sennheiser HD 280 Pro, Sony MDR-V600, etc.), and other audio hardware and software for sound playback.

Considering the perceived lack of sound quality MP3s provide compared to other audio formats, the inclusion of the visual equalizer thus served as a response to a broader criticism against digital music. MP3s have frequently been "singled out as particularly 'diminished' forms of recording" (Sterne 2006a, 339). Because the sound is compressed, and sonic data is removed in favor of making smaller and more transmissible files, MP3s are often seen as degraded when compared to compact discs or vinyl records: "the success of reduced fidelity media has been at the cultural expense of attention to quality, aesthetics and the ideals of accuracy and truth" (Rothenbuhler 2012, 39). For audiophiles and critics of compressed formats, fidelity, the truthfulness of the reproduction to the original, is what is at stake here.[5] Compression and other artifacts from the encoding process create a greater distance between the original recording and its digitized reproduction. The result is that the power of the sound itself is somehow diminished (McCourt 2005; Rothenbuhler 2012; Rothenbuhler and Peters 1997). Set aside for a moment the criticism that all recordings are already copies of a highly constructed "event" (i.e., studio sessions with multi-track recordings and other production interventions) whose own claims to truth are questionable. Instead, the issue over fidelity and devaluation is likely more a question of competing notions of value. Rather than promising the highest audio quality, the MP3 follows a trend in the history of recording technologies that focuses more on portability, easy storage, and exchange rather than higher fidelity (Sterne 2012; Rothenbuhler 2012). Digital music is part of a historical mode of listening—what Daniel Guberman (2011) calls the era of "post-fidelity"—where audio quality is only one among many factors that determine a user's attachment to a format (and no longer the primary one, as was the case with most formats leading up to the CD).

Winamp's media interface, with its visual and sonic features, can thus be seen as an attempt to persuade (largely male) audiophiles of the benefits of digitally compressed audio files. The discourse of the loss of fidelity was, at least at the time of Winamp's launch, a hurdle digital music had to overcome among some audiences. By giving users the ability to manipulate a visual representation of the sound spectrum, Nullsoft was trying to engage listeners with the sonic aspects of the music and to provide them the opportunity to improve and personalize the sound. MP3s may not have offered the highest quality sound around, but with Winamp it was at least sound that could be bettered. Though it's hard to say with any certainty whether the male users in the forums used Winamp in similar ways as early hi-fi users, and the discourse in Nullsoft's marketing is less explicitly gendered than the hi-fi advertisements Keightley examines, the design of its features suggests it is attempting to appeal to the same culture of audiophiles. The spectrum analyzer and the EQ sliders were skeuomorphs that generated a visual illusion of high fidelity; they position Winamp as a multisensorial media player, one that might be just interactive enough to convince skeptical audiophiles the computer could be an acceptable device for music playback.

Along with the Spectrum Analyzer and the EQ sliders, early versions of Winamp extended digital music's visual interface by including "visualizations" (see fig. 4). Abstract, computer-generated graphics that played along in real-time with the music, visualizations have their roots in the "demoscene," a computer art subculture that combined programming skills, art, and eventually music (Carlsson 2009; Green 1995; Maher 2012). In the mid-1980s, as home computers gained prominence, hobbyists and hackers started experimenting with the computer's capabilities by "cracking" software—removing its copy protections to share it more widely or simply for the technical challenge (Carlsson 2009, 16). To call attention to their cracks, users started attaching short audiovisual animations or "signatures" called demos to the cracked software (Carlsson 2009; Green 1995). Gradually, demos evolved into an art form of their own. They were disarticulated from the practice of cracking but still required artistic and technical skill. The community that formed around these demos—largely white middle-class teenage males from northern Europe and the United States (Carlsson 2009,

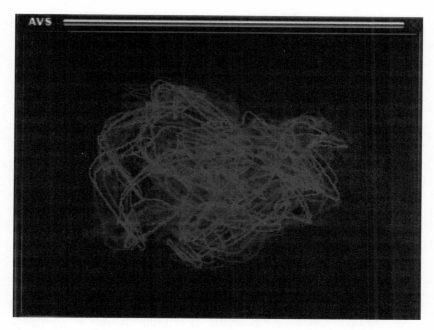

Figure 4. Winamp visualizer (version 2.0). Winamp's visualizer added abstract visuals that changed according to the characteristics of the music.

17)—produced thousands of demos and even held rave-like "demoparties" and psychedelic coding competitions.

Many demoscene participants went on to work in videogame and software industries. Jeff Minter, who also designed some of the visualizations for the Xbox 360, had developed what he called a "virtual light machine" (VLM) in 1990 through the demoscene (Minter 2005). Minter used it primarily to project visuals at parties, raves, and even a few concerts, but he worked over the following decade to develop commercial uses for his software (e.g., Atari). Although Minter didn't go on to work for Nullsoft, Winamp's visualizations owe a large aesthetic debt to work like Minter's and that of other demoscene participants. In Minter's own account of the history of visualizations, he describes a run-in with a Nullsoft employee who "apologized for 'borrowing' the techniques I'd used on the [Atari] Jaguar VLM for their own visualizations" (Minter 2005).

Visualizations added to the "pleasurable" aspects of music listening by triggering both visual and aural interaction. As Michel Chion (1994) has argued about sound and film, imagery and music have a particular way of working together that results in a different experience than if both were taken in independently. Since visualizations are tied to the musical attributes of the song, visualizations promote the act of watching while listening to music. Like music videos, laser light shows, and other visual paratexts, visualizations act as meta-artworks that use sound as the basis for an additional artistic statement. The visuals refract and reflect the sound and enhance the audiovisual experience. Again, Winamp may not have been the first program to use visualizations, but it helped popularize a stylized way of seeing sound on the computer, a stylistic interpretation of sonic characteristics rooted in demoscene aesthetics that asked users to consider what there was to see in what they were hearing. Visualizations offered another way to "listen" to music, one that entailed watching a cascade of colors, lines, and shapes moving in time with the beat and in tune with the pitch. They ushered music into computing environments in a visually particular way.

Winamp's various windows came wrapped in a graphical casing called a "skin." Users could choose from several different skins, each of which gave the player a unique look (see fig. 5). Nullsoft designed several standard skins, but there was also a subcommunity of Winamp users who designed their own visual faceplates for the music player. Unlike a home stereo, Winamp came with hundreds of skins to which users had access to customize the look of the program. Along with Winamp's other key features (visualizations, EQ controls, playlists), skins can be seen as part of a larger move toward mass customization in consumer marketing (Andrejevic 2002, 253–58). More important, although Nullsoft didn't sell these "skins," the user-generated designs were an early instance of what would become a more comprehensive integration of user labor into future music services (as is the case over the following chapters). The transectorial mix of software and music opened up new opportunities for hobbyist software developers to work and rework music's paratexts through their programming skills.

Although we should be skeptical of claims promising greater interactivity (Andrejevic 2007), especially when the actual amount of power and control afforded to users is still relatively limited and when that interactivity was tied to gendered and classed conceptions of hi-fi audio manipulation, Winamp's modular interface encouraged a high level of interaction with the music. Even though the interface was another layer of data between users and their information, the ability to directly manipulate these features made it seem as though users, not the computer, were responsible for affecting the music's look and sound (S. Johnson 1997, 21). Instead of putting a CD in the stereo and walking away, users could now play with

Figure 5. Winamp skin. An example of one of the hundreds of "skins" users designed for the program that mimics the front panel of a traditional stereo system.

the look of the device through which they played music (via skins), the sound of the music (via the EQ and spectrum analyzer), and the look of the sound (via visualizations). This modularity helped "sell" the digital dimensions of digital music; Winamp's flexible and customizable design was further support that computers were not just abstract machines but tools for personal expression and self-fashioning through music.

Taken together, these features were some of the first components of the re-tuning of music's interface. Though "skins" were the most visible and direct manifestation of this process, features of Winamp's like the equalizer window, visualizations, and playlist capabilities played a crucial role in reestablishing the music commodity's paratexts in digital form. Users were constantly tweaking and altering the interface and experiencing music's sonic and visual micromaterials in the process. Through Winamp's interface, music as a digital file became visible, audible, and realizable as a distinct musical experience. Winamp's interface was one of the first to show users what music looked like on the computer and what they could do with it and to it. It gave digital music digital packaging.

Despite some of the new practices Winamp encouraged, the program was also weighed down by the design of previous audio technologies and previous music playback conventions. Winamp's volume sliders, for example, could have been blank boxes to which users could assign a numerical value that would dictate the volume. The play and rewind buttons could have been a scroll wheel, with the ability to set the direction and playback speed of a song. All these options are possible within the digital realm (and can be found in alternative software) but they are not options Winamp espouses. Instead, the software is designed to mimic the interfaces users had experience with via existing sound playback devices.

These skeuomorphic choices are, like the "files" and "folders" on the "desktop" of our computers, only one possible system of expression among many (Manovich 2001, 70). Culturally, however, there is a certain weight to this particular organization, one that depends on familiarity, habit, and practice. Such is the influence of skeuomorphic interfaces (Bolter and Grusin, 1999; Hayles, 1999); they integrate not only past design features but also past practices and previous ways of thinking: "We tend to fashion objects skeuomorphically. Once thought is given material substance, it is not always clear what is a skeuomorph and what is not" (Gessler 1998, 231). Skeuomorphic design is, in these respects, conservative as a design strategy. By depending on a logic that uses familiarity with previous ways of thinking, previous ways of seeing as a way to make the new seem less new, skeuomorphs perpetuate old patterns, practices, and conceptual frameworks, even if the technology itself has progressed beyond it. While Nullsoft's marketing stance positioned Winamp as an upstart technology set to reconfigure listening practices, the program wouldn't have been as successful had it tried to completely reinvent some of the more fundamental elements of music playback and consumption.

Winamp's features evidenced a tension between newer and older ways of handling music. Take, for example, the kinds of formats Winamp was able to play back. Even though Winamp played a range of file formats, the program was primarily designed for MP3s that users found on the Internet (Frankel et al. 1999; Winamp 1997–99). Winamp could play audio from CDs, for example, but this was initially an arduous task. For the first few years of the software's existence, playing CD audio required the use of an obscure plug-in called Nullsoft CD/Line Input Player v0.100 (see "Advanced Winamp Configurations Guide" in Frankel et al. 1999). This would likely not have stopped knowledgeable computer users, but the fact that CD compatibility was a plug-in, a technical afterthought, suggests that activities like managing and playing CD audio were not motivating forces in Winamp's initial design. Early versions of Winamp also omitted many of the CD handling tools now common in media players. Users, for example, could not "rip" or "burn" CDs solely through Winamp until the launch of Winamp 5, in 2003 (five years after its initial release). Even then, the extent to which users could take advantage of these features depended on which version of the software (free, full, or pro) they had signed up for.

Winamp's features and skeuomorphic interface suggested that its designers saw the program originally as a stereo system: it was a playback device, not one for encoding or converting.[6] It was an audio operating system but one that was read-only. They optimized Winamp's features to enhance the playback of audio via computer-based sound files. They did not, at least initially, expect that a large use of digital music players would involve importing audio from CDs or older recording formats. Despite all its other features, Winamp's basic offering to consumers was not designed for managing and maintaining CD audio. Pulling audio from, or storing songs on, CDs was by default "unthinkable" through its interface. Even as Winamp's designers transitioned users toward new modes of consuming music, they treated digital music on computers as a separate trend from CD audio. The result was an interface that, at least initially, allowed for limited traffic between the two formats. Winamp's privileging of the playback of already-existing digital files over conversion reflected its ambivalent position between more traditional music commodities and music's future formats.

Features like playlists, spectrum analyzers, and other tools for manipulating music playback on the computer succeeded because they solved technical problems through cultural means: they made new technology feel familiar and less alien through aesthetic and design-oriented solutions. They brought a new materiality and vocabulary to music (e.g., playlists, visualizations, skins, spectrum analyzers), though these echoed audio technologies, features, and designs with which users were already familiar. They also brought a whole series of computer-related practices to music; collecting and playing now involved clicking, scrolling, dragging, dropping, cutting, and pasting. They made the digital nature of music on computers seem more material. Winamp was a specific application for the playback of music, but it was also a cultural interface that mediated users' early relationship with digital music. Winamp's media interface—its playlist windows, spectrum analyzers, and alternate modes of visualizing, hearing, and manipulating music—sold Winamp as a useful media player and "sold" the digital dimension of music on computers. In doing so, Winamp's features ultimately acted as some of the earliest building blocks for the commodification of digital music.

RE-TUNING THE COMMODITY

Contrary, then, to claims that digital goods are intangible or immaterial, the digital music commodity has many micromaterials to explore. The software interfaces that package digital music, like Winamp, are particularly important parts of this materiality. Interfaces are the sites where users and cultural products meet. They contribute to both the use and exchange values of digital commodities, even if it might seem that Winamp's interface innovations exacerbated the threats presented to music's status as a commodity.

After all, Winamp took advantage of the fact that music, as a digital file, existed as individual units to be moved, played, and used separately. The software, which was largely free, dispensed with the traditional packaging of the music commodity and added new kinds of visual and paratextual information that seemed to have little to do with selling songs or with traditional industrial concerns (copyright, royalties, etc.). Winamp's conception of music represented a splintering of the music commodity and a reconfiguration of the traditional affordances associated with music. Although Winamp had technical limitations to the kinds of music it could accommodate, it made no distinction as to the source of the files. It was a free piece of software that let users play an assortment of files, regardless of whether they had paid for them. Copyright-infringing files were just as welcome as any other type. In this light Winamp seemed to operate on a model wholly removed from music as a commodity. This is what drove Frankel's belief that Winamp—and the MP3 movement it supported—might potentially disrupt the traditional music industry.

But Nullsoft's faith in the power of its own software and the digital music movement surrounding it celebrates the power of change new technologies offer at the expense of critically considering how the logic of commodification was already at work in Winamp. Software like Winamp, and digital files more generally, only really disrupted a particular form of the music commodity (viz., the CD) and a particular way of playing it (viz., on CD players). The larger marketing efforts that fed music's commodity status didn't simply disappear with the advent of digital files, leaving the music commodity as nothing but pure use value. Recorded music files on computers, even in their most primitive forms, were still commodities in many senses. They were still songs that had value in relation to other forms and formats. The sound, as well as the artist and production team that created that song, still held residual cues to the commodity realm in which that song circulated. Winamp helped re-tune music's interface, but this did not necessarily threaten music's status as a commodity. Just as an instrument can be tuned in a variety of tunings, each offering its own interesting and unique tonal character, so, too, can the music commodity be disaggregated and repackaged in differently saleable forms. In other words Winamp provided a vision for music's new format and new ways of playing it, extending the music commodity into the digital realm. Ostensibly a technology for playing music on the computer, Winamp's interface and the features it promoted were an important representation of digital music at a time when the form and format of music were in question.

The re-tuning of music's interface represents a temporary and transitory point in time where the music commodity faces a moment of uncertainty, though this uncertainty is only conditional. Periods of technological change and innovation present opportunities for some actors as they present challenges for others. With music adrift and circulating relatively free of paratexts on the Internet and on computers, there were contesting views on the status and character of the digital music commodity. These conflicting views (e.g., regarding different formats, different software, different services and business models) were just as likely to further the interests of the dominant players in the music industries as they were to challenge them. Winamp, as I'll argue for the case of Napster as well, served a dual function in this respect. Its role was not solely to liberate music from the confines of its commodity status. It should also be understood as a starting point for the commodification of digital music. Despite Nullsoft's anti-corporate and anti-industrial marketing rhetoric before, and during, its time at AOL, Nullsoft provided a coherent vision for how digital music should look, sound, and feel on computers and how these qualities might make music sellable in its digital form.

Winamp's interface rebuilt music's materiality for its digital context. These micromaterials wrapped music files on computers in a package that made them seem as usable, functionally and aesthetically, as other versions of the music commodity. Beyond its interface Nullsoft helped commodify digital music in less subtle ways as well. The program generated more than fifteen million users in less than two years and many more in the years following. Winamp helped ignite an interest in digital music by selling users on its vision of computers as advanced and interactive stereo systems. Even though the program was primarily offered for free, it still hinted at the lucrative possibilities of an emerging digital music market. Many users "donated" money to Nullsoft—enough to fund server costs and other frills for Frankel until he sold the company to AOL—and even those who did not had spent money on related commodities like computers, Internet connectivity, soundcards, and speakers. Nullsoft further catered to this market as the software evolved.

In addition to charging for different "lite" and "pro" versions of the software, Winamp also started linking its software back to familiar outlets for the music commodity. Version 2.10, for example, included a mini-browser window (see fig. 6) that provided "information and web links relevant to the various MP3 files" a user was playing (Frankel et al. 1999, 57). The default browser page was Amazon.com, where users could buy a CD of the very file they were listening to (the irony of being sent to buy something users already owned in another format was obviously lost on the browser technology). The minibrowser also linked to other established music resources (rollingstones.com, MP3.com, etc.). Although such an innovation could be expected of Winamp after its merger with media giant AOL, the release date for version 2.10 was several months before the acquisition. As such, the minibrowser suggests the software and the music files it facilitated were already linked to a wider market place of commodities.

Even a feature as basic as playlists uncovers roots of digital music's commodification. Playlists represent a way of regrouping music that has become unhinged from its original context. If Winamp's ability to mix and match digital music files across a wide selection of artists, genres, and albums called the very concept of the "album" into question, then playlists

Figure 6. Winamp's integrated browser (version 2.10). Winamp version 2.10 included a browser that linked users to Amazon.com.

emerged as a new form of ordering the music commodity. Playlists capitalize on songs as individual units, confined by no preset order or classification. Playlists support the idea of songs as individual units (commercial and aesthetic) while simultaneously recognizing that they take on other meanings when part of a larger whole. By regrouping and ordering music, playlists recontextualize the individual songs that make them up. Originally a technical solution for cueing up digital music files, playlists have become the primary way to package the digital music commodity that is widely used in digital music stores like iTunes or services like Spotify (Drew 2005).

The ways listeners experience music depends on what they can do with it. Winamp drew on familiar practices and designs, and in doing so, it engaged in recontextualizing the music commodity for the digital realm. Winamp's interface and features made possible the playing and ordering of digital music in such a way that it could be repackaged as a new version of the same old commodity. Winamp's approach to music playback was a statement about how music should look, sound, and behave in its digital contexts. The features Winamp put forward as central to handling digital music, then, were simultaneously claims to reconsider practices of music consumption. Even though the program's designers did not intentionally set out to create a market for the sale of digital music files, Winamp's re-tuning of music's interface created an environment in which the commodification of digital music could take place. By creating a distinct experience for music on the computer that was different enough from previous formats to feel novel yet similar enough to ease users through the transition, Winamp hinted that music as a digital file was ready for commodification.

There is little doubt that the splintering of the music commodity into individual data files has presented challenges for players heavily invested in the sale of recorded music and for notions of musical value more generally. The album has been the dominant form of music consumption since the rise of the $33\frac{1}{3}$ rpm vinyl LP in the 1950s (Keightley 2004, 378–90). Although a long line of technologies, such as jukeboxes, 45-rpm singles, recordable cassettes, and radio, has challenged the "age of the long play," these technologies often supported, rather than opposed, the more economically and symbolically dominant album format (Keightley 2004; Powers 2014). But the modularity of digital music, through playlists and other forms of recombination, has sparked another round of the "death of the album" debate.[7] As Gerald Marzorati, a critic for the *New York Times*, notes, the "big album" (i.e., albums that were conceived of and understood as albums in their entirety, such as some of those by the Beatles or Bob Dylan) does not travel well to new technologies like digital files and the Internet. An album is, Marzorati goes on, "ultimately a matter of giving yourself over to somebody else's choices—this song, then this one, because it was conceived to be heard that way. The digital revolution promises precisely the opposite: you get to pick and choose, quickly, effortlessly, endlessly. What do you want, want right now? It's the ability to gauge and provide just that that's killing the Big Album" (Marzorati 1998). Rather than fear over visual or sonic inferiority, the death of the album discourse suggests that the disaggregation of albums into individual files disrupts not only the economic strategies of the music industries (Banerjee 2004) but also patterns of listening that have long been fundamental to the music commodity.

Even if we accept the premise that the album is dying, however, the death of one iteration of the music commodity does not necessarily mean the death of the music commodity more broadly. Winamp's disaggregation of the album format, while it partakes in the same logic that drove mix tapes and mixed CDs in the decades preceding it (Drew 2005; Drew 2014), did so in a way that presented new avenues for the repackaging and repurposing of the music commodity. Winamp's interface allowed a disaggregation of music but also provided a way to reaggregate it in other ways. Without the explicit intention of commodifying music into playlists, Winamp nevertheless created features that later became central to the digital music commodity.[8]

The music industries have faced several similar transitory moments since the introduction of sheet music, and the antagonism and disorder that gets created in such moments is, as is clear from past experience, not inherently disruptive. In most cases each new threatening technology is ultimately tamed or co-opted while the structure of the recording industry and its major players remains relatively unchanged (Chanan 1995; Garofalo 1999; McCourt and Burkart 2003). Software like Winamp, whose technical design encourages users to reorganize music into playlists, manipulate it with equalizers, and visualize it through abstract graphics, may have added to the chaos of this particular transitory moment. However, it also signaled the potential of a variety of new services surrounding the digital music commodity. Winamp was not the only technology involved in this process, and subsequent chapters examine other key developments along the road to commodification. Because of its early popularity, however, Winamp played a particularly crucial role in transitioning users from playing CDs on their stereos to playing digital music files on their computers. It freed the recorded music commodity from some of its confines and at the same time laid the groundwork for the commodification of digital music.

Neither Winamp nor the moment surrounding it, however, fundamentally changed the idea that recorded music was still a commodity. The question facing those interested in profiting from recorded music in its digital form—and here I include not only record labels but also artists and a host of other actors—was not whether digital music could be a commodity but how to proceed with its commodification. The answer to this question was not one that would come exclusively from the music industries. Instead, it would take a tense mix of industrial desires and the everyday labor of users and hobbyists working to shape digital music into a usable and valuable form. I turn now to explore this part of digital music's history by looking at a key feature on which Winamp relied for handling, sorting, and seeing digital music: metadata.

A BLACK HOLE

At the time of its launch, in 1996, the TuneBase 2000 probably sounded like a futuristic device. Its name called forth images of a yet-to-unfold millennium; its features promised a new world of sound entertainment. A combination of hardware and software, the TuneBase 2000 helped consumers play and organize their CDs in mega-CD changers (the multi-disc CD and DVD players that were gaining prominence at the time). The TuneBase 2000—which held hundreds of CDs—was the cream of this particular crop (Wilson 2000). What set the TuneBase 2000 apart, however, was not the number of CDs it could hold in its tray. Rather, it was because the device was essentially a small computer loaded with a database of information that included album names, track titles, and cover art for hundreds of popular CDs (Culbertson 1997; Wilson 2000). When users inserted a disc into the CD player, the TuneBase 2000 would "recognize" it, call up its associated information, and display it on a TV screen (Culbertson 1997). While the US$2,500 device was geared toward rich audiophiles, Scott Jones, CEO of the company behind the device, hoped that falling prices and technological advances would lead to mainstream adoption. Plus, he argued, it was meeting an important new demand: "These mega-changers have no idea what's in each individual slot. If you look at CD number 63, track 5, it becomes a black hole. No one remembers their CDs by number" (qtd. in Pletz 1998).

Today's users of music on computers do not need to remember CDs or digital files by number; instead, they have metadata. Among other things, metadata—the data about the data on CDs or in digital files—tell users what song they are listening to, which album it is from, and the name of the artist who is singing or playing it. Traditionally this information came from the packaging on CDs or albums, but the migration of music onto computers and computer-based devices created, in Jones's words, a "black hole": a space where no light seeped out, an information dead zone. A touch hyperbolic, the metaphor rightfully points to the critical role that information *about* music plays in our experiences of music. Metadata help users recognize, sort, collect, and use digital music. Metadata are both functional and aesthetic. They can be loaded with cultural cues and artistic flourishes or coded with technical instructions and marketing messages. Through software players like Winamp, they provide necessary information about music's sonic content, re-tuning music's interface by making it more recognizable, sortable, and usable.

Building on the previous chapter's focus on music's visual and sonic transformations through programs like Winamp, this chapter looks beneath the digital music commodity's surface to consider the music file's internal structure. I review efforts, like the TuneBase 2000, that sought to enhance the music experience through metadata. In particular, I trace the evolution of the Compact Disc Database (CDDB) and ID3 tags, two instrumental information technologies for shaping and presenting digital music on computers (the former added metadata to CDs in computers; the latter embedded metadata in MP3 files). Despite their prevalence and importance, it is easy to underestimate the significance of the CDDB, ID3 tags, and the metadata they provide. Technically speaking, they represent only minor feats of innovation—matching CD contents to an online database or providing labels for digital files.[1] Like Winamp, ID3 tags and the CDDB grew out of programmers' desire to solve a specific technical problem. They were practical solutions for music that had been stripped of much of its paratextual context. Metadata are micromaterials that work quietly in the background, and when they work properly, most consumers barely notice their presence. For many users, digital music has never looked otherwise. Yet metadata from ID3 tags and the CDDB, like the interfaces through which music comes to us, are crucial to how digital music works on computers. They have grown from basic tools for categorization to central components of the digital music ecosystem that hold various other technologies in place and help them interact. The re-tuning of music's interface, through metadata, illustrates how materiality is ever-present in seemingly immaterial digital objects. Metadata may never garner the attention that Napster or iPods have, but the CDDB and ID3 tags are keystone technologies that contribute to the commercial development and the social life of the digital music commodity.

Given the role users played in developing the CDDB and ID3 tags, these services also reveal the conflicted nature of digital commodities. The CDDB and ID3 tags incorporate users in the making and maintenance of metadata, implicating their labor in the production of digital music as a commodity. Metadata capture user labor in circuits of cybernetic commodification (Andrejevic 2007; Mosco 1996). However, by allowing users to re-tune unauthorized downloaded files, metadata also trouble the standard logic of commodification. Through ID3 tags and the CDDB, users played an active role in adorning unauthorized digital files with metadata, and their interventions helped make digital files look, sound, and act like proper commodities.

GETTING META ON METADATA

If you've still got a computer with a CD drive, try a little experiment. Load an audio CD into the drive and watch what happens. Typically, within seconds of doing so, your media playback program (Windows Media Player, iTunes, etc.) will flash the name of the CD and the artist, a list of songs, their various lengths, and other details on your screen. It's a process that occurs so quickly, it's easy to forget that a relatively complex set of connections, calculations, and processes are going on. To the unaware or the simply uninterested, it's as if all the information was already there on the CD, ready to be revealed onscreen. The data, however, isn't on the CD or anywhere on the computer. As proof, repeat the same process. Except this time, make sure your computer is not connected to the Internet. Instead of an informative layout of song names and album titles, all that appears is the most unimpressive of lists: track 01, track 02, track 03 . . . (see fig. 7). The reason for the unhelpful metadata here is because the data about the CD resides not on the CD itself but on a large Internet database that hosts and provides a wealth of information about any particular CD and populates your music player via your online connection.

The data that describe the music on CDs or in digital files—the data that turn track 01 into a more useful label—are commonly known as metadata. The term surfaced in the 1960s, but the topic's rise in prominence over the last several decades coincides with the digitization of data (not just music but of all kinds of resources) and the need for librarians, archivists, and hobbyists to organize electronic resources and Internet-based information (Campbell 2007; Dempsey and Heery 1998; Greenberg 2003a, 2003b; Mathes 2004; Vellucci 1999). Metadata have several key functions, including describing the attributes of a resource, characterizing its relationships to other resources, and supporting the discovery, management, and use of a resource (Vellucci 1999, 205). Metadata are "structured" data, and their

Figure 7. Music without metadata. A screenshot of the contents of a CD without proper metadata in iTunes Media Player.

main purpose is to support the functions associated with the object that they describe (Greenberg 2003a).

Although metadata technically exist for nonelectronic resources, such as the "bibliographic data" and "cataloguing" schemes for physical resources like a book's Dewey Decimal number or Library of Congress designation, there are disciplinary debates among scholars of information science and library studies about whether metadata is a strictly electronic affair (for an overview see Greenberg 2003a; Vellucci 1999). While largely a matter of semantics, the disagreement begs the question: what, if anything, is new or different about digital metadata from the forms of paratextual information that came before it? Like bibliographic data and cataloguing once did, digital metadata engender novel sorting and ordering practices. However, the sheer scope and scale of resources that can be tracked and the attributes that can be assigned to them multiply significantly when metadata is in digital form (Poster 1990, 96).

Digital metadata also open up the classification process to a wider group of participants. Metadata were historically the province of professional database managers (librarians, archivists, etc.) and technical metadata creators. Standards-setting bodies like the International Organization for Standardization (ISO) traditionally governed metadata categories and techniques. Authorial, top-down metadata standards like MARC cataloguing practices in place at most libraries are a good example. MARC, or MAchine Readable Cataloguing, refers to a metadata schema that codifies what elements of a resource should be defined (author, title, type, etc.), how to define them (last name, first name, or the syntax for writing out dates and titles), and how to apply the schema in practice (Greenberg 2003a). MARC allows library users to search a library's vast holdings, obtain a call number, and track down the precise location of a resource. These are highly structured classification schemes; they are generally static (i.e., slow to respond to changes to individual resources), and they require highly specialized training/education in classificatory systems, information standards, and in making sophisticated metadata-related decisions. MARC is only one of dozens of metadata standards just as the ISO is only one of the standards bodies charged with developing and maintaining metadata standards. The Dublin Core Metadata Initiative, for example, is an organization trying to fuse the benefits of universal cataloguing techniques with the flexibility of more user-generated metadata in order to address the challenges posed by the variety and scale of documents and objects found across the Internet.

In other words the Internet and the scores of digital objects it contains have spawned new labeling challenges and techniques (Greenberg 2003a, 2003b). Authorial top-down metadata schemas like MARC now mingle with more colloquial and user-generated labeling systems, like those found on sites like Flickr, YouTube, or the CDDB.[2] On these sites users can add tags, keywords, and other metadata to categorize and sort digital media in ways they see fit. They may not be as clearly or systematically organized as systems like MARC, but these classification systems are nonetheless highly useful and customizable. Often referred to as "folksonomies" (Mathes 2004; G. Smith 2008), these user-built and maintained repositories of knowledge are easier to use and more participatory for larger audiences (almost anyone can enter a tag or keyword, whereas learning the Library of Congress Subject Headings list takes more time and effort). Folksonomies can suffer from a lack of consistency, universality, and accuracy when compared to more formal metadata-generation techniques, but the effectiveness of this kind of organization has led to impressive communal resources like Flickr, Wikipedia, and the Internet Movie Database (Mathes 2004).

Metadata for music thus operate within a wider realm of digital objects linked by information that simultaneously describes and constitutes resources. They also operate within a longer history of the standards that have shaped the music commodity itself. The Red Book Standard for the compact disc, for example, is perhaps the most familiar. The Red Book, which takes its name from the red-bindered document published in 1980 by Sony and Philips that outlines the CD's technical specifications, outlines the three main "areas" of the CD: a lead-in area, a recordable area, and a lead-out area (Pohlmann 1992, 50–52). It doesn't, however, provide much in the way of metadata, at least as defined above. This lack of a defined metadata schema for music on CDs is what makes the transition to digital music files such an interesting and unique case. Metadata for digital music evolved quickly and through an odd mix of user groups and industry players, and it also evolved into a thoroughly integrated schema that is integral to how music works on computers. Music was ahead of other cultural commodities in fully exploring and making use of the possibilities metadata could provide. It was better able to provide a consistent—or at least recognizable—experience between its digital and nondigital forms, and metadata were a key reason for this.

Most of the digital music metadata that users encounter comes from the CD Database and ID3 tags. The CDDB provides metadata for CDs in computers, while ID3 tags embed metadata in MP3 files. Although they work on different formats, they serve similar ends: both help users and producers discover, label, manage, and embed digital documents and files with paratextual information. Given the expanding size of today's music libraries and the increasing storage capacity of computers, metadata provide essential navigational and archival functions. The mass accumulation and hoarding of digital music is a common practice, if not an inherent feature of music as a digital file (Burkart 2008, 4; Sterne 2006b, 831–32), and metadata are crucial for managing the resulting mass of files. Metadata were solutions for music that was moving from one format to another. They were further evidence that the CD was not designed with computers in mind and that computers were not originally envisioned as consumer audio devices. Metadata helped re-tune the music commodity as users put CDs in their computers and ripped music from its discs.

Metadata's grander promise is to give us better control over our information. Users could choose, for example, to leave their music unlabeled in a collection full of track 01s and track 10s, but this prospect is as daunting for the use of music as it is for its cultural significance. Metadata not only endow files with information; they afford users a measure of ownership and control over those files. Metadata open up a series of connections and possibilities for digital goods as cultural objects and as commodities. Without metadata about your musical data, digital files would make pale commodities: barely usable and faded versions of recorded music's previous formats.

ID3 tags sprang from the work of Erik Kemp, who created a program called Studio 3 for making and identifying MP3 files (Nilsson 2006a; Potts 2002). The MP3 format didn't originally allow for this functionality. The Fraunhofer Institute and the MPEG consortium were more interested in compressing audio for easy transmission to radio and television broadcasters than in making a new kind of recorded music commodity (Dowd 2006, 219; Katz 2004, 160; Sterne 2012). Given the MP3's open source structure, as well as its associations with "piracy" and file sharing (Dowd 2006, 220), the MP3 had much less industrial support, at least from the recorded music industries. As a result, creating the tools to properly sort and label music fell to users or amateur developers like Erik Kemp.

The first version of ID3, released in 1996, was a relatively simple affair: a 128-byte tag appended to an MP3 file to which users could add the track name, artist name, and album title. Other users began building on Kemp's idea and adding complexity to the type of data ID3 tags could store (track numbers, longer field entries, etc.). In 1998 another programmer, Martin Nilsson, created ID3 version 2 (Nilsson 2006a), which allowed users to add a huge variety of extra tags to their files (ratings, embedded pictures, production credits, tempo, etc.) and even to create customized fields of their own. The current version, ID3v2, is the de facto standard for MP3 metadata in most software players (iTunes, Winamp, etc.), and its utility and flexibility is largely thanks to a disparate group of users and programmers who contributed to the file specifications.

Similarly, the CDDB grew from the work of a hobbyist programmer and, subsequently, its users. In 1993 Ti Kan developed a Winamp-type media player called XMCD. In addition to letting users play CDs—something that computers at that time were still not adept at—XMCD matched CDs with information in a database file on the user's computer (Fry 2001; Kan 2004). XMCD calculated that a disc had, say, thirteen songs and that the first song lasted 3 mins., 42 secs.; the second one 2 mins., 48 secs.; and so on (Fry 2001). With this information, and with the assumption that no two CDs had the exact number of tracks with the same lengths in the same sequence, XMCD set about finding matches within the database file. Once XMCD found a correct match, the program displayed the artist's name, track title, and so forth to the user (Fry 2001; Van Buskirk 2006).

The service caught on, and users were soon emailing Kan details on hundreds of CDs to add to the database. In 1995 Kan's friend Steve Scherf moved the database to an online server so that users could add new or edit existing entries directly instead of emailing them to Kan (Fry 2001; Van Buskirk 2006).[3] In other words, if the data for a particular CD were not available, users could enter the information themselves and send it back to the database, which would then be available for the next user who might load in that same CD. Thanks to the diligent work of these early users, the number of entries to the database grew rapidly. By August of 1998 the database had approximately 1.2 million entries and was receiving two million connections a month, making it the most extensive service of its kind online (O'Malley 1998; Pletz 1998). As long as users were connected to the Internet when they placed a CD in the disc drive of their computer, musical metadata would feed back to their software media player.

At this point Kan and Scherf sold the CDDB to electronics manufacturer Escient LLC, which began licensing the database to producers of software programs like Winamp and MusicMatch Jukebox. As we will see, this growing privatization of the database was controversial given the substantial proportion of the database that was made up of user-generated entries. Nevertheless, Escient pressed on with commercial opportunities and later spun the database into its own company, Gracenote CDDB, which it sold to Sony in 2008 (who then sold it late in 2013 to Tribune). The service boasts more than 250 million users in more than two hundred countries. It powers more than two thousand applications and is used in hundreds of millions of consumer electronic devices, from car stereos to mobile phones to digital radios ("Sony Corp of America to Acquire Gracenote," 2008; Gracenote 2008, 2010). The CDDB now also tracks consumer preferences, collects sales/play count data, and offers sophisticated recognition technology (e.g., waveforms, sonic cues, audio fingerprinting) to identify files (Dean 2004; Palenchar 2002).

In many respects the CDDB and ID3 tags are simply the next iteration of music's paratextual information. The music commodity, after all, has long had what we could anachronistically call metadata. With the advent of recorded music came packaging and cataloguing features with which to distribute that music. Album art, liner notes, band photos, inserts, and so forth all contributed to the shape and materiality of the music commodity over the last century. CDs, tapes, and records each have their own kinds of metadata. Even the grooves of a record could be considered a form of metadata since they denote track numbers and lengths. While CDs, tapes, and records have individual conventions for presenting this paratextual information, metadata have typically remained *outside* the actual media. Song titles, artist names, and production details are generally found on the packaging (on record sleeves, liner notes, jewel cases, etc.) or on the media itself (i.e., stamped onto the actual plastic discs or cassettes). The information contained on the CD, tape, or record was almost entirely audio data. Metadata for digital music, however, are embedded or networked into the individual file itself (as explained further below, ID3 tags embed metadata into the MP3's file structure while the CDDB links the audio information on CDs to a networked database). Both the CDDB and ID3 tags are designed for an era in which we are increasingly likely to encounter music that has been distanced from its packaging.

Of course, digital music is not the first kind of music that has been able to leave its commodity wrapping. While the gramophone was not conducive to quick copying, the advent of tape and tape recording machines in the 1960s made it possible for the reproduction of entire albums, stripping songs and sounds from liner notes and other packaging in the process (Drew 2005). As users recombined their favorite songs to share primitive mix tapes and "playlists" with their friends, they also created their own versions of metadata. There is a world of wonderful metadata associated with tapes, ranging from the intensely personal drawings, writings, and scrawlings of friends on mix-tape covers to the near exact album replicas of professional bootleggers (Heylin 1994; Moore 2004). This trend continued (and accelerated) once music went digital: blank CDs and CD burners took up where tapes left off (Drew 2005).

However, the metadata for both mix tapes and CDs, if present at all, is almost always tied to the packaging in which the format arrives, not the media itself. Take the packaging away, and you also take away most of the relevant metadata. There are notable exceptions. Most CDs contain some minimal embedded metadata in the form of a table of contents (TOC) that allows computers and other devices to recognize the start, end, and duration of each track. The TOC tells users that a disc has twelve songs and displays the length of those songs, but that is its descriptive limit. This is why a typical CD player displays "Track 04—3:49" as opposed to "'Stop Whispering' by Radiohead from *Pablo Honey.*" This "limitation" was built into the original Red Book standard. While the TOC did not provide very rich information to CD users, it was through the information in the TOC that software like XMCD and, later, the CDDB matched a CD's contents with its associated metadata. Despite its limited descriptive capabilities, the TOC acted as a (virtually) unique identifier that allowed the CDDB to link CDs with a whole range of other metadata.

The original CD also included industrial-purposed metadata like the international standard recording code (ISRC), which was a means of uniquely identifying sound recordings internationally for rights administration and royalty collection (Pohlmann 1992, 92–99).[4] Like the Universal Product Code (UPC) on the back of most consumer goods or the International Standard Book Number (ISBN) for books, these kinds of metadata are crucial for tracking and describing products, but they have little bearing on how consumers handle their music. This is yet another reason for distinguishing CDs as digital music from music files on computers as digital music commodities. While the sounds on CDs may have been as digital as the sounds in digital music files, the digitization of music's packaging is what led to radically reconfigured practices of producing, distribution, listening, sorting, and collecting music.

Other than technical forms of metadata like the TOC and the ISRC, the record labels and technology companies of the mid-to-late 1980s were more focused on using advances in CD technology to stuff them with interactive bonus content and other audiovisual extras (e.g., exclusive video content, games, audio remixes) than to provide basic organizational metadata. Through a host of "rainbow book" standards,[5] projects like David Bowie's *Jump* (1994), Peter Gabriel's *Xplora1* CD-ROM (1993), Prince's *Interactive* (1994), Brian Eno's *Headcandy* (1994), and Todd Rundgren's *No World Order* CD-I (1993) were attempts to create "enhanced" and "interactive" music products that took advantage of the new environment the computer provided.[6] These experiments were more about selling additional entertainment content than providing metadata proper, but they did belie an interest on the part of record labels and technology companies in using computers to provide more information about the music in their music products. They were one possible way the digital music commodity could have manifested itself, though most of these expensive endeavors met with limited commercial success ("Ziggy on CD-ROM" 1994; Trachtenberg 1996a).

Eventually, Sony and Philips realized the need for more basic metadata on CDs. In 1996 they extended the Red Book standard to include CD-Text—a function that embedded data about the artist, the album, and individual tracks onto the CD itself ("Sony, Philips Agree on CD Text Function" 1996; "CD Text Specifications Announced by Licensors Philips and Sony" 1996). CD-Text was clearly an attempt to address the increasing use of CDs in computers and other visually powerful devices and to overcome the CD's lack of built-in metadata. It was also an admission that artists, manufacturers, and consumers had an ever-growing interest in linking information about the music to the music format itself. Unfortunately, CD-Text was introduced more than a dozen years after the original CD, and it was not backward compatible (i.e., discs with CD-Text could display metadata, but the hundreds of thousands of discs produced before 1996 could not). CD-Text was also a Sony and Philips-based standard, so not all companies rushed to add it to their CDs. While most Sony-produced CDs post-1997 have CD-Text capability, many others do not (for an unscientific check of CD-Text's diffusion, grab a handful of nearby CDs and see if they have the CD-Text logo).

CD-Text took cues from an earlier Sony product: the Mini Disc. Launched in 1992, Mini Discs (MD) had a user table of contents (UTOC), which, unlike the TOC on CDs, included metadata for track name, disc name, and the date recorded (Minidisc.Org 2009; Pohlmann 1992; Tsurushima et al. 1996). It was a small innovation and one that is barely mentioned in the engineering publications on the development of the MiniDisc (see for, e.g., Ishida et al. 1993; Pohlmann 1992; Tsurushima et al. 1996). But even the earliest MD recorders and players could label audio material and display metadata (see the instructions for the first MiniDisc player, the MZ1, archived at minidisc. org 2009). This meant that even when users ripped songs from CDs, they could still identify and sort them. MiniDiscs did have copy protection schemes that prevented users from replicating them digitally, but the MiniDisc allowed for the translation of music from the CD (without metadata) to the MiniDisc (with more metadata). In other words users could see what they were hearing. They could select songs by name instead of by number. Although the format never took off in North America for music consumption (Dowd 2006; Trachtenberg 1996b), the MD and its UTOC were precursors to the idea that digital files, wherever they went, should carry information normally found in the music commodity's packaging.

For major labels and technology companies the improvement of metadata on CDs or increasing their usefulness on computers ultimately took a backseat to the development of higher quality audio formats. In the late 1990s, while software like Winamp and Napster were hastening the development of a digital music commodity, most major technology and music companies were still hedging their bets on disc-based products. Sony and Philips had put major resources into releasing Super Audio CDs (SACD) in 1999 and the DVD Group (a consortium of tech companies including Toshiba, Pioneer, and Sony) developed the DVD-Audio (DVD-A) standard to launch in 2000 (Legrand 1999; Traiman 1999). Like the earlier efforts with CD-ROMs, the record companies saw these formats, unlike lower fidelity and definition MP3s, as value-added formats that provided higher quality audio, visuals, extra data, and other "interactive" functions (McCourt 2005, 251). Given the high cost of the new hardware for SACD and DVD-A devices and the lack of perceived difference between these high-quality formats and regular CDs, neither format took hold with consumers beyond niche audiophile groups (Legrand 1999, 2004). As I mentioned in the previous chapter, high-definition formats are part of a long line of music-industry developments (and, indeed, media industries innovations) that chase a "dream of verisimilitude": a quest to make media experiences ever closer and truer to actual lived experience (Sterne 2012, 4). This quest for high-quality experiences, however, ignores the equally significant history of media innovations that focuses on increased mobility, portability, and convenience.

In this light it is unfair to say that the major record labels were unprepared for music's next format change. In reality the labels, technology companies, and artists were working hard to develop the next commodity-revitalizing format of music, but their efforts were misplaced. They spent most of the 1990s experimenting with enhanced CDs and other rainbow-book technologies, assuming that the future of music lay in the ability to enhance audio quality or the interactivity of CDs (bonus footage and material, games, etc.). They put their resources toward developing and improving a technology they knew and understood, one they could control in terms of manufacture and distribution. Focused on these initiatives, they failed (or were unwilling) to recognize that the real growth in music on computers was going to come from separating it from the disc entirely and giving users a new interface with which to manage their collections, through technologies like Winamp, the CDDB, and ID3 tags.

The CDDB and ID3 tags, then, are an evolution of the informational aspects of the music commodity. As with previous forms of musical metadata, the CDDB and ID3 tags serve important functional roles for finding, sorting, and classifying music. But digital metadata play a significantly greater role in shaping our experience of the music commodity than what came before them. Digital metadata are more thoroughly embedded and networked into the commodity itself. In the case of ID3 tags the paratextual information is literally embedded into the file itself. In the case of the CDDB the information is encoded in a file that resides in the CDDB's database, but it is networked to the file through the TOC and other properties of the CD. This marks a key difference between digital and analog metadata. Digital metadata are part of the product experience and are intimately tied to digital music's form and functionality. They travel with the files and shape digital music's use. The CDDB and ID3 tags are integrated and integral technologies: they describe the information that accompanies music and prescribe particular ways of classifying and sorting it. While all paratexts shape the meaning users make from the media objects around them and prepare users for their encounter with the text (Gray 2010), metadata are unique in that they insinuate themselves into cultural commodities and exert structural effects on the files and formats of cultural content.

DESCRIPTION AND PRESCRIPTION

Metadata's integral and integrated nature has significant effects on the ways digital music appears and works. Metadata are not, after all, organic or natural characteristics of objects (Coyle 2005, 160; Manovich 2001, 224–26); they are highly constructed with specific purposes such as classification, archiving, and accessibility in mind: "Cataloging appears to be routine work so long as one believes that the materials just have a regular structure which can be trivially read off. But on inspection, it appears that this regular structure is the output of the work of catalogers, not the input" (David Levy, qtd. in Campbell 2007, 15). Defining which metadata are relevant, which are not, and who has the right or the ability to inscribe those data all influence the process of finding and handling any given resource. As much as metadata and cataloguing rest on the assumption that documents have concrete attributes that can be transcribed, ordered, and retrieved (Campbell 2007; Manovich 2001, 224), the categories cataloguers create are subjective and highly cultural. Like any system of classification, as Pierre Bourdieu (1991) might argue, metadata are both descriptive and prescriptive. The labels we assign to categorize the things around us are descriptive, but they also set up modes of perceiving those things. Labeling and classification are a kind of *performative utterance:* "a prediction which aims to bring about what it utters" (Bourdieu 1991, 128). Although sorting an album by artist or title seems like an innocuous act—one that borrows from a century's worth of music-collecting practices and technologies—it also prescribes how users access and experience their music. ID3 tags and the CDDB are highly structured systems of labels and names that set out the categories that constitute the digital music commodity.

Initially, the fields of the CDDB were relatively basic (e.g., song title, artist name, album title, release year), but the number of fields expanded as the database grew (e.g., credits, label, web URL, notes, beats per minute). Users could submit information about a CD by entering it directly on the CDDB's website, though users generally did so through their media software programs like Winamp. This information is never "embedded" into the CD, though once entered into the database, it can be used to recognize other queries for matching discs. Metadata for MP3s, in contrast, reside in frames that are located at the beginning of the file.[7] ID3v1 only allowed for a fixed amount of characters and fields in a 128-byte tag, whereas ID3v2 had variable length "frames" that allowed for tags that included lyrics, the composer's name, the date recorded, comments, pictures, album art, or other icons (for a full list of frames see Nilsson 2006b).

Aside from metadata used to sort and organize music, ID3v2 also contained metadata that could tweak the actual sound of the audio file. The "relative volume adjustment" frame let users align the output volume of their files while the "equalization" and "reverb settings" frames colored the frequency and echo of the sound. Metadata, in this case, was acting not only on the file but on the sound itself. These informational changes to metadata fields resulted in material differences in the sound files. ID3v2 also came with a "Music CD Identifier" frame that was specifically designed for users looking to link MP3s with CDs. The frame's design allowed users to dump data from a CD's table of contents into the file or for software programs like Winamp to embed this data automatically during the import process. The Music CD Identifier frame also enabled MP3 files to access the CDDB. This frame provided a tight connection between CDs, MP3 files, and the CDDB. Although it is unclear to what extent there was a formal affiliation between the CDDB and ID3 communities—Steve Scherf and Ti Kan were among the contributors to ID3v2 (Nilsson 2007) though they were hesitant to get involved with anything associated with MP3s (Howison and Goodrum 2004, 12)—they were linked by virtue of the similarity of their services.

The frames and fields of the CDDB and ID3 tags are a series of culturally inflected categories and attributes that are tied not only to technology but to the social setting in which digital music evolved. At the time—and certainly for the largely white male group of developers involved in these projects—rock, electronic, pop, and hip-hop were among the most prevalent genres in the digital music sphere. The majority of MP3s that needed metadata or CDs that got looked up on the CDDB reflected the tastes of a certain subset of young, tech-savvy music listeners. CDDB categories and ID3 tags were thus designed with these genres and listeners in mind. Although they were flexible enough to meet the needs of other genres, they were best suited for these particular cases.

Nowhere is this more evident than in the case of classical music. Although sales of classical music in digital format are starting to grow more steadily (Shugold 2005; Tsioulcas 2007), classical music's move online was slower than other genres (Gracenote 2007; Singer 2007). While there are various plausible explanations (e.g., demographics, fidelity), classical music faces fundamental informational challenges that do not apply to other genres. Metadata, despite its flexibility and expandability, was not designed with classical music in mind. Sorting music by artist, by album, or by song title works for genres like pop, hip-hop, electronica, or rock, but fans of classical music require fields like composer, conductor, orchestra, and soloist to make sense of their compositions (S. Brown 2008). The length and format of classical music compositions also poses problems: how, for example, should users sort movements or suites from the same piece? How can users distinguish between multiple performances of the same piece by different orchestras? Users with a library full of multiple versions of Symphony no. 7 in D Minor need added mechanisms for finding the piece they want to play.

These are just some of the issues that confounded classical music users trying to sort and play their digital collections on computers. Jazz listeners voice similar complaints about the bias inherent in metadata. They describe the difficulties of trying to include all of an album's session musicians and the problems presented by reissues with different release or record dates (Bremser 2004). Gradually, iTunes and other media players have improved their metadata capabilities for niche genres (e.g., iTunes included a "composer" category in 2004). There are also a growing number of stores and other online resources that cater to this market (Tsioulcas 2007). The CDDB even launched a "Classical Music Initiative" in 2007 that focused on displaying complete and consistent classical metadata across a wide range of devices (Gracenote 2007). Still, the issues metadata pose for jazz and classical music highlight the problems that arise when databases and tags built for certain resources start accommodating objects that require different sorting strategies. They remind us that ID3 tags and the CDDB are built on culturally inflected categories and attributes that are tied to the social setting in which those technologies evolved. They also suggest that metadata make music behave in ways that affect the usability of digital music.

The ways metadata condition a user's experience of music become increasingly evident as a host of new recommendation technologies emerge (Pandora, iTunes Radio, Spotify, etc.). At a local level these services use metadata to trace out aesthetic and other connections between sounds and songs. But metadata also plug users into a vast repository of commodities on the Internet, where the act of listening to a song triggers algorithms and advice to purchase similar sounding songs, related merchandise, and other linked media properties. If a user plays a song by, say, Texas-based instrumental rock band Explosions in the Sky, recommendation engines can not only tell users that they might also like Lymbyc System (another Texas-based instrumental band) or Do Make Say Think (a Canadian band in the same genre), but they can also direct users to check out a DVD of Friday Night Lights, a football film with a soundtrack that features the music of Explosions in the Sky. Some of these services use their own databases— Pandora, for example, has dozens of musicologists and "record geeks" coding songs with thousands of attributes (Platoni 2006)—while others, like Songza, Spotify, and iTunes Radio make use of a combination of proprietary and user metadata. Metadata affect how users sort and sift through their collections, but recommendations based on, and enacted via, metadata affect what genres and artists users are exposed to in the first place.

Given the size of today's music libraries and the availability of new music more generally, recommendation engines are increasingly central technologies for helping us discover new music and rediscover old favorites buried within our multigigabyte collections. With the parity of streaming services and their catalogues (see chapters 5 and 6), proprietary recommendation algorithms and other novel uses of metadata become key strategic means for differentiation among the services. Metadata are keystone technologies that make establishing these connections possible in the first place. They extend the reach of our music files, both within our libraries and outward to other commodities beyond it, and link them to a wider network of goods and practices.

This is where metadata's informational inconsistencies become truly visible. Many users have likely run into some of these limits, be it with bands that have multiple potential spellings (e.g., Guns and Roses vs. Guns & Roses), those that begin with common articles (e.g., is the Strokes listed under *T* or *S?*), or the alphabetization of artists by first name rather than last. Additionally, incorrect metadata—mislabeled by well-intentioned users or never properly labeled in the first place—can and do find their way into our libraries. Dates can be wrong, names can be misspelled, and albums can be assigned to genres that make little sense. Since many data-fetching and recommendation processes are automated, inaccuracies propagate widely and quickly. The problem is only compounded by the mobility of the digital music commodity as music is transferred to digital players that have their own sorting eccentricities. At the most basic level, incorrect metadata can cause problems when trying to locate and play back music, especially in massive libraries. More troubling, with metadata integrated into sound files and networked to databases outside of the product, decisions and recommendations based on improper metadata become a regular feature of the music experience. Metadata are an imprecise art, yet the way they describe music prescribes how users experience their music.

The persistence of flawed metadata for digital music has spawned a secondary market of software like FixTunes, Media Monkey, and TuneUp that help users correct messy metadata. These automated reconstruction programs condense and expose a process that occurs continually with digital music: software fetches information from databases that colors and codes our digital collections and the songs that get recommended to us. Metadata's networked nature means that the information that constitutes our libraries comes from a source outside our collections, as well as from our own curating. Whereas data used to be part of music's packaging, metadata are now integrated in the media and networked to databases outside of the product. Databases like the CDDB act on our collections from afar in conjunction with our own actions. This is not simply a question of the difficulties users face in finding their music. It is a reminder that metadata are micromaterial paratexts that change independently of the product to which they are attached. In doing so, they alter the materials and modes through which users encounter that product. Metadata are a user's personal notations mixed with a file's individual history. They are hybrid labels based on information from automated services and from our own inscriptions; they are the material manifestation of memory, preferences, circulation, and information.

Metadata, then, cover digital files in a layer of highly specific attributes through which listeners interact with, label, sort, and handle their music. Through ID3 tags and the CDDB, metadata are embedded and networked into the very files themselves. While the devaluation narrative suggests digital files are "just data, metadata, and a thumbnail" and are inherently less valuable than tactile counterparts (McCourt 2005, 250), metadata instead embed the music commodity with different kinds of value. Metadata may be less materially material than the sleeve of a vinyl album, but they still package music with a look that we recognize (album covers, song titles, etc.) and provide it with a functionality we understand (i.e., I want to play song X from album Y). As part of the re-tuning of music's interface, they rebuild music's emotive context on its new platforms, with features that are specifically useful for those platforms. They make digital music more material than it might otherwise have seemed, adrift without its paratexts. Metadata are what turn a hard drive full of data into a personalized, customized, dynamic collection of music. Metadata are simultaneously part of the digital music commodity and about it.

Metadata let users add ratings to their music, track how many times a song has been played, see how recently a song has been played, and tag tunes with other commentary. Advanced metadata make digital music libraries searchable, not just alphabetically or by date but by multiple, customizable variables (tempo, mood, favorites, etc.). Users with a richly tagged library can even delegate the task of music selection to the computer itself. Software players can generate playlists and other user-specified groupings based on tag information. When users can sort digital music in these ways, it starts to act like music with which they could build a collection. When they can organize songs into temporally, behaviorally, or spatially distinct playlists, users can create new histories around them, ones not based on the wear and tear of album covers or scratches on a disc but ones still intimately tied to use and meaning. Ripping audio from a CD may strip music from its original context and leave it bare in a new environment, but metadata ensure digital music files will never be immaterial.

As with the interfaces of software players like Winamp, metadata are essential to digital music's materiality, embedding familiar attributes of the music commodity while at the same time suggesting new uses. This is not to suggest that people buy digital music for its metadata. Rather, they buy digital music because of what they can do with music in that format, and much of that functionality depends on metadata.

This insight is important across a range of digital objects. In an era of digital commodities, in the absence of traditional markers of packaging and materiality, it falls to the labels themselves to give the commodity its shape as well as its use and exchange value. Embedded or networked into files, metadata contextualize digital objects. Instead of assuming digital objects are immaterial and intangible simply because they are code, we should focus on how their micromaterials—their digital paratexts—condition the ways objects perform, how they look, and how they are received.

HOUSES THAT MUSIC FANS BUILT

While record labels, CD manufacturers, and technology companies spent much of the mid-1990s struggling to make CDs and other music formats more interactive, info-loaded, and high fidelity, it was hobbyists and technologists experimenting with their own alternative ways of linking music and data that developed the default standards for digital music's metadata. This marks another major difference between traditional metadata and the ID3 tags, the CDDB, and digital metadata more generally: their development depended heavily on the work and participation of its users. Erik Kemp's initial tagging strategies were rudimentary compared to what subsequent programmers and ID3 users would add. The CDDB went even further by building user contributions into its very functionality (to this day users have the option of submitting metadata to the CDDB's servers). Both of these developments happened either outside of, or in conjunction with, more commercial efforts. The story of metadata, then, is as much about users and their role in the commodification process as it is about industrial and technical innovation. Metadata services raise important questions about what kind of "work" users do on behalf of digital commodities as they contribute to the creation and maintenance of metadata technologies.

I put the word "work" in quotes because debates in media studies rage on about whether or not to classify user-generated contributions as work (see, e.g., Arvidsson and Colleoni 2012; Fuchs 2010). As users play an increasing role in providing content for sites like Facebook, Twitter, YouTube, and others, the line between audiences as laboring viewers or listeners and audiences as creators or producers blurs (Coté and Pybus 2007). The commodification of user content and communication is part of a turn toward "platform economics," where Web 2.0 services and other such sites put the products of the cultural commons in service of economic profit (Jakobsson and Stiernstedt 2010, 2012). These economic models both foster and depend on various levels of audience labor, creating spaces in which complicated networks of sociality, connectivity, and economic activity combine (Bolin 2012; van Dijck 2011, 2009).

It is clear that users, individually and collectively, contributed a good deal of time and energy to developing digital metadata. They worked as they tagged files, labeled their CDs, and helped compile the CDDB's vast database. They also worked at developing and expanding the file structure for ID3 tags, adding new means of classifying and categorizing sound files. While folksonomies are often treated as inherently empowering and part of the wider Web 2.0 trend (see, e.g., G. Smith 2008), the CDDB and ID3 tags also show how dependent folksonomies are on what Maurizio Lazzarato calls immaterial labor: "the labour that produces the informational and cultural content of the commodity" (1996, 133). For Lazzarato immaterial labor was an attempt to conceptualize what's at stake in the labor that takes place *around* cultural commodities that make them so highly desirable, including the fashioning of tastes, preferences, and styles. The work of immaterial laborers, then, is the work they do to fix these cultural attributes of a product. Users, especially early adopters and heavy users, provide much of this immaterial work, free labor they perform without any kind of formal economic recompense (Terranova 2004).

Take the case of the CDDB. Escient's acquisition of the database in 1998 was controversial. The CDDB began as an open-source, user-generated metadata storehouse that was free to all users and developers. After the purchase Escient released an updated version of the database called CDDB2 that was incompatible with the classic version (CDDB 1999b). Initially the company promised to keep the service royalty free for developers and users (CDDB 1999b; Chalmers 1999), but subsequent changes to the licensing agreements banned unlicensed use of the service (Chalmers 1999; Dean 2004; Hemos 1999). Consumers could still access (and contribute to) the database for free, but software developers like Nullsoft had to pay licensing fees to incorporate CDDB2 functionality into their products. Alternative, open-source, and spin-off databases like Freedb and Music Brainz emerged in retaliation (Chalmers 1999; Dean 2004), but, in a move that further exacerbated the situation, the CDDB2 license gallingly stipulated—at least originally—that software companies must not offer access to databases other than the CDDB in their product (see, e.g., the case of *CDDB vs. Roxio* as described in Dean 2004; Gracenote 2001a). What had once been a free and open-source resource for developers and users became Escient's licensable property. The situation was akin to a private company acquiring a resource like Wikipedia and then changing the terms through which users and developers access and contribute to it. Escient was using a moment of technical change to exert greater commercial and economic control of its product and to exclude "nonindustrial" options from competition. Through licensing restrictions and technical design, the company sought to establish sole control over the provision of musical metadata.

Reaction in the tech press to this corporate appropriation of user content was predictably negative (Dean 2004; Hemos 1999; Lemos 2001; Swartz 2002). Here was a "house that music fans built" yet one in which they no longer felt welcome, a publicly compiled database put to private ends (Dean 2004). Instead of a powerful and productive folksonomy, one in which users collaborate to create new and unexpected uses for technology and knowledge, the story of the CDDB seems like a clear case of the exploitation of free or immaterial labor, the appropriation of user-given labor and content into existing corporate structures.

However, while the immaterial labor argument explains how certain companies and technologies profit from the value of user contributions, it only explains so much. First, as David Hesmondhalgh (2010) argues, we should be wary of overusing terms like *work* and *exploitation* when discussing user contributions to the cultural industries and its products. After all, users who contribute data to social network services or who help create metadata are hardly working or being exploited when compared to the workers in foreign factories responsible for building the hardware on which our digital lifestyles rely (Hesmondhalgh 2010, 271). Even the scores of unpaid interns that fuel the North American cultural industries are clearer examples of exploited labor than everyday free laborers who give content, ideas, or labor to various online and digital services (Hesmondhalgh 2010, 279). The work of adding to information in a database, and the subsequent reselling of that freely generated information for a profit by a commercial company, while certainly evidence of the centrality of information in communicative capitalism, rests too uncomfortably in the realm between hobby and labor to critique it solely on these grounds.

Second, and perhaps more important for my argument, focusing on immaterial labor steers us away from another layer of the commodification process that is taking place here. Since user contributions took place "within a field that is always and already capitalism" (Terranova 2004, 80), user involvement implicates them in the commodification of music in its digital format. In other words, just because users helped develop the CDDB and ID3 tags, this did not mean the services were exempt from larger flows of capital or commodification (van Dijck 2009). In fact, the work of users in this case ensured that digital music looked and acted like other formats of the music commodity that came before it.

The case of the CDDB and metadata, then, is not simply about immaterial labor and the problems surrounding how corporate entities profit from user labor. Rather, it highlights how users' efforts to make a cultural good more usable in its digital form has led them to take part in the process of commodification, both explicitly—by creating tools that ultimately make the commodity a more sellable thing—and implicitly—by creating tools that eventually allow for greater data tracking, surveillance, and cybernetic commodification in general. If we frame the issue solely as a battle over content ownership between Gracenote CDDB and its users, we miss an important insight: one of metadata's key functions was to ready digital music files for their moment as commodities. Digital files, as unlabeled chunks of code, are a tough sell. Tagged with a name, an album cover, production credits, and other information, they become sellable packages. They can be presented in online stores, organized by genre or other useful groupings, and sold in a variety of ways. The CDDB and ID3 tags brought value, in a corporate sense, to digital music by making it recognizable, sortable, and searchable.

The CDDB transitioned CDs to computers and helped sell the idea of computers as a playback device for music. Regardless of who was contributing to or controlling the CDDB, the database's underlying purpose was to make discs recognizable in a new environment and endow digital music with attributes that distinguished the experience of music on computers from that which came before. Without software to automatically recognize and label CDs, users would have had to fill in song names, album titles, and artist names every time they inserted a CD into their computer (as they had to with early software players before Winamp). This task became exponentially taxing when multiplied across multiple CDs. Faced with interfaces and other hardware for which the CD was never initially prepared, the CDDB was a new way to deliver old information. The privatization and commodification of the database itself, in other words, was secondary to the way metadata was already at work in the commodification of digital music. By developing metadata's abilities to label, sort, and use digital music, users were also contributing to digital music's ability to act as a commodity.

The CDDB and ID3 tags reveal commodification as a thoroughly cultural affair and not solely an industrial activity. Both technologies depended heavily on the work and participation of their users. Kan, Scherf, and Kemp may not have been driven initially by profit, but their desire to transition music to a new environment—a motivation shared by users and designers of services like the CDDB and ID3—directly addressed many stumbling blocks to digital music's commodification. As users helped develop tools to manage, organize, and experience digital music through ID3 tags and the CDDB, they were contributing to its commodification, long before the database itself was commodified. As co-developers of metadata, users share a responsibility for readying digital music for its moment as a commodity. In addition to whatever creative and empowering benefits folksonomies bring, the user-generation of metadata actually implicates users in the process of commodification. In an environment where users are producers, users also take part in the process of commodification. The line between user-generated content and user-generated commodity blurs.

However, the re-tuning of music for its new environment also muddies the very notion of the commodity itself. One of the reasons metadata became such a pressing need was the marked increase in the circulation of unauthorized files or legitimate files that had been separated from their packaging. As users ripped music from their CDs or found files through sites like Napster, they used the CDDB and ID3 tags to replace missing paratextual information. As much as user contributions to the CDDB and ID3 helped establish a digital music commodity, they also let users repackage downloaded music *as if it were* an authorized commodity. Like CD counterfeiters who meticulously copy the album covers and other details of the duplicate CDs they're selling (Straw 2009), users contributing metadata were reducing the distance between raw digital files and music commodities. Through metadata they made ripped and (potentially) infringing files seem as authentic and useful as legitimate music commodities. The CDDB and ID3 tags simultaneously built the infrastructure for a legitimate digital music market while allowing users to disguise massive quantities of unauthorized files as legitimate commodities. Metadata helped dubious digital objects parade as sanctioned commodities, even if they were acquired without direct payment.

Whether used to add context to purchased files or to cloak unauthorized ones in the guise of commodities, metadata incorporated users' labor into wider circuits of cybernetic commodification. Mosco (1996, 151) and Andrejevic (2007, 3) define cybernetic commodities as those that are valuable both as commodities and as objects that produce information that can be further commodified (e.g., television ratings, loyalty cards, and database marketing). In an information economy information is both an end commodity and an enhancer of the value of other commodities (Poster 1990; Schiller 2007). Metadata are part of the increasing commodification of information and the push to track the "transactions of everyday life" (Poster 1990, 43, 69–98). They contribute to the ongoing monitoring of consumer tastes, behaviors, and customization preferences for the purposes of profit and surveillance (Andrejevic 2007; McCourt 2005, 94). It is a participatory form of surveillance in which consumers willingly share their personal information as a condition of use of certain new technologies (Andrejevic 2007; Poster 1990). Despite rhetoric that digitization will free music from its commodified form, music as a cybernetic commodity offers greater organized technocratic control over its distribution and consumption (Burkart and McCourt 2006). Whether or not this capture of user contributions is defined as work, the centrality of these contributions to the end product suggests a heightened dependence on users in the very creation of the commodity form.

This is yet another distinguishing feature of digital metadata: they amplify the importance of a resource's paratextual elements. Metadata are a key technology for tracking and surveying the flow and use of digital objects. Unlike TiVo or ratings, though, users contribute metadata knowingly in the hopes of making digital commodities more usable. Metadata turn objects into "codejects" and "logjects" (Dodge and Kitchin 2009, 1348–51): objects that are dependent on code to function and that are constantly tracking their own histories and logging other usage information (e.g. TiVos, smartphones). Metadata are at the heart of this process; they are responsible for storing and shuttling information between various pieces of technology. Computers, smartphones, and other portable devices all rely on the instructions and cues from metadata to sort, organize, and present music to listeners. These same devices can also track what users are listening to and what they think of what they are hearing. User contributions to metadata databases, as well as their everyday use of these logjects, further integrate users into circuits of cybernetic commodification.

Just as TiVo was a "quantum leap" in the ability of producers to monitor viewers (Andrejevic 2007, 11), Gracenote transformed the CDDB from a user-generated database for identifying CDs to a massive information repository that stored precious data on the listening habits of a valuable audience. Gracenote seeded and licensed the database into a wide variety of audio players. With thousands of users connecting to the service each time they inserted a CD into their computers, Gracenote had a rich source of business analytics, which they provided to record labels, about which CDs were popular (i.e., which ones were getting the most requests for metadata), which they commercialized in the form of one of the first digital music "countdown" charts and other research services (Gracenote 2001c). They also tracked how the bonus content on CDDB-enabled CDs was being used, helping record labels hone their multimedia marketing campaigns. By 2001 Gracenote was working with close to four thousand partners worldwide, servicing more than one million consumers daily, and managing more than thirteen million songs in its database (Gracenote 2001b). A true cybernetic commodity generating a variety of business analytics, the CDDB provided Gracenote with insights into the tastes and behaviors of millions of users.

Gracenote also used the database to assist the major record labels in their battle against piracy and file sharing. After Napster's court injunction in 2001 (discussed further in the next chapter), the company faced the monstrous task of removing all copyrighted material from its servers. Gracenote partnered with Napster to help weed out hidden unauthorized tracks with misspelled labels (e.g., Boys 2 Men, Boys To Men, Boys II Men), since Gracenote's database had already logged many of these inconsistencies. After this experiment Gracenote continued to develop technologies for tracking files found on peer-to-peer networks for the purposes of providing metadata and facilitating rights payments (Dean 2004; Gracenote 2001b).

By 2004, helping companies identify copyright infringement in online spaces was quietly becoming part of the company's mandate (Dean 2004). This particular usage of the database, and the networked nature of many metadata services, hints at the privacy challenges metadata present. Beyond just private and personal labels for ordering our music collection, metadata can provide publicly visible documentation about the histories and origins of digital files. Metadata for downloaded files reveal marks left by other users, just as metadata that users input themselves add their own personal inscriptions to the files. This information colors a user's collection, contributing to how files look and work. Moreover, metadata offer visible evidence of the highly mobile and circulatory nature of digital commodities. They present a history that is perpetually subject to revision as new tags get added and old ones overwritten.

MAKING TECHNOLOGY BEHAVE

Escient LLC, the electronics manufacturer that first bought the CDDB in 1998, was also the same company that produced the TuneBase 2000, the device that tried to solve the mega-CD changer's black hole problem. Escient prided itself on "simplifying notoriously complex home electronics," and CEO Scott Jones was fond of claiming, "We make technology behave" (Culbertson 1997). Escient's acquisition was part of this strategy, and, like the TuneBase 2000, the company hoped the CDDB would bring order to our music collections.

By the same token, metadata can be understood more broadly as a technology that brings order to misbehaving music files—files that were stripped of their context, complicating the process of commodification. Metadata are not just data about data. They are data that describe an object *and* data that serve a broader purpose for that object. They underpin the everyday practices of digital music and present digital music as a commodifiable object. They provide functional features (helping users sort, locate, retrieve, and use resources more effectively and efficiently), and in doing so, they link a particular song and file to a wider network of goods and practices. They connect one bit of information to the rest of the info sphere. Part computer database, part CD player, the TuneBase 2000's rich interface promised to simplify multidisc changers to make CD collections behave. In a related way metadata from the CDDB and ID3 tags also helped impose a kind of order on digital music files, making them usable by giving them a more coherent commodity form.

Escient and Gracenote had a very particular vision for the way digital music's commodity form would take shape. Take the example of the *Bowie at the Beeb* CD, which Gracenote helped design in 2000. The project, led by Gracenote's chief technology officer, Ty Roberts, was an attempt to show the possibilities metadata might offer for record labels interested in digital music. Before working at Gracenote, Roberts had sat on an RIAA technical subcommittee during its push against piracy, and he was the owner of a multimedia/CD-ROM development company called ION, where he worked with record labels to create enhanced CDs for computers that kept the digital content secure (CDDB 1999c). Building on these earlier experiences, Robert's Bowie CD featured what Gracenote called "CD-Key" technology. When users inserted the disc into computers, CD-Key identified the disc as a legitimate copy and linked users to a site where they could download exclusive extra content. A primitive form of the kinds of technological protection measures certain record labels and technology companies have been experimenting with since the turn of the millennium, initiatives like this and others for Reeves Gabrels and Geddy Lee highlighted Gracenote's desire to provide extra content as a reward for authorized forms of purchase and consumption (CDDB 1999a; Gracenote 2000).

In these efforts the CDDB reinforced the importance of the CD commodity. As much as it contributed to the shape of the digital music commodity on computers, the CDDB's reliance on CD technology meant that it had one foot firmly in the past. The CDDB was a transitional technology, but the initiatives the owners pursued under Gracenote's direction were geared toward ensuring the relevance and value of the CD as a commodity form. This is echoed in the way the CDDB handles mixed CDs. The database does not work very well, if at all, for mixes. Because much of the recognition technology relies on the TOC listings, a user-generated mix causes trouble for the software. As a result the CDDB does not label the songs on a mixed CD properly; it does not make it easy for users to sort, and it does not provide other extratextual information like album art. The CDDB affords a lesser status to mixed CDs than to official ones. It helps perpetuate an old way of seeing the music commodity even as it makes digital music more visible on the computer. Gracenote was expressing a certain vision for the future of digital music: one built on trying to authenticate legitimate music purchases and on enhancing the content of the CD commodity. Gracenote was using a moment of technological change to extend its control over the music product. This control was written into the database and the metadata that constituted it. Technologies like CD-Key and Audio Fingerprinting were as much means of serving metadata and bonus content as they were a means of encouraging the purchase of a legitimate CD.

Metadata for digital files were not a given. Although they are part of an ongoing process of the commodification of culture and the informationalization of the cultural commodity (Schiller 2007, 101), metadata still needed to be re-tuned for digital environments. Album art, liner notes, track names, production credits, and the like all contributed to the shape of the music commodity over the last century. The CDDB, ID3 tags, and metadata more generally carry on this legacy. The development of digital metadata was the result of conscious decisions to reembed music with information from its previous formats and to present it in ways that seemed new and novel. Whereas information was previously "inseparable from the 'packages' in which it was delivered and the package had a price tag" (Poster 1990, 73), the package was now made up of layers of information that were embedded or networked into the commodity. Metadata now acts as the cover, the case, and the liner notes.

Although they can be seen as the next iteration in a long line of information that has traditionally accompanied and shaped the experience of music, metadata contribute to the development of the commercial and social life of the digital music commodity. They lead users to music, tell them about it, tweak its sonic character, describe how fast or slow it is, how much other people liked it, and how much they liked it the last time they listened to it. Metadata tie together disparate songs in our collections and point us outward toward a whole world of sonic links and other commodities. Without metadata digital music is just data, just sound created from bits and bytes. This sound is very powerful data on its own, but it takes the work of metadata to give music the context necessary for collecting it, using it, and interacting with it.

As users put CDs into devices like the computer or ripped discs into their component songs, they shed the descriptive skin of music's packaging. In the absence of this information, users and companies co-developed technologies to recreate that information for digital files. Built and expanded by users, the CDDB and ID3 tags were not solely industrial efforts. Users were partly responsible for the functions metadata provided and the ways in which the technology functioned. As such, users were also partly responsible for the commodification of the digital music commodity. ID3 tags and the CDDB not only helped users organize and sort their music in ways that were both familiar and useful, but they also advanced an idea of what music on computers should look, sound, and act like. They re-tuned music's materiality and made digital music behave like a commodity.

Given the contributions of users and industry to the development of the CDDB and ID3 tags, metadata challenge existing theories of commodification. They speak to the conflicted nature of the digital music commodity. Metadata simultaneously supported and subverted the emergence of the digital music commodity. On the one hand, they presented digital music in a commercially recognizable and useful form. As users began labeling their digital files and making music intelligible in its new environment, companies like Apple, eMusic, and many others could legitimately start treating digital music as a commodity, too, subject to prices and practices that governed other commodities. On the other hand, metadata also served a crucial purpose for the hundreds of thousands of downloaded files that were circulating in unauthorized settings. Metadata helped organize and personalize swathes of files that lacked much of their contextual information. They disguised unauthorized files as legitimate commodities and let users partake in commodity experiences despite the fact they had not acquired the music by industry-sanctioned means. There have long been pirated goods and knock-off brands, but the prevalence of file sharing has led to digital music libraries constituted by hybrids of authorized songs and disguised or conflicted commodities. While tech companies and record labels employ metadata to track, surveil, and provide authority to the music commodity, users deploy metadata to personalize their libraries, to disguise unsanctioned commodities, and to create a sense of cultural ownership over their music.

Digital music's conflicted status, then, comes from the ways it has been made to act and look like an industrially sanctioned commodity even as users were explicitly turning toward freely downloaded music services to remove themselves from authorized modes of consumption. But as companies like the CDDB explored the cybernetic potential of the data they were collecting and managing, they also struck upon the seeds of what would become a critical component of the digital music commodity: the gathering of user labor and data as a means of both subsidizing their own service and as an additional source of revenue for other interested parties. Though these insights seem commonplace now, in an era where much of our media habits are put to similar service, they were relatively underutilized in music at the time.

While the case of musical metadata hinted at these possibilities, the conflicted and cybernetic nature of the digital music commodity became much more apparent in a rather unlikely place: Napster, the notorious file-sharing network that is often blamed for destroying music's commodity status. With Winamp and metadata in mind, I turn now to explore the way Napster's interface and the kinds of metadata the service generated through everyday use would prove to be instrumental in establishing a market for digital music.

This Business of Napster

NAPSTER AND ITS OFFSPRING

In the summer of 2000 Napster—the company that produced the epony-mous music file-sharing program—found itself in a conundrum. No, it wasn't that high profile musicians like rock group Metallica or hip-hop producer Dr. Dre had launched lawsuits against the service for copyright infringement and racketeering. Nor was it that a US district court judge had just ordered Napster to shut down its website. This particular dilemma was much smaller in scale, but it put Napster in the awkward position of having to admit to itself, publicly, what role it was playing in the development of music as a digital commodity. In June 2000 pop-punk pranksters the Offspring started selling Napster-branded hats, T-shirts, and stickers on their website (King 2000b; Lash 2000b; Menn 2003; Segal 2000). Like much of the music on Napster's network, the Offspring merchandise could be considered pirated. The Offspring had not asked permission to use Napster's logo or sell its merchandise and sales profits went to the Offspring (Lash 2000b; King 2000b). The band's prank, though serious, was as much about sustaining the Offspring's image as it was about revenue or revenge: "It isn't about making money. In typical Offspring fashion, they think it's funny to fuck with people. They think Napster's cool and want to see how cool they [really] are" (Lash 2000a). The Offspring wanted to see how Napster liked the taste of its own medicine: "It's all fair. We've already said you guys [can use] our stuff—we're gonna do yours, too. You shouldn't have any problem with that, should you?" (Mancini 2000).

A day later, Napster reacted in a manner that was decidedly uncool: they sent a cease and desist order (Lash 2000a). Chris Phenner, Napster's busi-ness development manager at the time, reportedly contacted the Offspring via email: "We noticed the sale of Napster-related merchandise on the

Offspring.com site, and wanted to ask for the removal of all offers relating to the sales of our merchandise. I . . . wanted to thank you in advance for your compliance in this matter" (Lash 2000a). Even though not everyone at Napster thought this was the best course of action (Menn 2003, 137), Napster had little choice. The problem was that if Napster knew someone was using its trademarks and did not actively attempt to prevent it, the company could have lost the right to defend the brand elsewhere (Menn 2003, 137). After some back-and-forth discussion—and some significant mocking of Napster from the press/Internet music community—the two parties resolved the situation amicably. Napster apologized for the heavy-handed letter and worked with the band to sell official Napster gear from the Offspring's store. All proceeds from the sales would go to charity (Howells 2000; Segal 2000).

This halfhearted controversy makes visible an image of Napster that is often overlooked: Napster as a company, as Napster Inc. Normally, Napster is either demonized by the major record labels and industry bodies like the RIAA or IFPI for unleashing a Pandora's box of illegal file swapping or lionized by users, techies, and cyberlibertarians for ushering in a new era of music discovery and listening. The squabble between Napster and the Offspring puts both these opposing views in check. Here was a company accused of pirating the music of thousands of bands accusing a band of piracy. Here was a potentially law-breaking idea appealing to the rule of law. Considering Napster's countercultural and anticommercial overtones, how could it exist as a rogue piece of software *and* still send a cease and desist order? The answer is because Napster was a business. Like other companies striving for success in the booming dot-com economy, it had a corporate structure, venture capitalist investors, business development managers, and lawyers. It had a brand, a logo, and trademarks it needed to protect. It even hoped to be profitable one day, primarily through mining the value latent in its community of users. From before the software was officially released to its final days, Napster Inc. was actively trying to establish itself as a key player in the music and technology industries.

If Winamp was a primary interface for playing and experiencing digital music on the computer, and metadata were key micromaterials for sorting, organizing, and using it, Napster was undoubtedly one of the primary technologies for accessing and distributing early digital music. In the absence of formal distribution outlets that weren't hindered by a small catalogue of music or by technical limitations, Napster emerged as a hub for circulation. It did so through its interface and through the metadata the service generated. In this chapter I explore Napster's business plans, its software, and the discourse around its user base to consider the program's impact on the commodification of digital music. Napster gathered and organized an audience and made the idea of digital music retail more than just a bubble beneath the surface. Through its interface and website Napster enabled a commodity community, a network of connected consumers, all trading in mobile digital goods. Participation in the network was as "free" as the music available through the service, but Napster Inc. and a host of other entities extracted value from the program's users based on the kind of community they represented. Whether it was media measurement companies like BigChampagne (a Nielsen Ratings type service for online media) or the RIAA, Napster's audience generated valuable information for those looking in on the system, and the models these early businesses established set the foundation for the much wider range of media-measurement and sentiment-analysis companies that exist today. By downloading infringing files "freely" on Napster, users may have thought they were acting against the commodification of digital music, but the ways they came together through the software created an institutionally effective audience that could be measured, tracked, and packaged as a commodified good. Like the CDDB, Napster showed the possibilities that lay in exploiting the cybernetic potential of the digital music commodity.

As music's re-tuning progressed, Napster's interface connected users in novel ways and presented them with a particular vision of the mobility and fluidity of digital files. It played up the social and technical features of music listening and placed a heightened value on the moment of distribution and the environments through which music circulates. Napster's interface, its never fully realized business model, and its idea of community became the template on which subsequent file-sharing programs and other social media were built. Despite its potential to help users skirt the regular chain of economic transactions involved with acquiring music, Napster actually helped shape the form of the digital music commodity more than it contributed to its undoing.

ORGANIZING AUDIENCES

Napster has been the subject of significant attention in the popular press. There exist multiple journalistic histories of the site's emergence and its impact (see, e.g., Alderman 2001; Ante 2000a, 2000b; Hartley 2009; Menn 2003; Van Buskirk 2009), so the general details are now familiar: in 1998, while at Northeastern University in Boston, Shawn Fanning started working on a program to facilitate finding MP3 files online. Like Winamp, the

CDDB, and ID3 tags, Napster began as a hobby project, but by January of 1999 Shawn had dropped out of school and was working on the program full-time with his uncle, John Fanning, and with a friend he had met online named Sean Parker (Ante 2000b). In May John incorporated Napster while Shawn finished the beta version of the software. The program spread quickly through the summer and fall of 1999. If Winamp irked the major record labels by promoting heavy use of MP3s, Napster infuriated them. By November of that year the RIAA had launched a lawsuit against the fledgling company (Sullivan 1999b). Prominent musicians started filing charges of their own against Napster and its users in early 2000. The legal battles ensued for several years. Napster was ordered to shut down in July 2001, but another court stayed that ruling, allowing Napster to remain in operation during the appeal process. As a last gasp Napster began talks with German media conglomerate Bertelsmann (BMG), but in early 2001 Napster was ordered to filter all copyrighted files out of its network. The company filed for bankruptcy in June 2002 (Borland 2002a). After a judge blocked Napster's sale to BMG, a company called Roxio that manufactures CD-burning software paid $5 million for the Napster brand, logo, and patent portfolio in an assets fire sale (Borland 2002b). Roxio turned Napster into a viable though relatively unsuccessful subscription service. In 2008 Best Buy purchased the beleaguered service for $121 million (BBC 2008), and in 2011 Rhapsody acquired Napster and merged its library and subscribers with its own subscription service.

Given its infamy, Napster has been the subject of a good deal of academic research.[1] Little of it, however, focuses on Napster first and foremost as a business and one that laid more of the foundations (along with Winamp and metadata) for a market in digital music commodities. It may seem counterintuitive that the program that the major record labels have so vilified as the culprit for declining revenues from music is actually one of the prime reasons why a market for digital music commodities exists in the first place, but for as much as Napster was chided for giving users unprecedented access to "free" music, it was also essential in organizing an audience for digital music. As a business, Napster planned explicitly on profiting from its user base; other companies in the music and technology industries realized these plans. Even though Napster may have seemed antithetical to traditional forms of commerce, Napster's conception of its users and discourses about Napster users from the press, academics, the courts, record labels, and other music technology companies combined to construct a hybrid collectivity that fused audience and community. Individual Napster users became a unified group of users: listeners and participants that could serve legal and commercial ends. Napster provided a space for an audience that engaged in community-like behaviors but one that was nonetheless built to be a commodity that would generate data, information, and patterns that could be sold or used in other ways by the community's creators.

Napster's user base fluctuated wildly during its brief existence, and its rapid growth caught many people—its creators included—by surprise (Varanini 2000). Although Shawn Fanning initially shared the program with only a handful of friends, some of these users began discussing the program on public Usenet groups and attracted more users in the process (Ante 2000b; Beuscart 2005). By October of 1999 Napster had approximately 150,000 registered users, with about 22,000 of those users on the system simultaneously (Menn 2003, 101; Spitz and Hunter 2005, 171). Estimates vary, but just six months after going live, Napster had somewhere between two million and ten million users (Giesler and Pohlmann 2003; Hartley 2009), and it was gaining more mainstream attention from websites and publications like *Webnoize,* MP3.com, and *Wired* (Reece 1999; Sullivan 1999a). The added attention from the court cases later in the year brought the program more users and more press attention, with some research claiming the service had between seventy and eighty million users exchanging billions of files at its peak (Logie 2006, 5; B.C.Taylor et al. 2002, 610).[2]

Many of the service's early users were based in the United States, but as the service grew, so did the number of locations from which its users came. Little academic research exists on the demographics of early Napster users, but a 2001 Jupiter Media Metrix report noted that Napster had more than a million users in Canada, Germany, and Italy and was in significant use in more than thirteen "wired" countries, including Brazil, Japan, Argentina, Denmark, and others (JupiterMediaMetrix 2001). The press release for the report described this as "phenomenal global growth" and, because of users' abilities to add songs from various local regions and cultures, "one of the few real-time global marketplaces of culture" (JupiterMediaMetrix, 2001, n.p.). These kinds of global metrics may seem unsurprising now in light of networks like Facebook or Twitter, but they were relatively unmatched at the time. And while Napster itself may not have reached more than a dozen or so "wired" countries, recent scholarship on file sharing has linked the practices that emerged around Napster to significant changes in the music markets of regions such as the Himalayan ranges of the Garhwal region in North India (Nowak 2014) and the Oceanian island country of Vanuatu (Stern 2014).

The quantitative growth of Napster's user base is less interesting than the qualitative issues it raises about notions of audience and community.

In some ways Napster was an early version of social media and user-generated content sites that later became popular, not so much because it had identical features to, say, Myspace or Facebook but because it seemed to serve similar ends. Napster allowed users to connect, to find content and make it available for others. It encouraged discussion among users, and it helped users insert themselves into the circulation of cultural content. It also took advantage of the free labor of its users and used the data they generated as part of its plans to grow and expand the service, a business model that is now applied across a good portion of the web's most popular properties. What is perhaps most interesting about the work Napster's users performed, though, was that it seemed to undermine, or at least trouble, the traditional economics of production, distribution, and consumption. While users of Facebook, Twitter, and the like support the companies that own those sites by sheer virtue of posting their opinions and sharing their data, one of Napster's primary uses was for the trading and sharing of copyrighted content. "Measuring" Napster's audience is important since it is at the heart of what Napster was trying to do and of what will ultimately be Napster's legacy. But quantifying Napster's users or measuring their value is complicated by the nature of their labor and the supposedly illicit nature of the practices in which they were engaging.

Dallas Smythe (1981), in one of the most enduring works on media audiences, famously argued that media produce an audience commodity. Speaking specifically of broadcast media, Smythe noted that TV programs are the free lunch broadcasters and advertisers give out in return for audience labor. As viewers view, they are at work. They are being produced as commodities that broadcasters sell to advertisers (Smythe 1981, 266). Smythe's work has been criticized, reworked, and updated by a number of scholars (see, e.g., Bermejo 2009; Garnham 2001; Meehan 1984, 2001; Mosco 1996; Murdock 1978). Eileen Meehan's study of the ratings firm AC Nielsen has been particularly significant in reframing the concept by turning attention to the work of measurement companies and technologies. Given that the audience is "knowable only through the ratings that measured it and those ratings were the outcome of corporate rivalries, alliances, and manipulations," Meehan contends that AC Nielsen and other ratings companies created a partial—and highly gendered and classed—version of what constituted the television audience in order to appeal to the companies who relied on that information (Meehan 2001, 215). The audience commodity actually had little to do with the people who watched television. Rather, they were a figment of measurement used to convince networks and advertisers of the desirability of their audiences.

New media extend and complicate this logic, as a host of social media sites and software applications cater to audiences who gather not just to consume but to produce. As part of the rise of "Web 2.0" (O'Reilly 2005), there has been an explosion of social media sites and services that make user participation and user-generated content a key part of their offerings. Instead of passive recipients of media, users are "prosumers" or "produsers" who make and take content almost simultaneously through social networking sites, blogs, and the like (Bruns 2006). If in Smythe's model the "free lunch" was the content viewers received, social media sites like Facebook or YouTube offer users platforms on which they can create their own content. The audience is doubly at work, producing the very content it consumes, making its own free lunch. As I noted in the previous chapter, however, users of these kinds of programs—from the CDDB to Myspace or Facebook—perform a different kind of labor than does Smythe's typical audience commodity since they willingly offer up a significant amount of the content that makes these sites run (Coté and Pybus 2007; Terranova 2004). Napster was a prototypical Web 2.0 company that relied on the labor and content of users but did so in a way that made it difficult to apply labor theories of value to account for the value generated through these user-based production practices (Arvidsson and Colleoni 2012; Fuchs 2010).

New media and the Internet not only make possible different ways of assembling audiences and putting them to work; they also allow for different means of measuring and representing them. On the one hand there are more tools than ever for advertisers or producers wanting to track consumer behavior and predict audiences. On the other hand audience fragmentation via a proliferation of niche media, as well as added audience agency through new technologies and formats of consumption (podcasts, DVRs, etc.), has made predicting audience patterns more slippery (Napoli 2011).

Philip Napoli (2001, 66) notes that any audience is a balance between the predicted (i.e., forecasts about the audience's size and behavior), the measured (i.e., what ratings firms provide), and the actual (i.e., everyone who is actually an audience member for a given media product—essentially an unknowable detail). Since companies value predictability, the value of certain new media audiences may increase or decrease depending on how predictable they are. Measurement firms still face difficulties reconciling the packaged, sellable version of the audience with the actual audience. But as the gap between the measured audience and the actual audience widens and traditional ad-supported models become less effective, new media companies have found other ways to extract value from users to manage this unpredictability, "such as audience members' personal data, research services, and various cross-promotional opportunities" (Napoli 2001, 71). New media producers rely increasingly on cybernetic commodities, on the ability to sell data about users of commodities rather than the sale of those commodities directly (Andrejevic 2007, 14; Mosco 1996, 151). The act of being watched becomes as valuable as watching advertisements used to be.

Meehan and Napoli circle around a similar insight: all audiences are constructed. Measurement technologies are quantitative constructions of audiences but also technologies that manufacture a particular kind of audience (Bermejo 2009). Rather than reporting some true total viewing audience, ratings companies and measurement technologies provide what Napoli, building on Ettema and Whitney (1994), has called *institutionally effective audience:* those that can be efficiently integrated into the economics of the media industries (Napoli 2011). What's perhaps most interesting in the case of Napster, then, is that most of its users were in many ways working to remove themselves from the institutionally effective audience, to evade the typical reporting statistics that accompany music commodity purchases (e.g., SoundScan and other technologies that track music purchases at retail stores). Napster's audience, in some senses, became a test case for how to account for what had previously been unaccountable and how to put that account in the service of further commodification. Moreover, Napster's own vision of, and use for, its audience was fluid and changed conveniently depending on the legal and publicity issues the company was facing. While Napster users may have thought they were outside the institutionally effective audience, they were central in spurring innovations in new media measurement techniques and tactics that now occupy a central place in the media and cultural industries.

Before considering the question of whether Napster's "audience" became an institutionally effective one, I first want to review the ways Napster's audience was constructed through press coverage and through Napster's own website and software. Much of the discussion around the software in the popular and academic press was loaded with heated rhetoric that either elevated Napster users to revolutionary status or disparaged them as an underground network of thieves (Logie 2006). Many journalists were quick to label Napster's audience as young and deviant, even though there was evidence that Napster's software was hardly limited to students or the under-twenty set (Jones and Lenhart 2004; Mann 2000, 57; Taylor et al. 2002, 615–16). Press coverage and court documents consistently applied labels like "teens" and "undergrads" to signify all Napster users and "'adolescent' served as a metonym for Napster users as a whole." Depending on the story and on who was telling it, these young users were "wholly integrated members of society ('music fans'), external threats ('pirates'), or both." The press discourse and that of the RIAA shifted between the terms *users* and *pirates* as it suited them, defining the latter in a "purposefully vague" way as part of a negative image campaign against Napster's audience (Spitz and Hunter 2005, 172–75).

The discourse that surrounded Napster users also positioned them as a virtual community,[3] a group that bonded as they engaged in digital exchange (Giesler and Pohlmann 2003; Poblocki 2001). While communities like the IUMA, or those that formed around Winamp, ID3 tags and Napster can certainly be described as virtual communities, their role in digital music's re-tuning has to be understood in terms of their economic as well as their social impact. The kinds of community at play, in other words, should not divert attention from the role the technology itself played in gathering and organizing this community into a useful economic entity. This becomes a particularly pressing question when we consider that Napster's purpose seems specifically tailored toward subverting the generation of economic value. Napster, after all, has roots in various computer and security hacking subcommunities. Before Napster, Shawn Fanning took part in an IRC (Internet Relay Chat) channel called woowoo (Menn 2003, 17). A resource for building software projects and sharing information on coding, the IRC was made up of a loose collection of hackers and coders (primarily young, white, US male college students). Affiliated with other hacker groups like ADM (Association des Malfaiteurs) and el8.org, the motives of the various woowoo members varied; some were "black hat" hackers working on viruses and other malicious code; others were using their "white hat" hacking skills to discover and make public security exploits in a variety of programs and websites (Menn 2003, 18–19). The knowledge Fanning gained, maliciously or not, about firewalls, about opening ports on remote computers, and about the technologies for securing machines, proved invaluable in designing Napster. So while Fanning wrote the bulk of the code for the program, he was heavily indebted to the help he received from woowoo users. Many of the members of that group went on to populate Napster's offices in California, as well as other start-ups and Internet security firms in the dot-com boom years (Menn 2003, 20).

Although Napster has ties to the hacker community, and can be seen as a kind of hacktivist project, the community that ended up forming around the software, as well as the individual motives of each user, was much more varied (including hackers and students but also mainstream computer users). Napster users were highly dispersed and took part in an imagined, networked, and activity-based community built on specialized loose ties (B. Anderson 1991; Poblocki 2001, 4). It had a frequently changing membership, and its members had little perception of the attributes, way of life, and historical experiences of other users. Napster users were drawn together by their illicit or anticorporate behavior. Many Napster users identified with Fanning as a young tech-savvy "revolutionary" (Taylor et al. 2002, 616). They regularly conflated the creator (a nineteen-year-old computer science hacker dropout) with the software (a program that could distribute copyrighted tracks for "free") and saw Napster as a tool of protest "against the rising prices for albums and concert tickets" and a broader regime of intellectual property (Taylor et al. 2002, 616). By "viewing Fanning/Napster as *revolutionary*, users understood this identity to involve fundamental social change oriented to justice and equality" (Taylor et al. 2002, 616; Tench 2001). As with Winamp, users, and not just the younger ones, were caught up in an idea about Napster that went far beyond the physical attributes of the software and tied in with a larger vision of computers as devices for personal liberation and self-expression.

For these reasons Napster and its users were frequently held up as an alternate kind of economy and community (Barbrook 2002; Giesler and Pohlmann 2003; Leyshon 2003). Building on the idea of "the gift" in anthropology (Appadurai 1986; Hyde 1983; Mauss 1967), critical media researchers argued file sharers were engaging in radical acts of civil disobedience, practices that might soon bring about a "Napsterisation of everything" (Barbrook 2002). By sharing files, ideas, and culture, Napster users were constructed as altruistic gift givers, even if some engaged in nonreciprocal forms of exchange (Giesler and Pohlmann 2003, 8). Rather than a private technology, Napster was a public library for digital files (Vaidhyanathan 2003, 180). The service seemed to be an extension of one of the Internet's original promises as a research network for the sharing of ideas and resources (Abbate 1999). Gifts, in this case music files, stood against the logic of commodity exchange (Leyshon 2003), so communities relying on gifts as their primary source of exchange were engaging in what Barbrook called "anarcho-communism" (Barbrook 1998). Napster was a transient space, a "temporary hypercommunity" in which to practice divergent social logics (Kozinets 2002). Napster was part of an "MP3 movement," a "rational revolt of passionate fans" against costly CDs and slow distribution channels (Vaidhyanathan 2003, 179). Users sought to free themselves from market relations, to remove themselves from the institutionally effective audience. But they did so not necessarily by taking music that one would otherwise pay for but by using software that was a blatant expression of difference in relation to social norms (Giesler and Pohlmann 2003, 9).

Napster, as a company, might not have been as politically motivated as some of its users, but it did connect communities of users through the circulation and exchange of free goods and provoked the formation of alternative legal and commercial frameworks for the distribution of digital goods. Lawrence Lessig's Creative Commons initiative or other copyleft movements, for example, offered users the ability to give their creations greater and looser permissions for their work, licenses usually precluded by traditional copyright law (Berry 2008; Lessig 2004). More radical hacker projects, like FreeNet, were explicitly designed to destabilize intellectual property norms and commercial transactions (Dyer-Witheford 2002). These initiatives were not affiliated with Napster, but they speak to the opportunity many saw to question the codes and conventions of intellectual property ownership and distribution as a result of digitization.

This alternative ethos behind the Napster software and its users is, in some ways, related to the free and open-source software movements (Berry 2008; Kelty 2008). These movements go beyond the simple promotion of free software, the sharing of source code, and the appropriation of unconventional perspectives on copyright law. They represent "a considerable reorientation of knowledge and power in contemporary society" by positing an alternative system for the "creation, dissemination and authorization of knowledge" (Kelty 2008, 2). By coming together as recursive publics—publics that are constantly and vitally concerned with their own existence and boundaries as a public and that speak to forms of power by working through alternatives to it—the free and open-source software movements deploy technical skills to advance cultural change. Though it was freeware, Napster's corporate plans and proprietary software meant that it was neither a free software initiative nor a recursive public (Kelty 2008, 61). Nevertheless, Napster was a venue through which many members of these movements worked out ideas about rights and values and what technologies might best support their ideological framework (Kelty 2008, 52).

The conception of Napster users as a community of rebellious gift-giving downloaders is an appealing one. But the program's user base did not emerge spontaneously around a piece of software. It was planned, managed, and cultivated. It was also substantially funded through several rounds of investment from high-tech venture capitalists and, later on, one of the major record labels. As much as some Napster users might have been exploring "new forms of social exchanges and cooperation," they were also a "clientele" (Beuscart 2005, S2). Even those many users who were solely seeking "free" music and not explicitly politically motivated took part in the service as clientele. Napster users, in other words, may have been acting disruptively, but by doing so collectively, they showed paths for building a digital music commodity. Further, Napster's anticorporate image was as much a marketing move as it was a desire to disrupt the music business. Nothing sells as well as appearing not to sell.[4] Using anticommercial messaging, Napster Inc. saw the community that formed around its software as a way to bring in revenue from advertising and other sources. This is not to suggest Napster was not disruptive or to dismiss all of the radical hopes for Napster's potential to create alternative legal and commercial frameworks for the distribution of culture. Rather, I am arguing that it is quite possible for commercial digital markets to exist alongside wide-scale acts of piracy (Dyer-Witheford 2002, 143). In fact, the interaction between these two poles might be, realistically, the more essential state for digital goods. Digital goods like music circulate regularly in both commercial and noncommercial arrangements. The case of Napster highlights how the former stands to benefit from the latter.

COMMODITY COMMUNITIES

Rather than a traditional audience commodity, Napster is closer to what Christine Fry (1977) called a *commodity community:* an audience that is very much a community but one that was built and maintained as such in order to serve as a commodity. Fry coins the term in an anthropological study about neighborhoods and residential units (retirement homes, adult communities, etc.) that are "intentionally planned, designed, and developed as an economic endeavour" (1977, 116). In these preconceived communities residential units are sold in conjunction with a "'way of life,' culture, and social organization which is an implicit, if not an explicit part of the deal" (Fry 1977, 116). Commodity communities rely on the culture of the community to attract interest, either from potential homebuyers or from those looking to invest in or extract value from the community. Through design of the environmental space (e.g., buildings, facilities, parks) and control of resources (e.g., education, recreation, transportation), developers must convince buyers and sellers of the type of community they hope to create. Commodity communities thus depend on a fairly long-term and structural involvement of those managing them. Developers become patrons of the communities they create. They are constantly shaping and trimming the community's features in order to enhance its culture and value (Fry 1977).

From very early on the people behind Napster had a vision of the role its users would play. Through its business plans, software, website, and marketing, Napster designed a program conducive to creating a community that could provide value and profit for the company. For example, an October 1999 strategy document that surfaced during the trial written by Napster's management team outlines the company's immediate goals: "Progress user base to X# of concurrent users. Get top tier VC [venture capital] funding. Perform tests to determine deal presented to Sony. Do a deal with Sony. Do a deal with other labels under similar terms. Determine whether to become a portal or intermediate infrastructure. Lather. Rinse. Repeat" (qtd. in Menn 2003, 102). The document, though short on specifics and long on irreverence, lays out a linear plan in which each subsequent step hinges on the ability to gather a large number of concurrent users. Only then would Napster be able to acquire seed funding and convince labels they were providing a worthwhile service: "We use the hook of our existing approach [i.e., free music] to grow our user base, and then use this user base coupled with advanced technology to leverage the record companies into a deal. The fact that we grow 4 or 5 million simultaneous users with millions of songs (through the inherently viral nature of the Napster concept) can hardly be ignored by Sony or EMI" (qtd. in Menn 2003, 102). Napster's strategy depended on more users and more files. Like broadcast media, Napster planned to use "free" content to grow and then leverage its audience. It also hoped that its underground status and its ever-growing network of users would help it spread virally.[5] Although Napster hoped to "ultimately bypass the record industry entirely," the company knew it could not get by without the major labels: "The key is to co-exist with the record industry, at least temporarily. The record industry is essential to our efforts" (qtd. in Menn 2003, 102). As such, it is not surprising that Napster was in discussions with the RIAA in an attempt to avoid litigation, though how sincerely the two parties engaged remains unclear (Ante 2000a; Menn 2003). Napster believed the audience it was gathering would be worth enough for the service to flourish, even though John Fanning had apparently received specific legal advice telling him that the business model was most likely illegitimate.[6] Twisting the adage "If you build it, they will come," Napster hoped that if they came, it would get built.

Under this strategy Napster set out to grow its community instead of profiting from it directly. In fact, Napster actively turned down opportunities for obvious revenue, such as its decision not to implement a subscription model or to include advertising in software or on the website (Menn 2003, 101). Napster also held off on selling merchandise, since it worried that significant revenue coming into the company would hurt its chances in court (Menn 2003, 138). This is why, when Napster reached a deal in the Offspring dispute, it donated the proceeds to charity (King 2000b; Mancini 2000).

Of course, Napster *was* taking in money, and this was part of the problem for those who opposed it. In the company's first summer, John Fanning managed to convince a few business associates to invest $350,000 in the system to build and maintain the infrastructure for a few months (Beuscart 2005, S7). In October 1999 Napster received $2 million from a few wealthy Silicon Valley "angel" investors, and venture capital firm Hummer Winblad contributed another $15 million in May 2000 (Ante 2000b). Though Napster was in talks with record labels such as Universal Music in 2000 for funding and partnership opportunities, the only label that took an interest was BMG. In October 2000 the label made a substantial investment to the site, apparently in an attempt to hedge its bets depending on the outcome of the court case (Menn 2003, 261). Although Napster was not profiting from its audience, it was using the promise of that audience as a hook to bring in financing. This level of investment in the company angered labels and artists like Lars Ulrich, the outspoken drummer for Metallica. Ulrich, despite being critically assailed by the MP3 and tech community for his stance against Napster, argued that Napster was not simply a benevolent new technology looking to set music free for listeners, like some digital Robin Hood. Rather, it was an organization that had serious funding behind it and every intention of being a profitable entity: "What people have to remember . . . is that Napster is a corporation, OK? They just got $15 million in funding from some of the major venture capitalists out here. They have all along, ultimately getting to the point where they could have a major IPO, which is the one option, or get basically bought out by an AOL type of company. So at some point there will be a major, major profit going on for the people who've invested in Napster" (qtd. in Alderman 2001). Regardless of whether we agree with Ulrich's "Napster bad" argument, his point that beneath the community was a commodity is well placed. If Napster users saw themselves as oppositional, Ulrich was asking what it was they were opposing. Indeed, as Napster's legal situation got worse, the $8 million infusion it received from BMG could be seen as exactly the kind of deal Ulrich was predicting.

Despite an abundance of press coverage during Napster's rise to cultural prominence and its ensuing legal troubles, these mundane details about the business aspects of Napster were rarely discussed (for exceptions see Ante 2000a, 2000b; Sullivan 1999a; Varanini 2000). The idea of Napster as a rebellious, young, and even "revolutionary" technological and cultural innovation (as described in Taylor et al. 2002) was so pervasive that the press largely overlooked Napster's commercialization strategies, and many of the company's business strategies, plans, and documents were never made public in early reports on the site/software (Menn 2003, 1). The legal and cultural issues the program sparked were of such interest to the media and scholars that they barely touched on what made Napster such a wholly ordinary case of start-up failure during the dot-com boom and bust. It was only by ignoring Napster's commercial nature that Napster could be heralded as a "sea change," a threat to private property specifically and capitalism more generally; only then could Napster be "a technological fetish onto which all sorts of fantasies of political action are projected" (Dean 2005, 62).

This is where the concept of the commodity community is particularly useful: it helps explain why the commercial aspects of Napster were relegated to the background. Fry argues that the term *community*, at least in anthropology and community studies, has long had an organic character. Hardly the crass stuff of corporate creations, communities arise from below, from the interactions among people and their environments. Communities can create their own commodities and carry out any number of commercial enterprises, but social organization itself is rarely considered a sellable or marketable object (Fry 1977, 115). This is part of the attraction of the commodity community for those who live there; it feels somehow "natural," a regular state of social organization that allows people to play out their lives and meet their needs. This naturalness is also precisely what appeals to advertisers, marketers, and other actors looking to benefit from that community. The more natural it feels, the more natural consumers will act. They will feel less like they are being sold something, less like they are being targeted, and more like the social organization they are taking part in is one of their own creation.

As early as November of 1999, Eileen Richardson, one of Napster's CEOs, was touting the idea that Napster was, at its core, about community (Sullivan 1999a). A key site for building this community was Napster's website. Napster.com was the prime location for downloading the application, but the site also had explicit mission statements about the revolutionary nature of the technology and the company: "Welcome to Napster, the future of music. . . . By creating a virtual community, Napster ensures a vast collection of MP3s for download" (Napster 1999). As the legal battles began, Napster mined this virtual community, not just for access to more MP3s but as a political and activist tool. Shawn Fanning and Hank Barry, another of Napster's CEOs, posted updates about Napster's ongoing court cases and encouraged users to "speak out" in support of Napster by writing to major record labels and the RIAA. They actively called on artists—"Are you an artist who wants in on the revolution? Click here to get your music heard on the world's largest online music community!" (Napster 2000b)— and suggested that users "buycott" CDs of musicians that supported the program (i.e., buy the music of bands that spoke highly of Napster or bands that were featured on the site). Napster provided addresses and contact information for users who wanted to mobilize and send letters to record labels or congressional representatives. They also created a forum for users to discuss strategies of resistance and how to stand up for "the future of person to person file sharing" (Napster 2000b).

As the court case progressed, the site's original focus on the software and the music was obscured by pleas to its community for participation: "We're still going strong but we need your help. Join the Napster Action Network now and make your voice heard. The only way to make a difference is to GET INVOLVED" (Napster 2001b). Like the rhetoric that underpins *MP3 Power! With Winamp,* Napster saw itself and its users as part of a broader movement. Napster, the computer, and the Internet were more than mere tools; they were means of self-expression and resistance against an out-of-touch music industry whose products cost fans too much and paid artists too little (Knopper 2009, 133; Mann 2000, 2003). From musicians like Courtney Love posting the questionable math behind record labels contracts (Love 2000) to fans incensed by high CD prices and the illegality of the Minimum Advertised Price scandal (Kot 2000)[7], Napster provided an outlet for expressing antipathy toward perceived forms of music industry exploitation. Napster users could help the cause by using the software but also by becoming even more involved in the software's future. They could be part of an uprising that pitted the forces of technology and everyday users against an industry that seemed anachronistic and fearful of change.

Despite Napster's desire to enlist users as potential allies in its legal struggle, the company also maintained a distance from its community. In 2000 Napster added a strictly worded copyright policy and a Terms of Use page to the website in an attempt to shift the responsibility of infringing files to its users: "Napster is an integrated browser and communications system provided by Napster, Inc. . . . Napster does not, and cannot, control what content is available to you using the Napster browser. Napster users decide what content to make available to others using the Napster browser, and what content to download. Users are responsible for complying with all applicable federal and state laws." (Napster 2000c). Additionally, as its partnership with BMG began to make headlines, Napster took pains to separate itself from the community. Take for example this Frequently Asked Question, to which Napster posted its blunt response: "Has Napster Sold Out?: No. We strongly believe that this partnership with Bertelsmann is an important next step for Napster. Napster is a business, and as such, we are taking steps to establish a business model, create value for our users and push the limits of our technology" (Napster 2000a). The admission of Napster's commercial intentions was likely sobering for users who believed in the image of Napster as an anticorporate and rebellious technology. Although the Internet Archive does not have records of Napster's user forums, discussions in the Winamp forums sum up the anger many users had: "Man, this is a bunch of B.S!!!! I can't believe they are doing this!! AGHHHHHHHH They have made me mad now. They say they are not selling out, but it seems like it to me. . . . Never thought it would come to this, but they claim the battle is not over and I hope it's not" (OneJ1Way 2001). Although Winamp forum users weren't as universally against a sub-scription-based version of Napster as OneJ1Way, it's clear that the dis-course on Napster's site and about the program more generally had created an organic vision of a community that stood for free music and against the traditional recorded music industries. Based on this vision, it seemed incom-patible to many that Napster would accept money from the very companies Napster users thought they were opposing.

As Napster's legal leash shortened, website posts to their users became even more antagonistic:

> Napster is continuing to comply with the District Court's injunction
> and to prevent the record companies from shutting down file sharing
> . . . we have implemented a range of filters designed to remove from the
> Napster service all copyrighted works for which we have received
> notice. We have recently enhanced those filters in an effort to screen
> out the wide range of variations in artist name and song title. . . . While
> many of the variations in artist and title names are the natural result of
> individuals naming their own files, some of the variations are deliberate
> attempts to evade the filters and share material over the Napster service
> that would otherwise be blocked. Napster's terms of use prohibit the use
> of evasive measures such as pig latin, napcameback, napsterdecoder and
> otherwise deliberately altering file names in order to evade Napster's
> filters. Users found to be employing such evasive techniques will receive
> a warning and those who continue to share such files will be blocked.
> (Napster 2001a)

Users that Napster had been courting as supporters were now liabilities. Napster was scolding users for evading its filters, even though users were simply trying to reembed the program with some of its former capabilities.

Napster users had to confront the idea that their community was far more planned and managed than they had assumed. The service ceased to live up to the expectations users had of it—expectations Napster itself had set.

Napster shut down its website in September 2002. All that remained was a logo and a graffiti-inspired message: "Napster Was Here." Even though Napster's relationship with its community was strained at times during the two-year period the site was online, the company was still hopeful that it could salvage some value from its audience. Before shutting down, the company encouraged users to sign up as "public beta testers" of a new version of the program and to wait while the details of the new service were unveiled (see, e.g., Napster 2001c). Although Napster shut down before it could truly profit from its commodity community, the company saw the community as a resource for garnering public support and for tactical activism.

That said, Napster's conception of community quickly spread to other sites and services. Napster's technology and template for community opened the door for a multitude of digital web services. While its immediate successors (like Gnutella, KaZaa, SoulSeek, and Limewire) used similar tactics and features to woo former Napster users, the tension that existed between Napster users as a dispersed but connected group exploring new forms of exchange and as a potential source of value presages many of the current popular models of online media interaction. Napster employees have gone on to work at some of the more prominent web properties (e.g., Sean Parker, a Napster co-founder, was also the founding president of Facebook; other employees like Jan Jannink founded music streaming service iMeem); and a variety of social networks and other "Web 2.0" services, following Napster's lead, position their users in a similar state of balance between community and audience. This is what makes Napster's case so relevant to the contemporary moment. Napster was a protobusiness that incorporated strategies and features that are now common in new media and Web 2.0 business models (Allen 2008).

In some ways Napster was rather unoriginal. Its business model was similar to previous forms of mass media. Like television and radio (as well as countless dot-com boom-era companies), Napster relied on providing "content" in order to attract an audience. Although the "free lunch" Napster provided was largely content it was not licensed to provide, the model of using content to aggregate an audience had clear parallels to other forms of media. The content may have felt "free," but it was put in service of creating value in other ways, for other interested parties. Despite these echoes of previous media forms, Napster was one of the first companies to design a piece of technology that realized the size and scale of community that was possible around digital music. It also offered a way of conceiving of collectivities and of managing their affective relationships with a business. Napster cultivated an image of itself as anticorporate and rebellious and presented Shawn Fanning as the youthful face of the company (Taylor et al. 2002). It used this representation to help strengthen and enhance the value of the community it was building. Through its website and, as I argue in the following section, its software, Napster gathered users who bonded over practices that felt as if they had organic origins within the community. The community culture was reaffirmed with each download.

COMMUNITIES OF CIRCULATION

Napster's software was an instrumental component for gathering and organizing its commodity community, but it did more than just collect a group of potential consumers. It showed the kind of value that could be gained and gleaned from acts of exchange. It made visible the mobile and fluid nature of digital music and illustrated in a compelling and powerful way one of the fundamental concepts of the Internet: that it is a thoroughly networked and interconnected space. By connecting users and making that connection visible through its interface, Napster was a vision of the Internet in miniature (Kelty 2008, 52). It brought together disparate and transient users with hard drives full of music and connected them in ways they had not been connected before. This ultimately had an impact on how users came to understand the act of file sharing and the nature of the digital music they were trading. Even after the company's demise, the community that came together through the software and the contexts through which those users experienced digital music files are central moments in the commodification of digital music.

Given the ability of users to circulate cultural goods at an unprecedented rate via digital networks, the Internet reminds us that the movement of music and the technologies that move it are central components of how users experience and understand music (S. Jones 2002, 215–16). Napster has a lot to tell us about the moment of distribution and the influence it exerts on both production and consumption. Interactions between Napster users revolved around the exchange and circulation of files, their community rooted in a kind of culture of circulation (Lee and LiPuma 2002, 192). The objects, ideas, and commodities that people exchange, as well as the technologies and paths that underpin that movement, create and animate different kinds of communities. As with the close reading of Winamp's interface in the first chapter, my analysis of Napster's interface, then, is less interested in a hermeneutic interpretation of the program's design than in the ways the program connects users and enables circulation of the music commodity. I will pay more attention to the surface of the object's interface, and the role Napster played in music's re-tuning, than to what Napster's interface "means." In other words, while the Napster interface might mean something, in the interpretative sense, it is also, at its core, a site of interaction between humans and machines that allows for a reconfiguration and "new forms of connection between consumers (and purveyors) of music" (S. Jones 2002, 222). Napster's contribution to the re-tuning of music's interface was the relationships between users and digital files that the software brought together and made visible and the kinds of circulation its features afforded.

The IRC discussions with other hackers not only helped Fanning create Napster, but they also framed the kinds of features Fanning built into the program. While search engines collect data by crawling the web at regular intervals (these were, at the time, daily or weekly), IRC channels kept constant tabs of who was online and connected to the group and who had signed off. Fanning built this insight into Napster: "My idea was to have a real-time index that reflects all sites that are up and available to others on the network at that moment" (qtd. in Menn 2003, 34). The result was that Napster—like today's instant messenger clients or social networks—provided a constant awareness of the presence of other users and of the contents of the network.[8] Napster's interface further reinforced this network awareness by providing a constant count of how many users were on the service and how many files they were sharing (see fig. 8).

By June of 1999 Fanning had a first version of the program ready. The next version came out shortly thereafter, and it contained the key elements that would define its interface over the next year and a half, such as the "Advanced Search System," the "Library," the "Transfer Window," the "Audio Player," the "Playlist," the "Chat System," and the "Hot List" (Napster 1999). Napster's near instantaneous indexing of all the files on the system meant that as users logged on, their shared folder was immediately visible to all other users on the system. Searches were quick and returned a dizzying array of files. Napster amplified the sense of limitless files by stuffing the search results window with entries. The text was a small but readable list, and the interface seemed maximized to show as many results as possible. By focusing on the vast amount of material in circulation, the interface heightened the affective experience of searching for and finding music. Each file query was an indication both of the amount of movement taking place

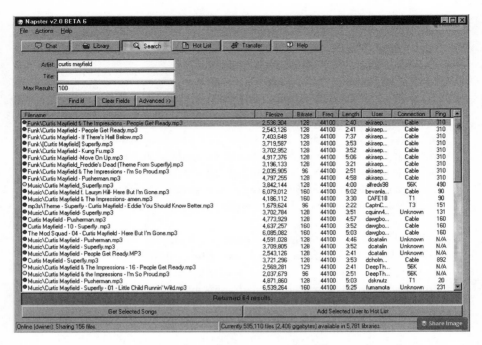

Figure 8. Napster main search window (version 2.06). The search window provided access to the program's features (search, hot list, chat, etc.). It also showed users how many other users were online and how many files they were sharing.

on the network and of the sizable amount of other users who were engaged in a shared practice. Searching simultaneously revealed the music that users were seeking and validated participation in the community.

In addition to indicating the availability of songs, searches returned other information about the file (e.g., bit rate, length of the song, frequency at which it was recorded, nickname of the user providing the file, and details about connection speed). While this string of information seemed like nothing more than minor technical details, the choice to include this meta-data was one of the ways that Napster brought its community together through circulation. It allowed users to peer, ever so slightly, into the lives and habits of other users as they browsed or traded. Each search for a file or artist returned a multitude of results, each one a partial glimpse into the library of another. To know that "dsknutz" had a T1 connection meant knowing that your download would be served quickly, but it also set up a hierarchy of users. In an environment where access to songs was governed

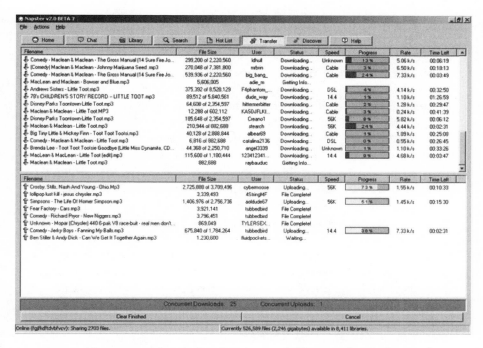

Figure 9. Napster transfer window (version 2.07). The transfer window made visible the idea of a networked community and put the act of waiting on display.

not by price but by how quickly one could move them onto or off of a computer, resources like these confer a certain status and reputation upon users with higher technical resources. Circulating files on the system was not simply an altruistic act of providing music. It was also an act of display, one where a user's tastes, preferences, and technical attributes were public and part of the movement of music through the community.

The transfer window kept users apprised of the status of files coming in and out of their computer (see fig. 9). While contemporary downloading software connects to multiple computers (and users) to download a single file, Napster worked on a one-to-one basis. If a user was downloading a file from, say, aoldude67 and the peer disconnected, the user would have to wait until the peer was back online or find another peer with the same file. Circulation, here, depended on the willingness of others in the community to stay online, creating a certain technical tangibility to the relationships between users. The transfer window also displayed the usernames of people who were in the process of downloading files, giving an ambient sense of which files were popular and the tastes of other users. As peers connected and disconnected, and music circulated, users left traces of their presence in the transfer window. Watching transfers take place made concrete the idea of a network of connected users.

Visible distribution through the transfer window also added an extra moment of anticipation in the consumption process. Susan Willis (1991) argues that the anticipation for the moment of consumption is a key source of our attraction to (and dependence on) the products of everyday life: "commodity capitalism fully develops the anticipation of use value while use value itself seems to serve no other purpose but to create the basis for its anticipation" (6). In other words waiting to consume is as important to commodification as consumption itself. Typically, in music consumption, the moments of finding a desired object and acquiring it are separated by time, though that time is greatly reduced with digital distribution. Napster, for example, had a combined audio library and music player; it essentially combined the acts of searching, collecting, and playing music (which, as I describe in the next chapter, becomes one of the central organizing principles of the iTunes Store). Even though Napster promoted near-instantaneous distribution and acquisition of files, the transfer window put the brief period of waiting on display and incorporated it into the downloading experience. Like the clear plastic packaging that envelops everyday products and heightens our anticipation and fetish for supermarket commodities (Willis 1991, 5), watching a file crawl or fly in through Napster was to anticipate the arrival of new sounds.

Beyond these functional aspects of the software, Napster also included community-oriented features such as Chat and Hot List to organize its audience (see fig. 10). Fanning included these features to differentiate Napster from other music sites at the time: "It was rooted out of frustration not only with MP3.com, Lycos, and Scour.net, but also to create a music community" (Varanini 2000). This claim may be slightly revisionist, given that Napster's legal status depended on showing substantial noninfringing uses of the software. Drawing on arguments from the Sony Betamax case in 1984, Napster might have been trying to position itself as a "community" as a way to show that the technology served other purposes beyond the circulation of infringing files. The failure of its ability to convince the courts of this is part of the lasting discourse that continues to surround contemporary file-sharing technologies.

That said, the Chat and Hot List features suggested the community aspect was not mere posturing. The Chat feature (fig. 10a), which drew on the functional and technical features of IRC, let users maintain loose ties on the network either individually or through group chat rooms (Poblocki 2001, 7). While all users saw nicknames pass by during uploads and downloads,

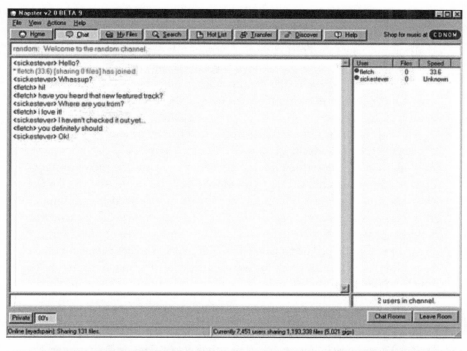

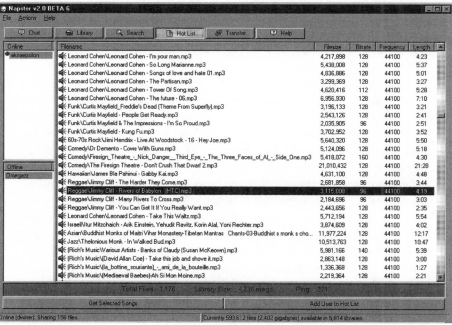

Figure 10. Napster Chat (top) and Hot List (bottom) features (version 2.0). These features enhanced the community aspects of the software and presaged many of the features of today's popular social media sites/programs.

chatting put users in direct communication with each other. Through this feature Napster's interface facilitated the age-old practice of sharing music and telling other people about it, enabling not just the movement of music but also the movement of discourses about music (S. Jones 2002, 214, 225).

The Hot List (fig. 10b) was another way for users to engage with other members of the community. It allowed users to compile a list of other peers to "follow." Each time these hot listed peers signed on, the (new) contents of their library became visible to users that were following them. Like the chat function, the Hot List not only facilitated more effective searching; it also focused users on the rest of the Napster community. It was a way of following users with particular tastes and a primitive form of music recommendation that helped users navigate the network. The people in any given user's hot list were resources for weeding through the massive amount of music on the network. By integrating the choices of other users into one's own process of searching for music through the Hot List, Napster reminded users that one of the most effective ways to find out about music was through other listeners. Instead of a world without gatekeepers, Napster suggested the best gatekeepers were other users. This insight underpins much of the MP3 blog movement and much of the social music software and recommendation engines that have developed in the last decade (e.g., SoulSeek, Spotify). Napster's software suggested that tastemakers are all around; they just need to be connected.

It was in these respects that Napster's primary innovation, as Beuscart (2005) notes, was more organizational than technical. Even though "the software was a substitute for the interactional and technical skills that used to be necessary [to download files]" (S5), Napster's main achievement was how it organized its user base through its software and website. While Napster's messaging through its website was an explicit attempt to build a community, the interface worked at a more subtle level. Software seems to act as if it is "visibly invisible" (Chun 2008, 300); it appears as a magical source that gives users the ability to manipulate virtual objects they cannot entirely perceive or to interact with other users they cannot entirely see.[9] Wendy Chun critiques this "sourcery" as a kind of fetishism (Chun 2008, 300); the power of software and its interfaces come from how they regularly conflate the categories of representation (what users see onscreen) and organization (what users can do with what they see onscreen). In this way Napster drew users together in a series of technical and social relationships through its features: relationships that were premised on the circulation of files and making that movement and connection visible to users.

Like other mass-mediated communities, one of the only ways users could understand each other in this relationship was *through* the interface and the partial glimpses and traces it offered of others on the network. Napster showed that digital music was readily available, highly searchable, and intimately social. Users could see file quality, speed of delivery, and the array of other users who were also interested in the same kind of music. It showed users, in real time, what other users had on their computers. It helped make tangible the intangible idea of a mass of connected computers by displaying the activities of other users and by allowing them to interact. It made the moment of transfer a moment of anticipation, and it let users peer into other user's digital closets.

This is where theories of the gift economy do not take us far enough. Optimistic hopes for the "Napsterisation of everything" (Barbrook 2002) or the redistribution of power often neglect the role of gifts or free software and content in drawing together a usable and valuable audience. Gifts, in other words, act as a way for users to engage in exchange outside of typical market practices while at the same time serving as a foundation for an effective type of business model with "free" stuff as its central promise.[10] The production, distribution, and consumption of free content can thus be foundational to both gift economies and innovative forms of online commercial exchange. Indeed, many emerging music services (Spotify, Rdio, etc.) are working experiments in the possibilities of commercializing "free" (T. J. Anderson 2014, 44). Contrary to conceptions of gift economies as inherently antagonistic toward commodification and capitalist forms of value creation, gift communities can and have played key roles in establishing the market for digital music commodities. The unsanctioned activities of individual Napster users were channeled toward the creation of a commodity community. The boundaries between market and antimarket activities are precisely what make digital music both a conflicted and cybernetic commodity.

NEW MEDIA MEASUREMENT

Even though Napster may not have profited directly from its audience, the commodity community it brought together presented novel opportunities for advertising, market research, and surveillance (McCourt and Burkart 2003, 335, 343). Mark Andrejevic uses the term *digital enclosure* to suggest how new media technologies have a tendency to create an ecosystem, while promoting added interactivity and control for users. These ecosystems depend highly on users surrendering private information and personal preferences to heavily monitored databases (2007, 2). Digital media, just like previous technologies of radio or television, generate important data about the behaviors and preferences of users. The difference with many forms of new media is that, rather than relying on crude measurement tools like phone surveys, people meters, and focus groups, digital enclosures turn the very act of consumption into a form of feedback that creates traceable and commodifiable information (Andrejevic 2007, 88).

As anticorporate as it seemed at first, Napster was a primitive digital enclosure. Napster's networked nature and the information that circulated through that network provided a highly usable database. Although Napster undoubtedly intended to use this data itself (Menn 2003, 122), it was ultimately too busy responding to legal charges to fully realize the benefits of its commodity community. Instead, a slew of other companies looking to leech off of Napster's community emerged to organize, mine, sell, or otherwise use this cybernetic information (J. Brown 2001). In doing so, they helped commodify an otherwise unsanctioned practice and laid the foundation for practices and techniques that have become central to contemporary new media measurement and online audience tracking. Despite users' attempts to remain anonymous through cryptic usernames or dynamic IP addresses, the data they generated by circulating files nevertheless acted as important sources of information for trend-hunters, audience measurers, and even for court cases against individual file sharers.

The music industries have traditionally relied on Nielsen's SoundScan and BroadcastDataSystem technologies (and the *Billboard* charts they help produce) to gauge the sales and popularity of artists. These charts and the numbers behind them drive investment and promotion decisions (McCourt and Rothenbuhler 1997). But the arrival of Napster meant that a significant portion of music consumption and circulation was occurring outside the traditional realms of retailers and radio stations. Although there had always been a gap between the measured audience and the actual audience, Napster and the file-sharing networks that followed it widened that gap substantially. While the circulation of copyright infringing materials through file-sharing networks was seen as a direct economic loss for some parties, for others it represented a missed opportunity to observe and capitalize on the latest musical trends.

BigChampagne is perhaps the best-known new media audience measurement company in the music industries. Founded in the late 1990s, it was also, for many of its early years, one of the most-cited sources on file-sharing traffic. The company used to provide data and charts detailing which files were the most traded on networks like Napster, KaZaa, and Limewire and which songs were trading well in particular regions. Although the company now emphasizes file sharing less as its primary source of data, BigChampagne continues to provide numerous research services to its clients, including charts, trend-watching and prediction, and music intelligence. BigChampagne's *Billboard*-like top-100 list, called the "Ultimate Chart," is compiled from online and offline sources such as digital music retail outlets (iTunes, Rhapsody, etc.), social networks (Myspace, Last.Fm, etc.), web portals (YouTube, AOL, etc.), and file-sharing sites. In 2011 Live Nation acquired BigChampagne, giving the latter access to a huge database of event, ticketing, and merchandising data. Its modest tagline, "Now You Know Everything," hints both at the promise the company offers clients and the promise new technologies offer for audience measurement (BigChampagne 2010).

BigChampagne's reputation as the *Billboard* or Nielsen Ratings (Howe 2003) of file-sharing networks owes a large debt to Napster's audience and software. Before BigChampagne got into the business of tracking file-sharing traffic, the company's founder was using the Napster network as a tool for direct marketing. In 1999 Eric Garland, an amateur musician and management consultant, hooked up with Glen Philips, the former lead singer of Toad the Wet Sprocket. Philips was starting a solo career, and Garland was helping him design a mailing list to keep track of his fans. Philips noticed that users were trading files of his old band on the nascent Napster service, and he wondered whether there was a way to convert some of his old popularity to his new project (Dansby 2008). Along with another friend, Garland and Philips built a program that "sent anyone sharing a Toad the Wet Sprocket song an invitation to join Philips' mailing list" (Howe 2003). Around 20 percent of users contacted ended up joining the mailing list, a significantly better response rate than the traditional 2 to 3 percent that many direct-marketing attempts achieve (Howe 2003).

Encouraged by this trial, Garland created BigChampagne and approached potential clients about conducting a more official marketing effort. The result was a promotion, in late 2000, for singer songwriter Aimee Mann. They sent any Napster user sharing Mann's songs direct messages through the chat feature: "I see you have some Aimee Mann songs on your hard drive. Aimee Mann has a new promotional song, go check it out at aimee-mann.com" (J. Brown 2001). Mann initially had significant reservations about Napster; it was her manager that suggested the promotion. The campaign resulted in seventeen hundred new members joining her mailing list, and it helped Mann and her manager see the service in a new light: "Really, I think that if we could have some kind of relationship with the people who are downloading the songs, we'd feel a lot better about [Napster]" (Mann's manager qtd. in J. Brown 2001). Other artists and record companies were also hesitant to work with the company. The record labels were especially afraid of promoting any legitimate use of peer-to-peer technology and of contradicting their no-tolerance policy toward file-sharing networks (J. Brown 2001). If companies dealt with BigChampagne in the early years of file sharing, it was usually in secret. It was a research strategy that "dare not speak its name" (Howe 2003).

As file-sharing networks proliferated in the wake of Napster and as the amount of information those networks generated increased, many of the major labels started using BigChampagne's information directly and indirectly to supplement their campaigns (see, e.g., Capitol Records' promotion for Radiohead, Led Zepplin's Reunion Tour setlist choices in 2007, and helping My Chemical Romance choose which singles to release from one of their new albums in 2004 in Mathews 2001; Lange 2009). They graduated from instant message marketing or "instant spamming" (Olsen 2001) to more sophisticated data collection, including partnerships with Clear Channel (2003), Billboard Radio Monitor (2005), and the recent acquisition by Live Nation (2011).

Like the difference Andrejevic (2007, 87–88) notes between telephone surveys and people meters, or the difference SoundScan boasted about when it introduced its product scanners in 1991, BigChampagne purported to measure what people were *doing*, not what they were *saying* or *thinking*. BigChampagne sells its data as a more accurate and comprehensive method of measuring online communities than methods like SoundScan that rely on sales. As Garland explained: "We seized onto P2P because it allows a singular opportunity to observe really intimate consumer behavior. You're not asking them what's your taste in music, games, books, what have you— you're looking in the pantry, straight into the fridge" (qtd. in J. Brown 2001). This intimate view comes not just from BigChampagne's technology but also from the interfaces and the technologies like Napster. Through these file-sharing programs, BigChampagne can participate directly in BitTorrent swarms and monitor trackers ceaselessly. They can collect information about each file uploaded and downloaded in real time and determine what's "popular" regionally through IP addresses, claiming to be better than 99 percent accurate at a country level and slightly less at the city level (Garland 2009a). BigChampagne's software is an overlay on top of all this activity, capable of recording and archiving the contents list of shared folders and P2P search queries.

For BigChampagne and other market research firms these connected and visible networks were like "gold mines" of data (Olsen 2001). This may seem unsurprising now, given the proliferation of work on new media-metric companies (see, e.g., Baym 2013; Bermejo 2007, 2009; Buzzard 2012; Hearn 2010; Napoli 2011; Turow 2006, 2011), but it is worth recognizing that Napster served as an early test case for how to mine large-scale online virtual communities for economically profitable data. Although the current crop of new-media metric companies have honed their information collection and analysis techniques since Napster, their existence and evolution points to an expansion of the institutionally effective audience for cultural goods. The data that Napster generated about its networked but individual users suggested a way to turn a community of file swappers into a cybernetic commodity. While traditional ratings companies typically set out to track the institutionally effective and commercially relevant audiences (Napoli 2011), BigChampagne built its business on tracking users that were in many ways working to remove themselves from the institutionally effective audience.

Marketing companies were not the only ones sourcing information from Napster's audience. User participation in the network also provided key data for the RIAA during its legal challenges against file sharers. Just as marketers used individual and aggregated file-sharing patterns to deduce tastes and preferences, the RIAA used similar data to root out copyright infringers. In a declaration made in a court case in 2003—the RIAA was challenging Internet Service Provider Verizon for access to some of its customer data—Jonathan Whitehead, VP of Online Copyright Protection at the RIAA, shared how the industry group was able to track down file sharers through the metadata that users made available, knowingly or unknowingly, through the files they had traded on the Napster network (Whitehead 2003; "How Downloaders Are Tracked" 2003).

One particular example involved a Jane Doe who went by the username "nycfashiongirl@kazaa.com." The RIAA had accused nycfashiongirl of sharing a large amount of copyrighted files through KaZaa (a post-Napster file-sharing program). The defendant's lawyers claimed that nycfashiongirl had used KaZaa primarily as a media player and that she had disabled any file-sharing access to copyrighted sound recordings (i.e., she may have downloaded files, but she did not upload—the digital age's equivalent of the "I smoked but did not inhale" argument). Through the use of KaZaa's software, the RIAA debunked this claim by accessing and analyzing nycfashiongirl's "shared" folder. Contrary to the claims that she had turned file sharing off, the RIAA team was able to access more than eleven hundred files (Whitehead 2003, 3; "How Downloaders Are Tracked," 2003). Looking at the metadata of those files, the RIAA was further able to determine that the majority of songs came from online sources or other KaZaa users and not from CDs that nycfashiongirl owned and copied into her shared folder, as her lawyers claimed. Most of the files in her folder included ID3 tags with comments indicating their original source—for example: "ripped by pbv," "Ripped by ATOMIC PLAYBOY 1999!," "Uploaded by Smog," etc. (Whitehead 2003, 6). Many files also included the URL of the website/archive from which they were downloaded and the name of the encoding software used. Some even contained statements encouraging further infringement, like "SHARE WITH OTHERS" (Whitehead 2003, 9). Recalling the micromaterials and categories provided by the CDDB and ID3, the "description" or "comments" fields seem innocuous enough; they are something that most users do not even see unless they have those fields enabled in their software player. But the RIAA's use of these rather harmless micromaterials doubled as a means of tracking circulation and even of establishing "criminal" intent.

Perhaps most damaging, the RIAA argued that the hashes from many of the files in nycfashiongirl's share folder indicated that the songs came from the original Napster network. Hashes or hash tags, the RIAA argued, are equivalent to the "fingerprints" of a file (Whitehead 2003, 12; "How Downloaders Are Tracked," 2003). They represent a "computed value based on the properties of the individual bits in a file" (Whitehead 2003, 12). File-sharing services make use of hashes to locate other versions of the same file, in case one user disconnects from the system and a new source file is needed to complete the download. The micromaterial hashes in nycfashion-girl's share folder matched those the RIAA found in the original Napster database years previously, so the RIAA argued that nycfashiongirl had been making these files available since as early as 2000. Given that the courts had already deemed Napster as infringing, the presence of Napster-era files in nycfashiongirl's shared folder only made the case against her harder to refute. Whether or not one accepts the RIAA's claims that it is possible to link a user name to a particular person's behavior through metadata, the declaration shows how deeply embedded music's micromaterials are and the extent to which new media audiences make available information that serves a variety of purposes, be it file sharing, marketing, advertising, or even criminal investigation. In this case, the RIAA was able to make use of Napster's audience data even though the service had been shut down for months. The traces its audience left behind were still in circulation. The RIAA used digital music's micromaterial traces as tangible proof, an "empirical remainder—a trace of physical evidence that can't be staged" (Andrejevic 2007, 38).

Napster's community provided a wealth of data for services and purposes other than those that were originally visible to Napster itself. Despite the claims that Napster was an empowering technology set to disrupt the music industries, the kinds of data Napster made available fit well into traditional commercial practices like audience measurement and became useful tools for legal pursuits like those of the RIAA. Even as Napster promised free music and a choice of whether to participate in the regular economics of the music industry, it also generated new kinds of information about music consumers and their patterns that fed back into the commodification process (McCourt and Burkart 2003, 346). A publicly accessible index of downloadable songs available to networked users wasn't just an ideal way of swapping files; it was also a well-sorted database for the purposes of advertising, market research, and other forms of monitoring. Companies like BigChampagne built viable businesses based on Napster's commodity community. Other entities, like the RIAA, used the data as means of tracking and punishing what it deemed illicit behavior (this despite the fact that RIAA argued vociferously in the Napster case and those that followed that peer-to-peer technology provided no legitimate or noninfringing uses). Napster's audience may have signed up for the free music, but in the process they were willfully submitting to a kind of monitoring that gave other actors on the network greater insight into their behaviors and preferences than ever before. The community commodity invites a multitude of relationships, some social and some commercial in nature.

This highlights a critical point about Napster and file-sharing networks more generally, one that often gets buried in a narrative about youthful rebellion against an out-of-touch industry: Napster helped organize a measurable audience. The RIAA and BigChampagne's early use of the metadata of Napster users laid the foundation for the new media measurement practices that take place today and are an increasingly important source of information for cultural industries producers. Though still largely underpublicized, companies like Webspins, A.D.D. Marketing, Media Defender, and others all work at providing comprehensive online audience-measurement and brand-management tools for record labels based on using data gathered from sources that are not sanctioned by the industry. Beyond music, we can look to more recent examples, like when the Australian broadcasting media giant Fairfax listed the monitoring of BitTorrent as one of its strategies for acquiring new content (Ernesto 2010) or the host of companies like Radian 6 or Sysomos that provide "sentiment analysis" by monitoring all kinds of signals and cues from social media and other networked audiences (Hearn 2010). There is a burgeoning industry of infomediaries building on BigChampagne's Napster-inspired technology and practices to monitor, participate in, and guide online feedback about an artist, an album, or any other entertainment property.

For labels and promotional companies that have spent millions to push the popularity of an artist or song, these kinds of services serve a rhetorical function. They justify decisions on which acts to invest in and which ones to ignore, and they rationalize risk in essentially irrational industries. Although the practice of audience measurement clearly does not begin with Napster, the file-sharing network stands out as a model for how audience measurement practices could no longer be based solely on institutionally effective audiences. To fully measure the audience, tools that could measure both industry-sanctioned and unsanctioned behaviors needed to be developed.

The info-mining companies that have emerged in the wake of Napster not only represent the commodification of an extra layer of information surrounding music; they also underscore the hazy relationship between sanctioned and unsanctioned economic activity within various media industries. As much as the labels, networks, studios, and industry associations shake their fingers publicly at the harm file-sharing networks are causing their businesses, they are less likely to admit the ways and the extent to which these antimarkets inform their own everyday decisions and investments. Writing about film distribution in the digital age, Ramon Lobato uses the phrase "shadow economies of cinema" to describe the informal, unmeasured, and unregulated circulation of audiovisual goods that has become an increasingly central aspect of cinematic commerce and culture (2012, 40). He details the vast infrastructure that supports pirate and other informal networks and the ways it overlaps with, feeds into and supersedes the one supporting the more legitimately sanctioned circulatory networks. There is, ultimately, a "slippery" distinction between shadowy and legitimate practices and a "great deal of traffic between the formal and the informal over time and space" (Lobato 2012, 41). Formal distribution and production channels often rely on informal ones for products, information, and profit. The resulting gray economies are neither cleanly formal nor informal.

The use of file-sharing data as a means of gathering market research is not the only example of the music industry's gray economics. The file sharing of market research is similar, in some ways, to the way that event companies like Live Nation or TicketMaster sell blocks of tickets to professional or semiprofessional secondary markets of scalpers who drive down the availability and drive up the prices of tickets for regular consumers

(Cloonan 2012). Although scalping is clearly publically frowned upon by artists and the event organizers, it is less clear what steps the event companies are taking to limit the practice given the value they are able to realize from this secondary market (Cloonan 2012). Similarly, we can look at how video-game publishers incorporate and resell the hacks and mods of amateur game enthusiasts after widely denouncing the practice and trying to limit it by means of technological protection measures (Dyer-Witheford and de Peuter 2005). Ultimately, these are all antimarket practices that are officially condemned but that unofficially add significant market value and ensure their own proliferation.

The kinds of data-mining practices file-sharing networks allow trouble the standard narrative surrounding file sharing's deleterious effects on the industry. Industrial uses of Napster's metadata helped turn a potentially economically threatening community of file swappers into a commodity that could generate valuable research information. In other words even though users of file-sharing networks were engaging in seemingly disruptive consumptive practices, they were nevertheless contributing to the further commodification of new media products. Not only was Napster a business; it was one that, despite public protestations from the major labels and industry associations about the unsanctioned behaviors it promoted, showed the media industries the wealth of consumer insights and data that could be gleaned from commodity communities.

NAPSTER WAS HERE

The summer of 2009 marked the ten-year anniversary of Shawn Fanning's release of Napster. The occasion generated a flurry of retrospective profiles in local newspapers and magazines (see, e.g., BBC 2009; Bruno 2009; Evangelista 2009; Hartley 2009; Van Buskirk 2009). In one, former RIAA president Hilary Rosen was asked about Napster's enduring legacy: "There's no question Napster galvanized the process in several important ways. . . . It brought consumers into the discussion for the first time. All of a sudden, record companies started hearing from music fans in a way they never had before. The 'customer' for record companies for many years were radio stations and record stores. All of a sudden record companies were on the hook from music fans" (Bruno 2009). Read through the analysis presented here, Rosen acknowledges that one of the software's most lasting impacts was organizational in nature. What was different about Napster were the novel and interesting ways in which it organized its audience through its software and website. Napster brought together a group of users via its interface and made visible the kinds of circulation and connections that were constitutive of the digital music commodity.

Napster's audience was not simply an organic oppositional community, though. It was a commodity community designed to provide value for its developers. Despite the troubled nature of the practices Napster promoted, the company hoped to build a business model off of its ability to gather and connect users. Napster did not profit from this commodity community in the long term, though it certainly benefited from the work of its users during times of legal troubles and via early venture capital funding. Other actors like BigChampagne or the RIAA, however, were able to mine the community and lay the foundations for measurement techniques that would follow. As much as the battle against file sharing wages on, Napster was the start of the music industries' incorporation of the unsanctioned circulation of digital commodities into everyday rhythms and decisions. There are now multiple ways to profit from the commodity communities that various antimarket entities like Napster create. Napster was a form of digital enclosure where music sharers who gathered under one pretense suddenly found themselves laboring under another.

Not only did Napster generate a commodity community that suggested the viability of an online digital music market; the way it presented digital music to its users also helped shape the emerging digital music commodity. Napster emphasized the fluidity and mobility of digital music and focused users on the act of circulation. Interfaces are not just mediators between users and the programs they use; they are ways of knowing about the objects the program acts on. Napster's interface showed users when uploads were completing and when downloads were arriving. Users could wait with anticipation for transfers to finish. Napster offered chats with other users and means of finding tastemakers among a huge network of users. Users could peer ambiently and actively into the tastes of others and, in doing so, realize the fundamentally social aspects of music consumption. Napster provided a means of searching for files with fine-grained technical details and made these characteristics part of the culture of music's circulation. It was a visual metaphor for how networks worked. These features and qualities helped Napster gather its commodity community and helped users feel part of a natural and organic community that was engaging in alternative (even subversive) forms of circulation and exchange.

The challenges Napster posed to the recorded music industry (and media industries more broadly) are substantial. But not all those changes have turned out to be as disruptive as early discourses around file-sharing technologies suggested. File sharing has proven to be, as Jonas Andersson suggests, both "uncontrollable and unyielding, as well as compliant and business friendly" (Andersson 2014, 1). As new streaming services emerge that offer a wide catalogue of music for a low monthly subscription fee or for free with ad-supported listening (Spotify, Rdio, Pandora, Beats, etc.), there is increasing pressure to mine and make use of the data gleaned by users of these services. Given the number of paid versus unpaid subscribers on many of these services, these sites must make up for their lack of revenue by monetizing data gleaned from users. Spotify, for example, has approximately forty million users as of this writing, of which ten million are paying subscribers (Spotify 2014). While Spotify promotes its model by arguing that it is shifting users away from file-sharing networks to a paid service, this logic belies the larger fact that the very rise of streaming services depends highly on the existence and utility of the commodity community.

Napster's innovations, then, are visible throughout digital music, even today. Sites ranging from iTunes or Spotify to the Pirate Bay and BitTorrent have all built into their services many of Napster's key features. In another of the tenth-year anniversary retrospectives about the company, ex-Napster CEO Hank Barry argued: "Without Napster, there is no iPod, period" (qtd. in Hartley 2009). Although Barry is likely referring to the fact that Napster's massive database of "free" music was one of the prime ways for consumers to fill the massive storage capacity of Apple's portable music devices, his claim should be further extrapolated. Napster did not just generate a community that helped boost iPod sales; it also organized users that were ready to take part in all manner of digital music and online media services. Napster's impact on the economics of the music industries is secondary to the audience it organized, the means through which it gathered them, and its community's interaction with music as a digital file.

Even though Napster 2.0 managed to achieve a sizable user base—just under one million at its peak—that paid regularly for music, it was only a brand name and logo-inflected shadow of its former self. Ironically, Napster's influence on the commodification of digital music was less as a legitimate subscription service than it was when Napster was giving away music for free to millions. Far from a rogue piece of software that destroyed the music business and turned everyday consumers into plundering pirates, the early version of Napster was a business that helped create a market for digital music commodities and a template for how new media properties might manage their affective and economic relationships with users. These users and their interactions would become key metrics for future digital market analysts and would help spark a variety of info-mining companies and technologies.

After Napster shutdown, its users continued to gather and circulate music and to engage with the digital music commodity, either through other file-sharing networks or through some of the more "legitimate" retail outlets that followed in Napster's wake. Although the major record labels and industry associations continued to wage very public campaigns against file sharers and the damage they had done to the value of the recorded music commodity, the contours of the market for digital music were already becoming clearer because of Napster's technologies and practices. Napster's informal market spurred the development of more formal distribution channels, including, as we are about to see, one of the most successful online retail efforts to date for digital music: the iTunes Music Store.

4 Click to Buy

Music in Digital Stores

SELLING MUSIC ONLINE

When I first visited the SightSound Technologies website in 2006, I was greeted by a monkey, or rather, a black-and-white animated image of a chimpanzee with its mouth agape and a club in its hands. There was an automatic sound triggered, too, one that sounded like a computer starting up. It was a short crescendo, a rising sting that suggested something big was about to happen. The not-so-subtle nod to Stanley Kubrick's *2001: A Space Odyssey* in the splash page, logo, and sound design were meant to signal an evolutionary moment of significant proportion. The monkey has a tool; it has evolved. The logo faded and a crunchy guitar riff segued into a brief video detailing the company's various contributions in the field of digital sight and sound technologies.

The first achievement SightSound claims is the sale of the first-ever digital music download online in September 1995: an album by Pittsburgh-based folk-rockers the Gathering Field (SightSound 1995). Users could buy the entire 634.2MB self-titled debut album for US$6.00, which took anywhere from twenty minutes to dozens of hours to download. Although Aerosmith had experimented with digital distribution for a song called "Head First" one year prior as a free download limited to CompuServe users (Haring 2000, 59), SightSound recognized the historical precedent they were setting: "That's right, the entire disc [is] sold, then electronically delivered via the 'Net to the buyer. You can make history too. Order your own copy . . ." (SightSound, 1995–2002). For SightSound, users who purchased *The Gathering Field* weren't just buying an album; they were taking part in a new way of buying music. Music retail was evolving.

SightSound—a "media eCommerce consulting" company with interests in audio and video distribution—hoped this new way of buying music would be exclusive to its company. Thanks to several patents it held, SightSound felt it had the sole right to sell and distribute digital music online. Company co-founder Arthur R. Hair had received a patent entitled "Method for Transmitting a Desired Digital Video or Audio Signal" in 1993 and a similar one in 1997, both for technology that facilitated the sale and download of audio and video files via phone lines and Internet connections (Hair 1993, 1997). In 1997 SightSound filed lawsuits against other online music retailers like CDNow and N2K that were starting to sell digital files of their own. The company sent letters to MP3.com (1998) and GoodNoise (1999), demanding a percentage from every digital sale those companies made (Lemos 1999). Since SightSound had patents on the technology for selling digital downloads, it argued the very *method* of selling digital downloads was, in essence, patentable. In other words, no other individual or company should have been able to sell digital music online without recognizing SightSound's patent. As one of the co-founders said bluntly in an early interview: "We own digital download. We have won" (Newman 1999). Although SightSound promised more music from more artists in the future, and later claimed to have sold the first film via the Internet in 1999, the company shut down its virtual music store a few months after *The Gathering Field* experiment.

Of course, if there's a current "winner" in the online music retail business, it's Apple and its iTunes Music Store. Launched in 2003, the iTunes Store sold one million tracks in its first week, five million by week 8 (Apple 2003a, 2003b). On the first anniversary of its launch the iTunes Store had sold more than seventy million songs and held more than a 70 percent share of the legal download market (Apple 2004). The store not only sells more music than any other digital retailer; it has been the leading music outlet in North America since 2008 and holds a similar position in most other global markets (Bangeman 2008; NPD 2012). Apple has also branched out beyond music, selling or distributing movies, TV shows, podcasts, apps, e-books, and educational content. When Prince launched *Crystal Ball* in 1998, selling music online was barely conceivable. Now digital music retail is a thriving commercial market and the fastest growing sector of the recorded music industry, representing close to 39 percent of global music industry revenues (IFPI 2014).

After Napster's rise in 1999, it was not clear there could be a sustainable market for digital music. Many labels, artists, and industry associations worried that the value of recorded music had been decimated by its widespread availability through outlets like Napster. But, as I have argued in the preceding chapters, technologies like Winamp, the CDDB, ID3 tags, and even Napster all helped make digital music more visible, audible, findable, and usable. Although Napster's original existence was brief, successors like KaZaa and Limewire continued to connect audiences with digital music through the early 2000s. Winamp remained a popular music client (though it faced increasing competition) and the CDDB and ID3 tags continued to provide necessary infrastructure for digital music's metadata. In other words, through industrial and technological development, as well as the work and contributions of everyday users, digital music files were gradually becoming valuable enough to be sold as commodities.

This chapter looks at the evolution of early online retail music stores dedicated to the sale of digital music commodities, from SightSound to iTunes. Although it was transectorial and disorderly, the rise of online retail in the late 1990s was also a series of struggles for control over the business of selling music and over the music commodity itself. SightSound's patent story, for example, is just one of the telling examples of how certain actors use moments of technological change to secure economic and cultural advantages through law, regulation, and/or technological design. SightSound's attempt to own online audio and video distribution as a business method was just one tactic among many that companies were using to establish control over this emerging market. By arguing that digital music delivery was a unique business solution, they were staking ownership not just in the music but in the very act of acquiring it. SightSound hoped to profit from music and from the means of selling it. That SightSound was actually remunerated US$3.3 million over the course of its lawsuits only illustrates how vulnerable the codes and conventions surrounding the movement and use of certain commodities are when the format of that commodity changes (Chang 2004; Valence 2000; Petzinger 1999).[1]

Apple's iTunes Music Store, though it has plenty of patents of its own, took another tact in its quest for control over music retail, one that involved both convincing users of the value of a digital music commodity and creating a network of connected hardware and software to manage musical experiences. The iTunes Store resolved much of the conflict accompanying the digital music commodity by hiding or masking the challenges of digital music and presenting it in a familiar and integrated interface. Beyond the "user-friendly" appearance of the iTunes software and store, the tactics Apple used to market individual songs and albums set the terms for the experience of digital music for artists, listeners, and other online retailers. iTunes presents a networked store, connected by various technologies and interfaces that dissolve the barriers between the personal collection and the retail outlet. The iTunes Store fused the moments of purchase and playback and reinforced the idea that our music libraries were not just repositories for our favorite songs and albums; they were commodified and networked databases designed to encourage even further consumption. While other companies sought to control digital music through overt legal strategies or digital rights management technologies, Apple used its proprietary technology as a building block toward much more subtle, design-inflected tactics for promoting the use of its software and devices.

More important, the iTunes Store was pivotal in promoting the very idea that digital music *could be* a commodity, a digital item with a price tag. Apple managed to commodify digital music and, more precisely, the experiences surrounding digital music such that people were willing to pay for files they could find readily for less (or free) elsewhere. Apple's "solution" was as much about adding value to the act of buying digital music as it was about re-tuning the music commodity. The iTunes Store navigated and incorporated different conceptions of digital music retail in order to promote its vision of a commodified digital music file. Through its interface, navigation, price, and methods of organizing music, the iTunes Store showcased the music commodity in its digital environment and sought to rebuild some of the value that drifted during the migration from music on CDs. In doing so, it did far more than resell music in the online environment; it promoted a kind of digital lifestyle management that embedded both music hardware and software ever more ubiquitously into everyday life.

CONTROLLING DIGITAL RETAIL

One of the underlying assumptions of this book has been that the transition to a new format of any given commodity temporarily calls into question the conventions and practices that accompany the presentation and sale of that commodity. Like other commodities that raced online in the mid-1990s, the de-tuning of music's interface was a transitory period (that is, arguably, still under way) where the business models, technologies, and social meanings that structured its sound, look, and circulation were catching up to the new environment in which music found itself. As digital music files began their diffusion, makers and manufacturers of music came face-to-face with how to present, market, and distribute the new format, how to re-tune music's interface. Simultaneously, users were reassessing what the recorded music experience meant, now that the commodity was digital. Each new business model had to address basic assumptions about music that were formerly taken for granted, as did each new device or space through which consumers could access music. Attributes such as price, appearance, availability, mode of distribution, and means of playback all needed to be revisited as the micromaterials, interfaces, and consumer practices around digital music crystallized. Parts of the music commodity had become candidates for re-tuning, though digitization was also an opportunity to extend control and enforce new limits on the music commodity.

This is precisely what was at work in the SightSound example, and its quest to own digital downloading is reflective of a much larger set of technical and legal conflicts that were taking place in the late 1990s. As "brick-and-mortar" outfits raced to bring their businesses online, they filed for a flood of software and "business method" patents (similar to the ones discussed in the SightSound example) to cover their seemingly new innovations.[2] The methods themselves were not entirely new, although the fact that they were taking place through computers, with software, and on the Internet gave them an air of novelty. Applications and awarded patents for business methods skyrocketed from mere hundreds in the 1980s to tens of thousands by 2010 (S. J. Frank 2009; Hall 2009; Hunt 2001). As a result large swaths of everyday Internet activity are now covered by business method patents, including methods of running an online auction (e.g., Priceline.com), online ordering (e.g., Amazon.com), online rewards programs (e.g., ClickReward), the use of electronic shopping carts (e.g., Open Market), and even the selling of digital downloads over the Internet (e.g., SightSound), even if users and businesses regularly disregard the need to pay licenses to the patent holders.

These various legal attempts to establish or maintain control in an emerging market underscore how the introduction of new technologies is rarely a stable and cohesive process. There is a certain "interpretative flexibility" that accompanies the advent of new technologies (Bijker and Law 1992; Oudshoorn and Pinch 2003, 3). For different social groups artifacts can present themselves as essentially different objects (Bijker and Law 1992, 76). Put simply, different people have different ideas about what new technologies should and could do. The result is that the uses to which new technologies can be put are generally in flux, though conflicting meanings and ideas generally stabilize over time (Bijker and Law 1992, 76–79; Pinch and Trocco 2002, 9–11). Interpretative flexibility, however, is not a completely open-ended process. It is tempting to portray the introduction of new technologies as completely disruptive: as a chaotic and disorderly moment where everything and anything could change and the power or market dominance of existing players is under threat (Christensen 1997). Despite the potential for change, new technologies are equally capable of further enforcing entrenched entities and sustaining traditional ways of

doing business (Christensen 1997, 9–15). The music industries, for example, have repeatedly faced flux, crisis, and technological change, yet market
dominance has generally remained concentrated in the hands of a select few
key companies (Garofalo 1999; McCourt and Burkart 2003).

The idea that new technologies engender chaos and disorder, as business
and industrial historians suggest, is actually a myth that conceals a process
of rational change (Gomery 2005). Industries like music or film depend on,
and invest heavily in, regular technological advances. They expect and plan
for change. They make it part of their long-term strategies. Or, as Charles
Acland notes about the rise of 3D technology in film and television: "the
language of 'game changing' is another way to talk about business as usual"
(2009). When looked at from a wider industrial point of view, what seems
like disruption turns out to be multiple small-scale struggles over the creation of markets, and the codes and conventions that govern the flow of
specific commodities. Furthermore, while the transition to digital files put
some aspects of music's commodity form into question, it is not as if new
technologies obliterated the idea of the music commodity entirely. As was
evident from Winamp, innovations are firmly embedded in past ideas and
practices, and there is much more to the music commodity than simply
format and packaging. Similarly, as the cases of metadata and Napster suggest, even users actively engaged in working against the commodification
of digital music are inadvertent participants in the process. By making
music sortable and organizable, users start to treat digital files more and
more like traditional commodities. Interpretative flexibility is not a blank
slate; it depends on the nature and preexisting conditions of control and
power that govern the commodity in question.

Just as there were several competing visions for "new" technologies like
the fluorescent lamp (Bijker and Law 1992, 81), multiple models for the sale
of the digital music commodity emerged in the mid-to-late 1990s. Each one
offered a particular conception of how music should be presented, distributed, and sold. Before SightSound, and before the advent of browsers,
countless smaller artists and labels were experimenting with the Internet as
a virtual storefront for the sale of physical CDs and other music commodities. Sites like the IUMA were thriving communities for marketing and,
secondarily, selling music and merchandise, but they were hardly fully
functional retail outlets (Dube 1997, 4). More polished online stores followed with the likes of CDNow, N2K's Music Boulevard, and eMusic
(launched in 1994, 1995, and 1995 respectively).[3] These companies set up
websites where consumers could order CDs or cassettes by phone, fax, or
secure email (Capuzzi 1996; Wickre 1995). Traditional retailers like Tower

Records and record labels like Windham Hill and ECM also jumped online with similar offerings in 1995 (Gillen 1995). Compared to "brick-and-mortar" retail stores, these online shops prided themselves on convenience, the size of their catalogues, and all the contextual information (e.g., biographies, reviews, editorial commentary, and other kinds of nonembedded metadata) they provided during the act of browsing. The mid-1990s also saw the rise of more general purpose online retailers, or e-commerce sites for other cultural goods like books (Bakos 2001). Although Amazon.com did not start selling CDs until 1998 (Brynjolfsson and Smith 2000), its dominance in the category of books made it a retailer on which many other sites and companies based their online selling models and mechanics.

Like Prince's *Crystal Ball*, though, these retailers only brought music partially online. Even pioneers like Amazon.com used the Internet primarily as a hub from which to sell traditional formats of their cultural commodity. While the sites listed above were all technically "online," these retailers were not actually selling digital music commodities. They were selling the music commodity, digitally. Around 1995, though, digital entrepreneurs started shifting away from these halfway models to fully digital ones. In the process a further re-tuning of the capabilities of the music commodity occurred. Along with SightSound's attempt to patent the actual business of selling digital music, companies like Cerberus, Liquid Audio, IBM, and the major labels used the transition to digital to impose greater control over the music commodity. Although the MP3 file format was rapidly gaining popularity, most of the early digital retail efforts involved other, more secure formats. For example, a British company named Cerberus launched a digital storefront in 1995 that offered more than thirty thousand tracks at prices that artists set themselves (Pride 1994; "Multimedia Business Analyst" 1995). One of the conditions of the launch, imposed by the record labels, was that the songs had to be "protected." To play the songs, users needed special Cerberus software with "Cercure" technology (Rosen 1994). Liquid Audio, N2K, and Capitol Records teamed up in 1997 for a similar experiment. They sold a digital download of the Duran Duran single "Electric Barbarella" that, like Cerberus's downloads, was encrypted with proprietary technology that ensured only users who purchased it through the Liquid Audio player could play it (Alderman 2001, 46; Haring 2000, 68–70; Takahashi 1997).

In 1998 IBM and the major record labels (the Big Five, at the time: Sony, Warner, BMG, EMI, and Universal) had an even bigger plan to create an all-encompassing secure music service that would display, sell, and distribute music online while respecting copyright and facilitating royalty payments (Rawsthorn 1998; T. Smith 1999). A trial of the project—known as Project Madison or AlbumDirect—took place with one thousand users in San Diego from June to December of 1999. IBM and the labels put a positive spin on the results (Nguyen 2000). Users and journalists were not as kind (King 2000a). Critics argued that the number of total downloads from the trial (four thousand) was miniscule and that this number was more than overshadowed by the amount of customer service that had to be provided to make the system function effectively. Also, the music was not much cheaper than what was available in stores; the digital rights management system IBM employed limited what users could do with the files; and users could only download full albums, not individual songs. One user even reported needing over two and a half hours to buy, download, and burn his first CD (Drummond 1999).

These companies were some of the earliest musical adopters of what's known as digital rights management (DRM) technologies, perhaps the most overt form of control that emerged during the transition to digital music. By encrypting the information in files and by encoding devices with instructions on how to use and not use the secured content, DRM affects the usability of digital goods. DRM is "an umbrella term for a family of technical applications and for the legal and commercial arrangements they require" (Gillespie 2007, 51). It enforces intellectual property rights for digital goods and acts as a strategy for "morselizing" digital data such that it can be packaged in various forms of digital commodities (Gillespie 2007, 55–56). Software and game designers seeking greater control of their digital content have typically used DRM. But as digital music took on some of the properties of software, music and technology companies also started using software strategies for controlling the movement and use of music. DRM helps establish "trusted systems" that reduce the complex and politically charged issues of copyright, fair use, and intellectual property to mere technical features (Gillespie 2007, 54). DRM takes arguments about how any given cultural good can and should be used out of the realm of public debate; through code, trusted systems impose conditions of use on users before they even have a chance to choose otherwise (Gillespie 2007, 55). In line with Galloway's (2004) insistence that "code = praxis," Lessig's (1999) caveat that code is law, or Sandra Braman's (2003, 423) arguments that technologies instill "regulatory-like" relations, opponents of DRM routinely point out how the infrastructure of the Internet and the design of the hardware and software that access it often set the rules for how we interact with cultural content (Gillespie 2007; Vaidhyanathan 2003; Zittrain 2008).

The rise of DRM is an inextricable aspect of the evolution of music as a digital commodity. In addition to disparate efforts to develop DRM technologies from Cerberus, Liquid Audio, and the like, there were also more concerted, industry-wide initiatives, like the 1998 Secure Digital Music Initiative (SDMI). The SDMI was a working group of representatives from hundreds of companies, including music labels, other kinds of content producers, technology companies, and other parties interested in creating a voluntary industry-wide secure format for digital music (Alderman 2001; Haring 2000; Lamy et al. 1998). Instead of Liquid Audio having its DRM and a2b having another, for example, the SDMI was supposed to be an open forum of like-minded players working towards a shared security protocol: "This initiative is about the technology community developing an open security system that promotes compatible products in a competitive marketplace. It's not about the recording industry imposing a standard on technology companies. We'll simply provide guidance on the needs of our industry and its customers" (Rosen qtd. in Lamy et al. 1998). Despite the RIAA's stated flexibility, it was quickly apparent that the SDMI had too many groups with too many divergent interests (Knopper 2009, 150–56). The SDMI's dream for a shared DRM technology was roundly criticized as an overt grasp for power: "The announcement was not at all about security or about piracy—it's about control. By implementing security, they maintain control" (Steve Grady, spokesman for GoodNoise, qtd. in Krigel 1998). Because there were too many competing transectorial interests and too few incentives to work together on a shared standard, the SDMI was destined to fail (Gillespie 2007, 149), an exercise in "vaporware"(Burkart and McCourt 2006, 107). The SDMI—which at least one writer lovingly referred to as Some Dubious Motive or Initiative (Haring 2000, 131)—splintered back into its diverse groups, officially disbanding in 2002 with little progress made save for some networking opportunities between some of the group's key participants (Knopper 2009, 156). The inability to find common ground was indicative of the challenges presented by a commodity that had become so transectorial in nature. Although the participants all shared a desire to see a market for digital music flourish, different sectorial values and methods clashed when it came to discussions about how best to foster and protect that market.

As a result of all these competing interests and conflicts for control, none of the online retailers that emerged during this period offered a business model or a product enticing enough to draw more than a few hundred thousand users. Companies like IBM, Cerberus, Liquid Audio, and others were imposing technical and economic conditions over the delivery and playback of music. There were companies, like GoodNoise, MP3.com, and RealNetworks that were developing different and less restrictive models, but they generally did so without the blessing, and therefore often without the content, of the major labels. There were also companies like SightSound fighting legally for business method patents that would make the very act of selling digital music proprietary. The result was a lack of technical compatibility, a lack of a comprehensive catalogue of music, and complicated or overpriced subscription plans. Add to this a good deal of tension between record labels and traditional retailers, both of whom were worried about their future roles as middlemen, and there was a clear gap in the digital music market.

The drive to control the sale and usability of the digital music commodity, which may have made sense from an industrial point of view, actually contradicted many of the possibilities users had seen from using digital music through venues such as the IUMA or software like Winamp and Napster. From "Electric Barbarella" to the SDMI, the early history of digital music retail is filled with overt attempts to sell music in ways that would allow the seller to control the shape of the digital music commodity and the markets that would grow up around it. But in most cases the integration of security and commercial options directly into software and files left users little flexibility for using the music in ways that were not prescribed by the various proprietary technologies at play.

The drive to control the usability of the digital music commodity then, through technological or legal means, was evidence of a paradoxical belief that no profitable digital market could be established without first limiting the *digital* aspects of the music commodity. It was a logic that assumed digital files, as infinitely reproducible bits of data, needed to behave more like physical goods before they could assume their role as digital commodities. For many music labels and technology firms, digital music's fluidity, modularity, and portability were problems, not opportunities. Instead of promoting digital music's benefits in their push to establish a market, many actors in the music industries were trying to impose a false scarcity (Gillespie 2007, 56). This is partly why Napster and other file-sharing software seemed so appealing. They offered music for *free*, in two important senses of the word. Users could get music without directly paying for it, and they were free to do what they wanted with the music files they downloaded.[4] With DRM-free MP3 files on Napster's network, users could play songs in any media player of their choice, burn them to countless blank CDs, and share them with friends. Napster delivered on the *digital* features of digital music (modularity, reproducibility, transmissibility, customizability, etc.)

that other services stifled in their efforts to maintain control. For the end user Napster did not require a complicated network of software and hardware; it did not require understanding proprietary formats or signing up to multiple services to access a breadth of musical choices. As even Steve Jobs acknowledged during the launch event for the iTunes Store, Napster had "demonstrated that the Internet was made for music delivery" (2003). While early online retailers jockeyed for legal, economic and technical control of the digital music commodity, users rallied around technologies that fully embraced the commodity's digital-ness.

FAIRPLAY

Napster's combination of a massive database of music coupled with multiple ways to recombine and play that music made these early retail sites seem destined for obsolescence and, along with them, the idea of paying for music. The launch of the iTunes Music Store may have done little at the time to change that idea, but it has over time grown to be the primary outlet for the purchase of digital music. While Apple did not completely set aside the quests for control pursued by earlier retailers, the ways in which it dispersed and masked this control from a specific technological limitation to a network of integrated technologies has had lasting impact for the development of the digital music commodity.

The launch event for the iTunes Music Store focused on a few key features, from Apple's twist on DRM to the store's pricing policy and its integration into the company's lineup of hardware and software. One of the most prominent features was Apple's proprietary DRM technology, a system called FairPlay. Given the limited success of previous DRM attempts, the move was risky. It was also necessary. Apple had been criticized by major labels and other content industry players for its much-publicized "Rip, Mix, Burn" campaign supporting its CD-burning desktops and laptops (see, e.g., Harmon 2002). Apple needed to address the record labels' concerns about security if it wanted access to their catalogues. But while FairPlay presented some of the same restrictions and limitations of the DRM that came before it, Apple's proprietary technology was just one way (and not even the most important) of shaping users' behavior with digital music files. FairPlay represents one step on a longer path of transitioning users from the kinds of hard technological locks other companies were imposing to more integrated and subtler forms of control through technological design.

All files purchased from the iTunes Store came in a protected AAC (advance audio coding) format. FairPlay prevented users from burning songs to more than a certain number of discs (as part of the same playlist), transferring tunes to other computers, and converting files directly into unprotected formats like MP3. Since FairPlay was proprietary, it also meant that only the iTunes software and iPod hardware could read the technology; users could not play FairPlay on digital devices other than the iPod or with other media players like Winamp or Windows Media Player. While these restrictions were similar to other DRM systems I have discussed already (e.g., Liquid Audio), they were notably more flexible (e.g., users could burn as many as five copies of a song/playlist). Most users, Jobs argued, would never even run up against the technology's "generous" barriers. In return for this slight imposition, users could enjoy the good "karma" that came from knowing that musicians, labels, and producers were being compensated and that the RIAA was not going to be knocking at their door (Jobs 2003).

While FairPlay was relatively lax compared to other DRM systems, the technology still governed the overall usability of the digital music commodity. When users purchase a CD, they are relatively free to use it how they see fit (play it in any number of machines, copy it for backup, etc.). There are regulations about how many times a CD can be copied, but these are generally hard to enforce, at least when one is engaged in private, non-commercial copying. In this respect FairPlay was far more limiting since each digital music file came with code that tethered the music to a specific set of uses and devices. Regardless of how generous Apple believed its system to be, music in the store came with an implicit assumption: your purchases will work so long as you use Apple products. This enforced interdependence led individuals and governments to launch lawsuits against Apple in various jurisdictions (BBC 2005; CBC 2006). The plaintiffs in these cases charged that Apple's use of DRM enforced a monopoly relationship between particular software and hardware (like with iTunes and the iPod) and that the practice was essentially anticompetitive. Although most rulings have found in favor of Apple, the cases underscore how the commodification of digital music has involved an unprecedented push toward tethering music to a network of technologies used to purchase, manage, and play it.

DRM not only regulates the kind of software and hardware that can access any given file; it also structures short-term listening and long-term collection practices. Customers who purchase DRM-encoded music only "own" digital music so long as the provider from whom they received it continues to support and update its technology. Take, for example, the cases of the MSN and Yahoo! music stores. Both stores relied on DRM that verified files before letting users play them. MSN and Yahoo! encrypted their files with digital "signatures" that allowed them to be played only on particular machines (those of the file's owner). After a few years of limited success in the market, both stores closed shop. In doing so, they left their customers with music files that were obsolete (Burkart 2008, 249; Sorrel 2008; Van Buskirk 2008b). With the stores out of business, the music could not be verified or played. DRM not only tethers users to a particular brand of software player or portable hardware player; it tethers them to a certain kind of technology that must always be present to unlock the DRM. There are technical work-arounds to these kinds of DRM, like burning to a CD and reimporting, but these methods take time and ultimately degrade the sound quality of a file. DRM technology implicitly discourages its own circumvention. Moreover, legislation like the DMCA enshrines circumvention of DRM as a punishable offense.

This kind of wiring shut with DRM has drastic "material, economic, cultural and . . . democratic consequences" (Gillespie 2007, 57). DRM acts as a kind of technology-driven regulatory strategy that chains consumers to "tethered appliances"—devices whose use is highly prescribed and limited by proprietary controls (Zittrain 2008, 106). In the case of music, those investing in DRM and tethered appliances in an attempt to make the digital music commodity profitable made music far less usable than it had ever been. Never before had the music commodity come with so many restrictions. When users purchased CDs, tapes, or records, they "owned" the album in perpetuity and were afforded a wide range of rights with that media. Although the combination of mechanical and publishing rights complicates the idea of ownership for analog forms of the music commodity, these formats at least came with a number of rights, such as the Right to First Sale, that provided relative balance between producer and consumer (Burkart 2008, 247). Users could also play previous formats where they wanted, as many times as they wanted. Of course, these formats may have degraded over time and through use, requiring replacement. But while digital files are more likely to disappear through hard drive failure or accidental deletion rather than degrade through use, DRM enforces a dishonest sense of material control over ownership by restricting the number of plays or the context of plays. DRM initiatives, such as those mentioned above, were more concerned with ensuring music was secure than they were about trying to create and sell a desirable commodity.[5] In this respect buying digital music at the iTunes Store or other outlets that support DRM was not the same as buying music in other formats. Rather, it was a statement that implicitly supported a certain vision of selling music, one that placed greater limitations on the form and the function of the digital music commodity. Music at $.99, in other words, came with its fair share of trade-offs.

While the evolution of digital rights management in the late 1990s and early 2000s fueled impassioned criticism and calls for more generative technologies (Gillespie 2007; Lessig 1999; Zittrain 2008), the debate around DRM is abating, at least in some respects. The iTunes Store, for example, stopped using FairPlay in 2007.[6] Prompted by competitive pressure from Amazon and other digital retailers, Apple managed to negotiate the right to offer DRM-free files from all the major labels. As of January 2009 almost all songs in the store were provided in DRM-free AAC format, as opposed to AACs embedded with FairPlay technology. While the files still contained custom iTunes metadata and consumer identification information that could be used to link users to the uses of their files, many of the formal restrictions about converting the files to MP3s or burning them to disc were removed (Apple 2009). Given the amount of user outcry against DRM, both Apple and the labels seemed to realize that explicit DRM was doing more harm than good or, rather, that DRM was not particularly effective at enforcing the particular forms of control they were seeking.

This is not to suggest that DRM is passé or no longer important. The publishing, broadcasting, and film industries are currently working through their own DRM crises as they attempt to figure out a viable model for selling e-books, video, and other media content online. Amazon, for example, sells its Kindle e-books in a proprietary format that limits their uses and reuses (Striphas 2010). New streaming music and video services also provide additional forms of control for content owners, since the content usually resides on remote servers. In these cases technology stands in as a form of regulation extending or sometimes even contradicting juridical law. Furthermore, there are other kinds of practices that "lock" consumers into specific technologies. While DRM provides physical or technical locks on digital goods, customer-relations management (CRM) is a subtler strategy that involves the collection of massive amounts of user data, purchase preferences, and customization options that are generated during digital transactions (McCourt and Burkart 2003, 94). This personal information is sorted, analyzed, and presented back to the customer as part of the appeal of a given digital music service. CRM technologies not only have implications for surveillance (McCourt and Burkart 2003, 101); they also create consumer dependencies since it becomes more and more difficult or time-consuming to switch to other systems. Google and Facebook, for example, are able to provide such relevant and useful services because of the amount of data CRM takes in about users across their products. Switching to another service thus comes with a cost to the user of having to regenerate all the data they had through the previous service. So while DRM as a technological fix may be less visible as an explicit strategy, music as software still relies on a variety of levels of control, many of which are enforced via the code or the interface. Music as software relies on a network of technologies to make it playable, and it is through this chain of affiliations that "locks" continue to exist.

The switch away from overt digital rights management, then, only made Apple's central strategy more explicit: a kind of digital lifestyle management that sought to bind user practices through a series of hardware and software innovations. Just as Apple's marketing campaigns position their products not as computers or MP3 players but as "digital lifestyle" devices for media creation and playback (Knopper 2009, 166), Apple has used digital music as a way to expand commodification over the music experience more generally. Whereas companies like Cerberus, SightSound, and others focused on controlling the flow of music by "owning" certain legal or technological aspects of the digital music commodity, Apple's strategy was a reengineering process that worked on the technical, cultural, economic, and aesthetic elements of the digital music experience. Their DRM technology was important but ultimately less significant than the digital lifestyle management they incorporated in the store through its interface, navigation, pricing strategies, and modes of organizing music for consumption. It was through these features that Apple contributed to re-tuning digital music's interface and embedded the iTunes Store and its related technologies into the everyday practices of music consumption.

INTEGRATED INTERFACES

Considering the fragmented state of the music retail sector, online and offline, that characterized the late 1990s and early 2000s (Zentner 2008), the iTunes Store was an attempt to resolve experientially the challenges posed by file sharing and the mixed economy surrounding music. Using interface design as one of its primary tools, the iTunes Store took the confusion and complexity that went along with finding, buying, and playing music online at that moment (difficult-to-use file-sharing software, DRM, competing formats, variable pricing, rival purchase methods, etc.) and tried to repackage these practices as one seamless activity. Apple's digital music system hid all the wires and guts of the music consumption experience and presented it instead as a coherent unity.

Like Winamp's interface, the initial layout of the iTunes Store drew on skeuomorphs and other cultural conventions that came before it. Users could rely on traditional "brick-and-mortar" retail categories (e.g., "Top

Albums," "New Arrivals," "Singles and EPs," "Genre") or check out some uniquely digital musical groupings (e.g., "Playlists," "Exclusive Tracks," iMixes). But the idea of "interface" was complicated by the store's networked nature. The iTunes Store is only fully understandable through the software and hardware with which it interacts. Whereas Winamp's interface was mostly a stand-alone application, the iTunes Store is connected to the Internet and other technologies. Apple blurs the boundaries between these various connections, a process that ultimately affects how users encounter and perceive the digital music commodity and how they engage in their everyday listening practices.

Graphically speaking, the iTunes Store was an extension of the iTunes media player. Launched in January 2001, the iTunes software jukebox may not have been as flexible or easy to customize as other players (e.g., Winamp), but iTunes combined all of its key features in one main window.[7] In one glance users could see the songs in their library, playback controls (play, rewind, etc.), a display that flashed metadata, and a sidebar with access to playlists (see fig. 11). Despite being warmly received at the launch event, iTunes only began its wider diffusion in October 2001 when Apple introduced the iPod. Apple's portable music device was initially mocked (Hartley 2009) but soon became the hottest selling piece of consumer electronics since the Sony Walkman (Kahney 2004, 13). Apple's stock price doubled in the period between 2000 and 2005 and rose sharply by almost 600 percent after the introduction of the signature device (Reppel et al. 2006, 239). By 2006 the five-year-old iPod held more than a 75 percent share of the portable music player market with more than sixty million devices sold (Levy 2006; Reppel et al. 2006).

I mention this rapid growth not to further fuel discourses about an "iPod revolution" that saw an "iPod generation" furiously investing in a device that "changed everything" (Hartley 2009; Kahney 2004; Knopper 2009; Levy 2006). Rather, these numbers indicate how the rise of the iPod acted as a perfect vehicle for the spread of the iTunes media player. Since Mac users could only load songs on their iPods using iTunes, more iPod sales meant more iTunes users. The iPod was a physical and portable extension of a user's music library that was designed to work seamlessly with the iTunes software. As millions of users flocked to a new portable device for managing their music on the go, they simultaneously became users of new software that organized, sorted, and presented their music collections.

Importantly, when Apple launched the iTunes Music Store in 2003, it did so as a revision to the iTunes media player. This is worth noting, and potentially surprising, since Apple had already established an online retail pres-

Figure 11. iTunes media player (version 1.1). The early version of iTunes was a simple interface, but it combined all its information in one main window.

ence with the Apple Store. Since 1997 the Apple Store has been a place for Mac users to order software and hardware online. The store has a working e-commerce framework, as well as advertising and promotional support. Apple could have incorporated the sale of music into the Apple Store; music could have been one of the many commodities available there. Instead, Apple embedded the music store into the iTunes media player software, an update that came during the release of iTunes version 3.0. After installing the update, users could simply launch iTunes and click on the "Music Store" icon in the sidebar (just like they'd click on "library" or "playlists"), and the iTunes Store would be available for searching. The store, in other words, appeared within the interface of the software program itself (see fig. 12). Thousands of iTunes listeners and iPod users instantly became potential digital music customers. Interestingly, early PC users who bought iPods had a slightly different experience since they were given a free copy of MusicMatch Jukebox instead of iTunes. This hybrid alliance between the iPod and MusicMatch Jukebox ended when Apple launched the iTunes Music Store. If Apple was going to be in the business of selling music, it wanted to control all aspects of the process.

Figure 12. The iTunes Music Store (version 4.1). The iTunes Music Store was embedded into the media player, allowing for an integration of listening and buying.

At the time, this tight integration between the store, the software, and the hardware was in stark contrast to most other online outlets. Most digital retailers made their sales through websites. Buying music at these "stores" was not much different from shopping at your local record store; you could browse and purchase music from the online store, but then the files would have to be downloaded and launched within a separate media player. Browsing and purchasing music, in other words, were distinctly separate from the act of listening. With iTunes Apple embedded the store *within* its software. Rather than opening a web browser and downloading music that could then be added to the media player, iTunes fused these separate moments of the consumption process. Users could visit the iTunes

Store and purchase music without ever leaving the media player's interface. It was, in some ways, the equivalent of combining a fridge, a grocery store, and the very dinner table on which the food is served. Technically, the store and the software were still separate. The store's contents, for example, were not stored locally on the user's computer; they were hosted remotely on Apple's servers and data centers. Functionally, however, the store appeared as an embedded part of the iTunes software. Apple's integrated-design tactic ensured that listeners could browse their own music and music from the store all from one program. This seems like a trivial detail now, given how many media content playback programs also allow consumers to purchase, but the iTunes Store was one of the first services to allow users to shop without ever stopping the very activity in which they were already engaged. By merging the store and the player, and by giving them a physical and portable expression through the iPod, Apple combined the act of shopping for and buying music with the acts of sorting and listening to it.

Because the store was embedded directly within the consumer's music-playback application, the software had numerous technical and design links that facilitated smooth and recurring movement between the contents of the store and a user's library. Since the store and the player shared the same overall interface, the practices for navigating the store were virtually the same as those for navigating the user's personal library. The search box that found files in a user's personal library, for example, was the same one users employed to find digital products for sale in the store. Additionally, when users sampled songs in the store, it played immediately within the iTunes software. Playing and finding digital music within one's personal library became synonymous with the activity of playing and finding music for purchase. Users who did decide to purchase a song could click a "buy song/buy album" button and their purchase could be downloaded to their library in one click.[8] The speed and relative ease of the process (compared to other online music outlets at the time) helped hide the more mundane and cumbersome details of payment and commerce that were taking place. The media player became a media store, but the design of the interface and the integration of personal libraries and the store itself made the act of paying for music nearly invisible. In an era when millions of digital music users were accustomed to downloading their music for free, Apple's design strategies tried, as much as possible, to downplay the act of paying for music.

The store, housed within media-playback software with which the user was already familiar (iTunes), made for a relatively seamless transition from digital-media user to digital-media consumer. The "buy song" button represented an advanced blending of leisure and consumption that was

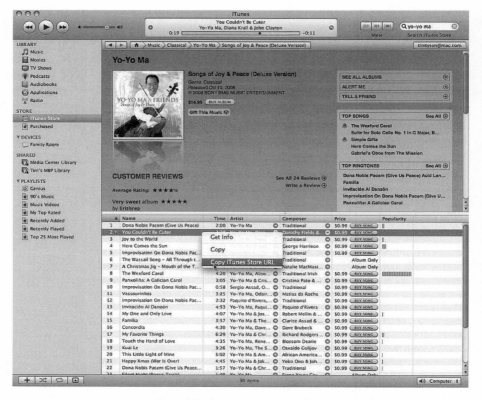

Figure 13. "Buy Song" and quick links (version 8.0). The "Buy Song" buttons facilitated easy purchases at the store while the quick link arrows (small gray buttons on the right of the Artist and Composer columns) allowed for traffic between a user's personal library and the store.

possible in the digital realm. It was a subtle reminder that digital music was a commodity like any other. This logic was perhaps most evident in the hyperlinks that appeared beside each and every song in a user's library. Whether purchased from the iTunes Store or not, every artist name, song, or album title that appeared in a user's music collection had a small gray arrow beside it (see fig. 13) that linked users to the iTunes Store. Technically, the links take users away from their personal libraries and to the store where they can buy the song or album in question. Symbolically, they serve as reminders that our libraries are constituted by commodities. Regardless of how users obtained the songs that make up their libraries (burned from discs they owned, discs of friends, file-sharing networks, online stores, etc.), the iTunes software presented them as commodities linked to a store full of other digital objects for sale. Design features like the linked arrows meant that every instance of using the player thus potentially became a visit to the store. Users' personal libraries were not just repositories for their favorite songs and albums; they were networked and commodified databases that encouraged even further consumption.

PRICE, OWNERSHIP, AND VALUE

Another crucial piece of the store's offering was price. For $.99 a song or $9.99 an album, users received a speedy download of a working, virus-free file that came with digital album art and accurate metadata. Jobs claimed during the launch of the store that Apple's "99¢ solution" would be *the* model for selling and distributing digital music files online in a post-Napster landscape (Jobs 2003). Apple hoped the price point was high enough to start generating revenue for digital music yet low enough to appeal to customers who were getting accustomed to "free" music. Even though the original Napster had folded before the iTunes Store launched, it was unclear whether the existence and popularity of the service had literally devalued digital music to the point that it might never be possible to charge for it again. This is what Tim Anderson identifies as the "problem of free music" (T. J. Anderson 2014, 36). After Napster, a host of record executives and technology companies realized their key struggle would not be about shutting down file-sharing services but about finding a marketable alternative to the free music many users had grown accustomed to, something that would be better than free (T. J. Anderson, 2014, 38). Napster and its legacy had occasioned a "breakdown in common-sense assumptions about the status of music as property" (Friedman 2005, 195), so Apple's pricing decision had more than just commercial implications. It was tied up in larger questions about value and ownership in the age of digital music. Apple's price was an attempt to navigate different conceptions of how goods should circulate on the Internet and various ideas about how users relate to digital music.

At the time of its launch Apple's "99¢ solution" contrasted sharply with the subscription models other online music providers were pushing. Both PressPlay and Rhapsody offered subscription models in which consumers paid a monthly fee for access to all the music in a store's database. Users could access millions of songs for a price that hovered around the cost of one CD per month. But these songs were essentially rented, since users could not access any of the songs if they cancelled their subscription. Users only "owned" the music if they paid an extra premium to download

individual songs or albums. Although subscription services gained popularity from 2000 to 2010, as I discuss in chapter 5, the download model on
which iTunes is based still accounts for about 70 percent of global digital
music sales (IFPI 2013a).

The iTunes Store, unlike streaming or subscription stores, charged users
a price per purchase, be it a song, an album, or a playlist. Much like the
relationship with a traditional record store, consumers only paid when they
made a purchase, not on a monthly basis. The model is founded on the
assumption that "owning" music is still a relatively ingrained social practice. At the iTunes launch event, Jobs reached back through a century's
worth of commercial recorded music history—conveniently skipping
mixed tapes and CD burning—to argue that people still wanted to "own"
their music: "People have bought their music for as long as we can remember. . . . We think people want to buy their music on the Internet by buying
downloads, just like they bought LPs, just like they bought cassettes, just
like they bought CDs. They're used to buying their music and they're used
to getting a broad set of rights with it. When you own your music it never
goes away" (Jobs 2003). Jobs intuited that while consumers were ready for
the new format of digital music, they still had beliefs about acquiring and
consuming music that were not simply going to disappear in light of new
technology. Despite the somewhat intangible nature of digital files, Jobs
argued they were still commodities that users wanted to own. Jobs's decision to make permanent ownership a key selling point helped reinforce the
material aspects of digital music files.

Jobs's notion of ownership here revolves around both use value (what
one can do with the music commodity) and exchange value (a price one
pays, presumably reflecting the worth of the music commodity). But the
way Apple implemented its $.99 solution opened up questions of how these
two kinds of value typically get ascribed to the music commodity. Whereas
most music retailers traditionally set their own prices—prices that usually
vary based on the expected popularity of an album, its newness, the status
of the artist in question, and the dictates of the label—Apple chose a one-
price-fits-all model. Regardless of stature, celebrity, or style, every artist
appeared on the iTunes Store for the same price. Bob Dylan, Luciano
Pavarotti, Celine Dion, the Born Ruffians, and my friend David Myles: all
$.99. These artists may be "worth" different things to different customers,
but the lack of price fluctuation, at least initially, suggested they were all
equal economically. The fact that an unknown independent thrash metal
band could sell its song for the same price as a Rolling Stone's classic was,
in many senses, egalitarian.

For proponents of "long tail" and "frictionless" digital capitalism (C. Anderson 2006, 2009; Leonhard 2008), this "egalitarian" presentation went hand in hand with the promise of digital music to disrupt the business of music production and distribution more generally. Chris Anderson coined the term *long tail* in a 2004 *Wired* article to recognize how, in markets for digital goods where there are little (or relatively low) costs associated with product distribution and limitless space to display those goods, the future of business lies in selling less of more. Companies that trade in physical goods need to rely on promoting and serving up content that appeals to the broadest range possible (i.e., a short tail on a traditional demand curve), but those that deal in digital goods can significantly broaden the range and diversity of the content they offer and drastically increase their number of customers. Companies like Amazon, Netflix, and iTunes stand out as key examples for Anderson's argument that markets become less about the scarcity of a few highly desired products and more about abundance that benefits both producers and consumers (C. Anderson 2006, 11). In the long tail consumers get greater choice, and companies can cater to niche markets and still stay in business, and a host of new relations between producers, consumers, and tastemakers emerge (C. Anderson 2006, 63).

The realization of this long-tail economy is part of the promise of digital music outlets. No shelves and no warehouses mean fewer physical limits to the amount of products digital stores can offer. Lower barriers to getting products in the store should also mean an increase in quantity and diversity of cultural products available. Producers of goods can be in direct contact with their consumers, skirting the costs and limitations imposed by traditional intermediaries. Even the Future of Music Coalition—an organization that protects the interests of independent musicians—celebrated the iTunes Store's egalitarian pricing policy in its review of the store (Thomson and Zisk 2003). The original iTunes Store charged no premium for skill, popularity, or longevity; all artists played on the same $.99 field. Since all the music files Apple was selling were, essentially, megabytes of information, the iTunes Store positioned itself as a neutral purveyor of data and charged everyone the same price of transfer.

This optimistic outlook that long-tail economics provided has come into question as services that rely on long-tail content mature. Anita Elberse has criticized Anderson's work on economic grounds, collecting her own evidence from Rhapsody and Quickflix (an Australian equivalent to Netflix) to show that there is not necessarily as much profit in the long tail as Anderson suggests (Elberse 2008, 95). Despite an increased amount of choice, the prevalence for blockbuster hits remains, and pursuing the profits from niche markets will only work for certain kinds of (well-financed) retailers (Elberse 2008, 96). More fundamentally, though, long-tail economics assumes that we now live in an era in which scarcity is no longer an issue. As some of the research above indicates, digital rights management technologies and other technological forms of lock-in can create forms of scarcity even for digital goods. Long-tail economics also favors companies with significant enough resources to gain access to, and control, a wide variety of content. The current crop of music streaming services, the iTunes Store, and nonmusic services like Netflix all depend on substantial and costly content libraries (and even many of these providers have run into licensing issues that prevent some content from being available). For cultural goods scarcity is always an issue, be it technical or social.

Finally, long-tail economics rests on a deterministic assumption that new technology is all that is needed to level the playing field between producers and consumers in capitalist markets. Any notion of commodity equivalency offered by the fixed pricing scheme was quickly undone by some of the store's other features. Despite the hope for "shelfless" retail, the iTunes Store—which launched with two hundred thousand songs and now includes more than forty-three million tracks—showed how the challenges of "shelves" and intermediaries still remained. Not only were there back-end technical limitations, such as server size, bandwidth, and the number of connections the store can accept; there were also the more visible design problems with how to accommodate such a wide range of music. Limitless content in theory could not be presented as limitless in practice. Despite the amount of music the iTunes Store held, it had a relatively small "space" within which to display its contents. Apple and other digital retailers had to make choices with regard to the content they could offer. These decisions affected the images and links that appeared on the landing pages and structured each visit to the store. The $.99 fixed price may have exerted a leveling effect, but the landing pages acted as digital shelves that gave prominence to certain artists over others and that presented only a select number of total titles and artists. While the shelves of a traditional retailer could prominently display dozens or hundreds of albums, the original iTunes Store interface could only house thirty to forty thumbnail images per screen. Even though it's possible for users to segment their search by focusing on a particular genre or category, with each one leading to another page of thumbnail album covers, or to view more options through a combination of horizontal and vertical scrolling, screen real estate was still relatively limited.[9]

There were also structural barriers for independent or emerging artists trying to present their material in the iTunes Store. At the time of its launch the store did not include any content from independent artists. Apple lacked the resources to deal with small-scale transactions, individual musicians, and small labels. Even now, Apple only deals with record labels of a certain size. Smaller, independent labels can only access iTunes by joining an indie label aggregator like CD Baby or the Orchard. Instead of a disintermediation, electronic markets simply bring additional intermediaries or new roles for old ones (Bailey and Bakos 1997, 12). This is not to suggest there are no benefits for smaller artists and labels. Rather, it is to point out that the assumption that long-tail markets automatically provide greater diversity and opportunity needs to be put in the context of the industry's existing political economic structure. Assuming that new technologies will inherently disrupt or alter the balance of power in an industry downplays the power afforded to entrenched players in various fields, especially when dealing with access to cultural commodities.

Despite the promise of an "egalitarian" pricing scheme, not all artists were equally likely to be found or heard in the iTunes Store. During its early years (though it continues now), iTunes had a marketing and affiliate program known as iTunes 360, which Apple describes on its website as "a great way for content providers to increase their advertising budgets and maximize sales" (Apple 2005a). Apple's artist contract for submission to the iTunes Store also suggested that it favored the placement and presentation of certain artists if doing so helped increase sales: "APPLE shall have the right to determine which sound recordings, irrespective of any particular record LABEL or label affiliation, would best further the commercial purpose of the Online Store, and to promote such sound recordings more than others" (Apple 2005b). Although this suggested all artists had an equal chance to be featured on the site, as in other spheres of cultural production and distribution, marketers with the biggest budgets were able to shout the loudest. Better-known artists received the extra benefits of being featured and presented on the store's main landing pages, mimicking the shelves of traditional retail stores. While the price and limitless shelves of the iTunes Store were a source of optimism for independent musicians and organizations like the Future of Music Coalition, the long tail of the iTunes Store was in reality an incredibly crowded marketplace. The benefits of the digital store's lower cost of entry and greater potential audience also increased the competition artists faced just to be heard.

Apple's $.99 model offered a different perspective on music's exchange value, one that was potentially leveling for artists but one that was still intimately tied to the wider conditions of publicity and production that governed the music industry. Also, since the leveling occurred at such a

relatively low price point, many artists and labels found themselves struggling to match revenues from digital and nondigital sources. While retail
overhead costs may have gone down with the digital commodity, it's not
clear that many of these savings made their way back to the artists (Byrne
2007). Given that the iTunes Music Store was only one part of Apple's
integrated digital lifestyle management strategy, however, music was a side
interest for the company, what businesses call a loss leader: a commodity
that draws users in and steers them toward more profitable goods and services. Apple's standardized pricing positioned music as a (relatively) cheap
piece of software to drive sales of more profitable goods (Bangeman 2005;
Leeds 2005). Although Apple has generally been coy about the amount of
profit it makes from the music store (Cherry 2004; Hansell 2008; Orlowski
2003), the amount of money it turns over to copyright holders—approximately 70 percent of each $.99—already hamstrings the amount of revenue
the company can make from the store. This kind of loss-leader strategy is
possible because digital music is a thoroughly transectorial commodity; the
products of a certain sector can be the fuel for profits in another.[10]

Although Apple relented on its one-price-fits-all stance in 2009—the
store now sells songs at $.69, $.99, and $1.29, as well as in "virtual album"
bargain bins for under $5 or $6—the move to variable pricing has not
undone the notion that music was better understood as data, as cheaply
priced software. As with other commodities, however, exchange value is
only part of a commodity's worth and part of the reason users feel ownership of an object. Ownership and value are not just about the price users
pay for an artifact, or the means through which they acquire it (i.e., subscription vs. à la carte purchase). They are part of a much larger system of
meaning we accord to objects during exchange. Certain forms of barter and
other moneyless transactions can still be considered commodity exchanges,
with the moment of exchange itself being crucial to ideas of ownership and
value that accompany the objects in question. Ownership and value are
clearly linked to use value, to the nature of the relationships users form
with the commodities around them, and what they can do with them. But
financial ownership (via a defined moment of purchase for an agreed-upon
price) is only one way of obtaining and owning a commodity. This is central
to the "freemium" model that Chris Anderson proposes (C. Anderson
2009), where artists or services give away certain commodities (in the case
of music it might be songs or albums) in exchange for data (e.g., emails),
branding opportunities, relationship building, or the future sale of other
commodities. These are gifts with strings attached. Increasingly, the music
industries are trying not to compete with free, but to find the value that can

be mined from free (T. J. Anderson 2014). The price at which we acquire music, then, represents one reason among many that we may ascribe value to cultural goods like music. It simply marks that we paid a certain amount for it at a certain point in time and in a specific context; it denotes a relative exchange value.

There is, arguably, another form of ownership at play with cultural goods: what Gillespie and Burkart refer to as "cultural ownership" (Burkart 2008, 249). Since our relationship with music is as much cultural (i.e., it is wrapped up in identity, taste, pleasure, etc.) as it is commercial, it is possible for users to feel intense ownership over something for which they have not paid (Sterne 2012, 385). As music becomes part of a user's collection, it becomes part of that user's identity, part of their sense of self, part of their own mediated personal history—much like the way Benjamin (2009) describes the role of books. Just like financial ownership, this cultural ownership serves as a rationale for users feeling they should have a certain amount of control and rights over the commodity in question. While value can come from both financial and cultural ownership, the latter is clearly the more affective relationship between individuals and their commodities. This is precisely why I have focused so heavily on the aesthetic and affective features of the various software and technologies. As music circulates, detached from its price, these aesthetic and affective features become the key points from which value of the music commodity derives. A narrow focus on the economic aspects of the digital music commodity or on its remonetization (how it will sell, how much it should cost) provides only a fraction of the story. In fact, the experimentations taking place with free are precisely where new notions of value and new relationships with the music commodity are taking place (T. J. Anderson 2014).

Given this notion of cultural ownership, the emerging retail business models and economic imperatives that drive digital music's circulation may ultimately run counter to the social and cultural gratifications we seek from music (Burkart 2008, 249). Users of digital music find value in its unique properties: its searchability, portability, modularity, accessibility, and so on. Whereas with a physical record or CD, the collector's fetish is satisfied through packaging, album art, and other tangible elements of the commodity, the sharing and hoarding of digital files become key sources of user gratification (Burkart 2008, 248; McCourt 2005, 251). Value derives from how users use their libraries, personally and with others: "The value comes in communication and sharing cultural objects, and ideas and information about them" (Burkart 2008, 246). Unfortunately, as Burkart notes, the commercial technologies that facilitate digital music acquisition and playback often make the realization of this value impossible, or at least always perpetually unattainable (Burkart 2008, 247). Thanks to DRM or to the conditions of subscription services, most digital music retail outlets limit users' rights to music (right of first sale, personal use rights, etc.) and replace them with strict and conditional end-user license agreements. Subscription services reinforce the hoarding aspects of digital music but then trouble it by never giving users full control over their libraries. À la carte models offer users ownership over the commodities they purchase, though they are still governed by license agreements and proprietary technologies. In this "new technology regime," as Burkart calls it, the introduction of "usability problems" continually undermines the value and ownership of digital music (Burkart 2008, 247).

The truth is that the music commodity has, at least since the arrival of tape, never been something that could *only* be acquired through purchase. The same is true today. For the foreseeable future the digital music commodity will be available for "free" and for a price. In addition to file-sharing sites where users can own music without purchase, there will be streaming services where they can hear music but not control it, subscription models they can manage but never truly own, and à la carte download stores where they can own music but still face limits in its usability. Apple's pay per download model will be one among several models for accessing digital music. The price it charges is as much an advertisement for a particular way of buying music and a particular way of using it as it is about the value of the commodity. The price of a track is less about the cost of the labor required to produce a song, or host and distribute a file, and more about an ongoing campaign for the act of paying for digital music in the first place. By giving music a price, by presenting it in a store in a manner that is both familiar and new, the store tries to reinstill traditional models of ownership and value using new technologies. Rather than evidence of disruption, the $.99 solution is further evidence there were simply different visions of selling and buying music that were circulating.

REAGGREGATED COMMODITIES

If value and ownership depend as much on what users can do with a given commodity as on its price, then the way the iTunes Store groups and sells music is worth a closer look. Digital formats promote the *disaggregation* of music (Bakos 1997; Drew 2005). Although disaggregation poses challenges for the integrity of the album as dominant form of the music commodity, it also allows for alternate modes of presenting and retailing music that *reag-*

gregate it into new types of commodified packages. While à la carte purchasing and the $.99 solution are examples of economic modularity and pricing models that facilitated disaggregation, iTunes achieved reaggregation most prominently through playlists, a central feature in Winamp but one that was much more thoroughly commodified in the iTunes Store. In addition to grouping songs by album or artist, as one might find in traditional retail stores, the early iterations of the iTunes Store sorted and sold much of its content through curated playlists. There were seasonal playlists (e.g., the iTunes Essential Halloween Mix featuring songs about werewolves and other monsters—$24.75), yearly reviews (e.g., the "Best of 2005" songs playlist—$86.76), and iTunes Essentials (e.g., Essential Bob Dylan—$71.28). There were also partner playlists (such as Starbuck's Playing for Change: Songs from around the World for $14.99, or Nike's motivational sports/workout mixes), as well as playlists from hundreds of celebrities and well-known media figures.[11]

During the early years of the iTunes Store, Apple also let users participate in the playlist process through the use of iMixes: user-created playlists. Like celebrity playlists, iMixes varied widely in quality, purpose, and cost (e.g., The Seductive Mix—$38.22, Time to Chill 17—$19.80, and Frat Party 80s Style—$19.41). Users could create a playlist in their iTunes software using songs from their library or from the store. iTunes then bundled the mix into a playlist and made it available for other users to listen to, vote on, and purchase. This could possibly be read as Apple's attempt at developing a virtual community, like those that emerged around Napster or Winamp, but there was very little space for facilitating discussion among users, other than the comments section in the store or the voting mechanism to indicate approval of various mixes. Its community building functions were secondary to Apple's drive to put users to work in collecting and combining the various musical commodities in the store. At the start of 2010 there were around two million iMixes that had received eight million votes. While users created and voted on iMixes for a variety of reasons—self-expression, fun, fame, identity negotiation, etc. (Drew 2005, 547)—the end result was a reaggregation of songs that Apple then integrated into its retail offering. Users compiled the mixes, and Apple resold them.

Playlists and user-created mixes are hardly a practice exclusive to the iTunes Store or other digital retail outlets. Compilation albums and mix tapes have a long history, and the new kinds of playlists on the iTunes Store—the personalized mix, the branded mix, the celebrity mix, and the user-contributed mix—all borrow from older forms of mix-making (Drew 2005, 537–42). The difference, as Rob Drew notes, is that these new forms of commodified mixes are increasingly encroaching on previously uncommodified practices (Drew 2005). Home-taping or making mix tapes for friends were once seen as activities outside the industry or even activities that record labels actively sought to limit or restrict (McLeod 2005). Instead, iMixes represent an attempt to profit from a previously unsanctioned consumer practice (Drew 2005, 543–46). Users may have a myriad of reasons for creating an iMix, but they are still performing immaterial labor in service of selling more songs. Echoing Terranova (2004), Drew argues the iMix "commodifies a practice that music fans have enjoyed on an informal, one-to-one basis for three decades; it puts a price tag on the mix, turns mixers into labourers on behalf of music retailers and record labels; and it corrals the practice of mixing within proprietary digital formats and confines it to the limited repertoires of particular music retailers" (Drew 2005, 549). Just as the CDDB benefited from the public contributions of users to their privatized database, iTunes employed users as curators and packagers of digital music commodities. Apple not only benefited from the iMixes themselves (as commodities) but also from the community that formed through the act of creating, judging, and consuming those mixes. In other words, it was not just free or immaterial labor in action; the iTunes Store incorporated immaterial labor 2.0: profiting from "the networks that people construct and participate in," as well as the sale of individual goods (Coté and Pybus 2007, 99). The iMix community of laborers was a particularly valuable one since, like the obsessive updating of user profiles that goes on in social networks, iMixes needed continuous tending to reflect the ever-changing identities of those who created them. The result was a constant supply of repackaged user-generated commodities.

Apple's grouping and regrouping of digital files extended the commodity logic of the music product. It represented the "morselization" of digital data into ever more sellable bits (Gillespie 2007, 55–56) as songs on the iTunes Store were sold individually, as part of an album, or as part of a playlist. In the digital realm "one album becomes a long shelf of songs and products, each carrying its own release date, distribution path, and price tag" (Steuer 2006). A user may not be interested in buying the "Final Countdown" ($.99), by the band Europe, but may consider buying the "Definitive 80s" playlist ($34.99), which, incidentally, includes the former track. Playlists are presented as a new, or inherently digital, way for consumers to discover music. But at the iTunes Store they are also a way to splinter and then recombine the music commodity into multiple products. If music had traditionally been a commodity that was generally purchased once and consumed often, Apple's playlists acted as an attempt to sell the commodity multiple times in different contexts.

This strategy was taken to the extreme when Apple partnered with British rock band Radiohead to exploit the unique properties of the digital music commodity (Kreps 2008). Radiohead had long opposed having its music on the iTunes Store (Huhn 2006). The band argued it wanted to have control over the sale of its music and that Apple did not allow enough flexibility (Huhn 2006; Van Buskirk 2007a). But as a special promotion for the single "Nude," from their album *In Rainbows,* Radiohead offered users five different "stems" of the song through iTunes in April of 2008. Each stem was $.99 and had a specific instrument track from the song: one with just the vocals, another with the guitar, one with drums, and so forth. Users were encouraged to remix the song and post their new version to a website operated by the band. The initiative, in some ways, represented an open-source approach to making music. Rather than giving fans finished versions of songs, they provided them with a select set of raw materials with which to rebuild and reconfigure the band's sounds and instruments. As with some of the open-source software projects Kelty (2008) describes, the song's various iterations became part of a much larger recursive dialogue—a conversation that played out largely through the website where users posted their final remixes—about the value of the project and about users' skills and abilities with music and technology. Despite receiving virtually no radio airplay (only three of the 1,289 stations that Nielsen BDS tracked played it), the song and its various stems were downloaded more than sixty thousand times from the iTunes Store—propelling "Nude" into the *Billboard* "Hot 100 Singles" chart, Radiohead's highest debut single ever, and just shy of their highest position ever on the *Billboard* Hot 100 (Cohen 2008).

Radiohead had already made headlines with *In Rainbows* by offering the entire album for digital download on a "pay what you wish" scale in late 2007. Although exact sales figures are unavailable, it is clear sales of the digital version of the album eclipsed all other digital sales of Radiohead albums (Morrow 2009; Van Buskirk 2008a). They also sold close to two million copies of the album in (physical) retail stores shortly after its launch, and more than one hundred thousand fans bought copies of a deluxe box set version of the album (Van Buskirk 2008a). With "Nude" on iTunes, thousands of users were then spending $5 to participate in the remix project. Depending on how they are framed, these initiatives could either be heralded as an example of a forward-looking digital music strategy or be criticized as novelty tactics by a band that was already popular (and well-financed) enough to pull off such an experiment (Adams 2013; Garland 2009b). While I am sympathetic to both of these perspectives, they miss a more important point. "Nude" and *In Rainbows* illustrate the variety of ways in which the digital music commodity can be grouped, splintered, sold, and resold. Although this kind of splintering and repackaging may open up some novel open-source-like possibilities for musicians and for the user-communities that gather around music (a point I discuss further in my conclusion), these initiatives also point to the extent and the various layers at which digital music files can be commodified. Radiohead's initial resistance to appearing on the iTunes Store was because the band refused to sell songs individually, because it wanted to keep the album, as an artistic statement, whole (Van Buskirk 2007a). It is interesting that what finally brought the band to the iTunes Store was the complete implosion of their music—their album separated out not just into individual songs but into its discrete component pieces.

Playlists, then, are metacommodities. They are commodities that rewrap individual commodities into a bundle under the assumption that the new whole is greater than the sum of its old parts and that another new whole is only a recombination away. While this kind of organization was possible before with compilation albums, singles, remixes, and the like, the digital playlist engenders a kind of never-ending reflection on, and regeneration of, the music commodity. Each new ordering encourages a subsequent reordering. Each playlist puts old commodities into new contexts, offers consumers multiple ways to purchase the same product, and gives users another chance to participate in the process of commodification. From Radiohead's "Nude" stems to user-generated iMixes, playlists have expanded and exploded the form of the music commodity. Hardly a case of the death of the album, the splintering of the digital music commodity into single tracks has created a multitude of repackaging options for music. Single downloads and playlists have not supplanted the album as a means of ordering music, and why should they? All of music's various aggregated forms can invariably coexist as complementary avenues that support the purchase of digital music.

Apple's presentation of playlists has diminished slightly in its quest to compete with streaming services like Spotify and Rdio. Its iMix feature gave way to its "Genius" mix function, which has since become iTunes Radio. Both Genius and iTunes Radio are Apple's foray into personalized recommendations. The technologies work by collecting data and metadata about a user's musical library, sending that information to be correlated with Apple's databases, and then returning recommendations and predictions for future related listening, and ideally purchasing, opportunities. There are still playlists, bundles, and compilations throughout the store though the direct incorporation of user labor from user-generated iMixes seems to have shifted to a more indirect form of data/metadata collection based on user history with the software/store. Recommendations and curated playlists no longer come from individual iMixers but from an algorithmic equation based on a database of aggregate user practices, purchase patterns, and song ratings. Still, the playlist remains a key organizing principle for the presentation and discovery of digital music, either in iTunes or in the various related and competing services that have sprung up around it. Playlists have not necessarily supplanted the album as the primary means for ordering a collection of songs by an artist or band, but they have relegated it to one among many ways to consume popular music.

BUY SONG

iTunes is not just a specific application for the playback and purchase of music; it marks another key moment in the re-tuning of digital music to ready it aesthetically and functionally for sale in digital retail outlets. By giving music new micromaterials through design, navigation, pricing strategies, and means of organization, Apple sought to inject value back into the digital music commodity and, importantly, into the purchasing process itself. Rather than achieving this goal through strictly technological or legal measures, like Cerberus, SightSound, and Liquid Audio tried to do, Apple used a multifaceted lifestyle-management approach involving aesthetic, technical, and cultural means. From hyperlinks that directed traffic between a user's library and the store to "soft" DRM to seamless one-click purchase technology that allowed customers to charge songs directly to their credit cards, the store's design relied on reducing the distances between listening, consuming, and buying. It fused the moments of playback and purchase, reminding users that music's commodity status was only ever partially in question.

Linked and embedded as it was into music-management hardware and software, the iTunes Store is part of a larger network of technologies. The store relies on connections to iTunes and the iPod. Although this kind of technological affiliation was also true of CDs, CD players, and CD stores, the difference with iTunes is the degree to which Apple embedded its products into the music consumption process. In Apple's world, listeners now purchase, store, listen to, and carry music around with one brand. This is digital lifestyle management. It is the commodification of gadgets and the experiences they enable. It is the enclosure of music into a wider assemblage of interdependent technologies, a platform model of music sales. It is an attempt to control and commodify ever-greater amounts of the practices related to music (a strategy that is by no means limited to Apple, as Google and Facebook show). As the value of, and ability to profit from, the recorded music commodity comes into question, the rest of the music industries are shifting their attention to other aspects of the music experience (hardware design, peripherals recommendations, touring, etc.). This is most evident in the push on behalf of major labels (and some independents) to sign contracts known as "360 deals": contracts that give record labels a percentage of everything an artist does, from recordings to tours to merchandise, in exchange for a huge advance (Stahl and Meier 2012). These kinds of deals suggest there is less and less to be made from the sale of recorded music directly and more to gain from mining and commodifying the overall experience of an artist or brand.

The iTunes Store has implications far beyond music. We need only look at the evolution of the store itself for evidence, as Apple has applied its approach to music to a variety of other cultural commodities (television, movies, software, books, education, etc.). The iTunes software has evolved in step with these developments, and it now supports the playback of a variety of media. The original iPod has given way to a lineup of sibling devices including iPhones, iPads, Shuffles, and iPod Touches; music management is merely one among many functions these devices serve. The iTunes Store arrived as a music store, but it has become a media distribution outlet. As with music, all these other commodities are available in a digital store that presents, organizes, and sets the contexts for how users experience them, if not directly as users of the software, then indirectly as users of other stores that look to Apple's lead in terms of how to present and organize such a large swath of media commodities. These stores are embedded within the personal media libraries of millions of users. All aspects of audiovisual leisure are now also, potentially, instances of audiovisual commerce.

I have focused on the early development of the music store because this is the moment when Apple most clearly expressed its vision for the digital music commodity (FairPlay, $.99, à la carte, playlists, embedded in iTunes, etc.). Although this was only one way of understanding the digital music commodity, it quickly became the dominant means through which people paid for digital music during the first decade of the twenty-first century, and it continues to command much of the digital and total retail market for recorded music. The strategies Apple developed to create a viable market have served as a template for commodifying an entire ecosystem of digital commodities, including TV, video, apps, and books. Through its interface, Apple sought to rebuild many of the everyday sources of value that music listeners were accustomed to. It relied on traditional relations of ownership (e.g., à la carte purchase) and channeled collective free labor from users and turned them into new kinds of user-generated commodities (e.g., playlists). The iTunes Store shaped the way users came to conceive of digital music retail and their own personal collections of digital music commodities.

In 2003 *Time* magazine honored the iTunes Store as one of the "Coolest Inventions of 2003," alongside such notable technologies as the Nasal-Mist Flu Shot, the Toyota Prius, and the Robo-lobster—a crustacean-like robot the US Navy was using to scour the ocean floor for mines and other explosives (Taylor 2003). But as Apple celebrated the ten-year anniversary of the launch of the store, and news outlets continued to marvel like *Time* had in 2003 at the influence of the store on the media industries, questions were forming about whether the model of ownership and value Apple had been so instrumental in building was a relic of an entirely traditional way of buying music. Consumer interest in streaming and cloud-based services like Spotify, Rdio, and Pandora seemed to be reaching a tipping point. These new services presented a challenge to Apple's market share and to the iTunes Store's founding principle that users wanted, above all else, to "own" their music. Apple tried, through the design and features of its store, to provide an experience for $.99 that was better than free, but it began to face competition from streaming music services that argued that free was better than $.99. As the next chapter addresses, these new services further challenge the very idea of ownership, value, and what it means to maintain a music collection in an era of ubiquitous tunes and networked technologies.

Music in the Cloud

YOUR MUSIC. ANYTIME. ANYWHERE.

Researching a potential business idea in the late 1990s, David Pakman was curious about the music habits of college students. Pakman, a former employee at Apple and online music retailer N2K, remembers hitting on a key insight: "We went to college campuses and asked, 'How big is your music collection?' and they would say, 'Four gigs'" (Pakman qtd. in Marriott, 2001). Hearing younger users describe their music collection as a specific quantity of data instead of as a particular number of CDs or tapes, Pakman wondered if there was an opportunity to capitalize on people's shifting sense of ownership. Along with another former Apple employee he founded MyPlay.com in 1999—a music "locker" service that allowed users to store their music online and access it via the Internet from a number of devices. MyPlay offered about 250 megabytes of free storage, enough for about sixty MP3 files (Harris 1999). Users could also share music via streaming audio links and could add songs to their locker from the web through a special "Add to my locker" button. Claiming to offer the first-ever virtual locker, MyPlay's original website proudly promised: "Your Music. Anytime. Anywhere."

Despite this promise, users could not download songs from their locker, nor could other users download files from the shared audio links, features that seemed to gain it moderate support from notable music labels (e.g., Jive Records and Dreamworks Records) and other players in the music industries (e.g., *Rolling Stone*, Spinner). MyPlay was also attempting to pay licensing fees to labels and royalties to artists, though it failed to generate much in the way of profits from its streaming business. Labels and music industry executives, however, remained interested in the service because of MyPlay's Target Music Marketing program (Batson 2000). Although relatively common now, MyPlay was also offering one of the first direct music marketing programs that targeted users based on the music they kept in their locker, their listening and sharing patterns and the other kinds of data they made available through their profiles (Batson 2000). Labels hoped to use this cybernetic information to provide custom marketing campaigns and promotions to interested users. After MyPlay had attracted several million users, BMG purchased the company in 2001, just after its Napster purchase. Sony now runs it as a direct marketing site offering exclusive deals on Sony Music content (Kirkpatrick and Sorkin 2001).

Although downloadable *à la carte* options like the iTunes Music Store superseded MyPlay's locker/streaming model, the music industries are undergoing a renewed push toward services that make good on MyPlay's original hope to provide "Your Music. Anytime. Anywhere." This promise goes far beyond MyPlay though. "Anytime, anywhere" has operated as a key catchphrase for more than a hundred years in advertisements for various music technologies and services, including the Walkman, car radios, headphones, pocket radios, and suitcase gramophones (Gopinath and Stanyek 2014b). It is an "absolutely crucial discursive figure" that both describes and prescribes an "ideology of immediate and ubiquitous access to music," which is often tied to larger notions of freedom, immediacy, and the unencumbered individual mobility associated with modernity (Gopinath and Stanyek 2014a, 10–16). Greater control over the temporal and spatial aspects of music playback has been one of the longest-running promises of music technologies; MyPlay was merely one of online music's first manifestations of the sentiment.

The hopes for anytime-anywhere music, and MyPlay's services, have most recently taken shape in the metaphor of the "cloud." There has been a rise in the number of cloud-based music services: streaming, subscription, locker, and similar services that offer users access to massive libraries of music or storage space for hosting their own sound files in places other than their own hard drives. Instead of relying on users to download and manage music on their computers, these services give users access to songs via the cloud and allow them to connect to it from a number of different web-enabled devices. Recorded music has long been available as a service through radio, music via television providers, or direct-to-consumer record club subscription models (e.g., Columbia House). Even the portability and mobility these cloud services provide is part of a much longer history of a push toward mobile music (Gopinath and Stanyek 2014a). But the drive toward the cloud does represent something different. Part metaphor, part vision for the future business model of music, cloud music is part of a transectorial push to make digital files and personal libraries more readily available for users, more profitable for producers and rights holders, and more surveil-able for advertisers, marketers, and a host of other information intermediaries

In this chapter I want to build on Sumanth Gopinath and Jason Stanyek's excellent deconstruction of "anytime anywhere" by exploring the metaphor of the cloud. While their focus is on the long history of mobile music—whether that mobility comes from a clunky gramophone that could be moved around the room or from users circulating around various urban spaces with an MP3 player or smartphone—mine is on the specific ways computing and music technologies have converged to further complicate our understanding of the music commodity. The previous cases of Winamp, metadata, Napster, and iTunes have, to a large extent, envisioned the digital music commodity as something that resides locally, on the hard drives or devices of users. Though each contributed in different ways to music's re-tuning, the technologies also reinforced the objectness of music through the forms of ownership they provided; they focused on how users manage libraries of folders, fields of metadata, and store-bought digital files through the interfaces of their computer's software. The move to music in the cloud alters this relationship by calling into question these previously central features of ownership and commodity management. Rather than owning and keeping music on their own devices, users are outsourcing the creation, maintenance, and storage of their music collections to cloud-based music services.

While the metaphor suggests the cloud offers an infinite and omnipresent space where music is ever available, cloud-based services also act as transient and enclosed spaces where the music users "own" is always at an ethereal distance to them. Although music stored centrally on servers allows for unique possibilities for the mobility of music and its discovery by users, the push toward cloud music is part of a drive toward a "celestial jukebox" designed and managed by companies looking to control the shape and flow of the music commodity and the data that commodity generates. MyPlay, for example, was ostensibly selling users the ability to store *their* music in a location that was not theirs. This shift in location of the music collection, however, also allowed MyPlay to sell data about a user's collection to other businesses in the service of further marketing, promotion, and selling opportunities. Music in the cloud becomes something users access rather than acquire. While labels and tech services present the push toward music in the cloud as the definitive realization of a seamless "celestial jukebox," the reality is much more fractured, constrained, and grounded. Hardly a simple shift from music as a good to music as a service, music in the cloud represents a particular cultural model of music distribution—one that enmeshes users in a network of technologies and a process of continual commodification of the music experience.

The recorded music industries spent significant resources decrying file sharing and other technologies for illicitly obtaining digital music files as a threat and crisis to the value of recorded music. While I've argued throughout this book that this devaluation narrative ignores some of the new forms of value that have emerged around the digital music commodity, I recognize that these practices of music circulation present, on some level, a form of industrial crisis. The recent push toward cloud computing, however, suggests the crisis, if we have to use that word, is less about the question of whether or not users will pay for digital music files in comparable amounts to what they paid for CDs than about a changing relationship users have with music as a result of the formats, services, and technologies that now mediate everyday uses of music.

CLOUD FORMATIONS

The value of the commodity form of any type of media or cultural product depends heavily on the devices and technologies through which users access, display, manage, and use those products. The value of the compact disc, for example, was bound up in the affordances of CD players, portable disc players, car stereos, and so on. The commodity itself has value on its own, through its packaging, shape, and form, but its full value is only actualized through use. CDs were innovative because they allowed users to skip forward and backward with ease, to see the length of tracks clearly, and to listen to an entire album without changing sides. The drawbacks of CD technology—they are easily damaged, they skip, and they have other glitches—also form part of the experience of the format. As the technology to play, access, and manage CDs changed, so did the value the CD commodity offered users. In other words form and format are deeply entwined. As computers started to become a popular device for playing back CDs, users found new reasons for valuing the CD as a format for music delivery.

Take, for example, Will Straw's anecdote about the evolution of counterfeit CD manufacturers in Mexico at the turn of the millennium. Throughout most of the 1990s counterfeiters were highly concerned with mimicking the exact details of the CDs they were pirating (Straw 2009, 80). They sold copied music, and it was important that they sold it in intricately copied packaging. The replication of the commodity's packaging and paratexts was just as significant as the replication of the CD's content. Graphics, liner notes, and the rest were all meticulously counterfeited, suggesting the pirated music's worth came not just from the discount prices but from the fact that the commodity context remained intact despite its move to an illicit market. Around 2005, though, this practice changed. Instead of copying the commodity in its entirety, counterfeiters began using compact discs as mere vessels on which to store as much digital music (usually in MP3 format) as possible (Straw 2009, 80). Whether this was a signal of the compact disc's diminishing cultural relevance or part of its cause, it was evidence the CD had "lost its integrity as an artifact" (Straw 2009, 87).

The "end" of the compact disc was a function of the CD technology itself. As CDs became increasingly mobile through portable CD players, car stereos, and, eventually, computers, users left the CD's paratexts behind as they brought the plastic discs into new environments and contexts. This is especially true on computers, at least until technologies like Winamp and metadata arrived. However, as the computer evolved, the CD's capabilities expanded. Thanks to CD-R technology and CD-burning drives, the CD became as much a storage technology as one of presentation. Users employed CD-R discs to burn music as data files instead of straight audio files. In the process the CD lost some of its importance as a music format. It was a format for data delivery rather than music playback. CDs could collect and present hundreds of songs, when burned and played back on a computer, not to mention the wide variety of other digital documents they could hold. Music was simply one of the many digital things CDs could do.

The CD's storage capacity—which was initially one of its key benefits over vinyl or tapes—was part of the reason newer technologies with greater capacities displaced it (Straw 2009, 82). As storage vessel rather than music artifact, the CD brought about its own demise. Its mobility and capacity took precedence over its materiality. Although the CD provided important paratextual information that rivaled previous music formats, function ultimately superseded form. The technology became "little more than a temporary host for music" (Straw 2009, 85). The compact disc was relegated to a "technology of intermediate agglomeration" for the movement of music from older formats to newer storage technologies (Straw 2009, 83). Rather than a musical artifact of its own, the CD's purpose became to collect media and prepare it for other devices.

The move to cloud computing repeats and extends this process. The digital music commodity first emerged on the computer, but the rise of cloud-based services suggests the personal computer will not remain the central device for hosting, storing, and playing digital files for long. Just as the purpose of CDs shifted as they became playable in more places on more devices, the digital music commodity is taking on new roles as it moves from the computer to the cloud and all its associated devices. In the cloud the digital music commodity is immanently configurable; it is fluid enough to exist on a wide variety of media formats and devices. While it took twenty to thirty years for the CD to lose its artifactual integrity, the digital music commodity has diffused much more rapidly to a far greater range of devices and services. The integrity that the digital music commodity gained through the interfaces of programs like Winamp or iTunes, or in the meta-data from the CDDB and ID3 tags, de-tunes again in the cloud. New inter-faces emerge, but they originate from and are tethered to the cloud and thus propose a further reimagination of the digital music commodity. The cloud is a technology of presentation, storage, distribution, and consumption wrapped into one.

This is why the move to the cloud is not simply an extension of the anytime-anywhere drive that has long directed innovation in music tech-nologies. The cloud certainly promises to offer control over the when and the where of music consumption. But it also promises to free us from the cumbersome materiality of music commodity ownership and proposes a vision of music collection that relies less on the collection of physical goods than on the willing delegation of musical collection, curation, and discovery to service providers.

Cloud computing relies on large data centers to store, process, and pro-vide data to users and businesses on an as-needed basis (Jaeger et al. 2009). Imagine a diagram of the Internet showing a vast number of connections between an equally vast number of computers and other networks. The traffic, noise, and space between them create the cloud. Cloud services offer massive storage space for users' files, playlists, preferences, and informa-tion, as well as remote access to that data regardless of device or location. While we used to rely on our own gadgets for our computing needs, increasingly we shop portions of our daily activities out to the cloud (Horrigan 2008, 5). Cloud computing is the commercialization of services like data storage, information processing, and computational power (Jaeger et al. 2009). This marks a shift from using our own machines to control our data to trusting the network to store it for us (Hayes 2008).

Cloud computing is difficult to describe, in large part because it is not that different from a general understanding of the Internet as an interconnected network of computers where data resides. The term *cloud computing* itself dates back to the 1960s, where computer visionaries like J. C. R. Licklider and John McCarthy foresaw a vast network of connected computers that allowed access to all sorts of programs and services from all kinds of devices (Mohamed 2009). Some of the Internet's earliest founders and architects, like Vint Cerf or Bob Taylor, used clouds and other amoeba-like structures to represent their vision of a dispersed but connected Internet architecture (Scanlon and Wieners 1999). Even companies like Western Union were proposing cloud-like services as early as 1965 (Carr 2009). Cloud computing is most easily understood in relation to personal computing, the dominant model over the last three decades. In the former users access information and services through servers and other offsite terminals. In the latter processing power and key applications reside on the user's desktop computer. Since both models have played key roles in the evolution of computing, it's slightly disingenuous to label cloud computing as entirely novel. As one tech CEO noted sarcastically in an interview on the topic: "The interesting thing about cloud computing is that we've redefined [it] to include everything that we already do" (Larry Ellison, Oracle CEO, qtd. in B. Johnson 2008). Indeed, cloud computing shares many similarities with earlier models like mainframe computing or time-sharing, where the resources and computing power of one (usually large, expensive, and difficult to operate) machine were shared among a variety of users. Cloud computing, in other words, is a new name for a traditional mode of computing and for services the Internet has long provided.

Aside from having achieved a certain level of discursive purchase in tech circles, then, cloud computing is both a return to a much older model of computing and an experiment with various ways of commodifying computing services. Although the last two decades have seen similar attempts to make cloud computing more mainstream—under names like software as a service (SaaS), grid computing, utility computing, and others (*Economist* 2010; Hayes 2008)—it is only since c. 2005 that the idea has become technically feasible for a wide range of businesses and consumer products. Thanks to increases in computing power, the growth in high-speed data lines and wireless networks, decreasing costs for storage, and the proliferation of portable digital web-accessible devices, companies like Google, Amazon, Microsoft, and IBM have incorporated cloud computing as a focal point of their business strategies and have in turn introduced services that capitalize on cloud-based means of producing and managing content (*Economist* 2009; Horrigan 2008, 5).

Beyond more capable technologies, this newest push toward anytime-anywhere computing is also proving more successful than previous attempts thanks to the vigor and resources companies are now devoting to building storage facilities, the technical aspects of cloud infrastructure, and the hardware and software platforms used to access the cloud. On the business-to-business side companies like Google, Microsoft, and Amazon have started renting out storage space and/or computer processing to other businesses with far less powerful IT infrastructures. This arrangement allows companies to build applications that generate reams of data or that can perform high-level data analysis without necessarily having to invest all the capital such capabilities would require (Horrigan 2008; Mohamed 2009). It also signals that computing capacity is now a "tradable commodity" in its own right (*Economist* 2011). Amazon has one of the largest cloud infrastructures established, though Google, Facebook, Apple, and Microsoft have all invested in "billion dollar data centers" to add to their growing number of server warehouses (Jaeger et al. 2009; Miller 2013).

For consumers, cloud computing is also more prevalent and interwoven into everyday computing practices than it has ever been. A PEW Internet Research study suggested in 2008 that more than 69 percent of all Americans used some kind of cloud computing services, even though many of them were not aware of the term "cloud computing" or what it meant (Horrigan 2008, 7–8). Popular cloud-based email programs (like Yahoo and Gmail) and other cloud-hosted services (like Google Docs, Zoho, and other online collaborative tools) have crept into our online activities so gradually that most users barely stop to think that much of their data are already in the cloud.

The push toward cloud computing is also an attempt to open new revenue streams for the use of the data being stored in these cloud services, as the case of MyPlay.com suggests. The cloud has as much to do with marketing and encouraging an unhindered flow of digital data as it does with technical innovation. Google's cloud services are a prime example. As users send email through Google's free Gmail program, Google serves up advertising that matches the content of the correspondence. Similarly, the use of Google's document-hosting service, its chat feature, its Google+ social network, and other services give Google access to users' habits and practices that the company coordinates, manages, and sells for advertising purposes. The data Google gleans from the cloud is enough to fund the production of more cloud-based services that are mostly free for consumers. Cloud computing and advertising go hand in hand (Schmidt and Sullivan 2006). The more data that users share and upload to a company's servers and data centers, the more information they provide to package and sell off to advertisers or to exploit in other ways. What's new about cloud computing, then, is the extent to which cloud service providers have found ways to generate business models and profits, not just from renting storage and processing power but from utilizing user data, uploads, and behaviors as cybernetic commodities for further exploitation.

Thanks to the transectorial innovations discussed previously, music is now wrapped up in computer industries' push toward cloud-based service models. There are several emerging cloud-based music services that are popular, though the business models behind many of them are still in question (Wikström 2009, 106). There are Internet-based streaming services, like Pandora or GrooveShark, that build on the broadcasting model established by radio and by early Internet streaming audio services like Real Audio. Users can listen to songs of a certain genre or by a certain artist, though they do not usually have complete control over the exact songs they can hear.[1] Some of these rely on advertising; others allow users to upgrade to a premium ad-free version. Companies like Rhapsody, Rdio, Beats, Spotify, Napster 2.0, and eMusic provide a more formal subscription service, where users rent access to a massive collection of music for a monthly price. Some of these services, like Rdio and Spotify, offer free streaming of music limited to particular devices (e.g., computers but not mobile devices) as a way to transition users to paid subscriptions. In all cases users "own" and manage their music only until their subscription ends.

There are also social network sites like Myspace, Last.Fm, and Soundcloud that are hybrids of commercial broadcasting, social networking, and music magazines where communities form around the discovery and discussion of music.[2] Finally, there are "locker" sites like MP3Tunes, MegaUpload, Google Music, and Amazon's Cloud Drive that provide storage space for users to upload their own files. Increasingly, companies are providing cloud-based services that mix features from all of the above models. The iTunes Match and iCloud services, for example, allow users to access music files stored centrally on Apple's servers, as well as download local copies for their specific devices (computers, tablets, music players, etc.). Apple has fused streaming, locker, and music recommendation functions in one service, with parts of the service available for free and others available via subscription.

The move to the cloud thus introduces multiple arrangements for encountering and using the digital music commodity. While buying a digital song from the iTunes Store was in many ways analogous to buying an album at a physical retail store, the cloud presents songs as streams, as subscriptions, and as downloads. Music can be a file that stays on a user's computer and lingers on the hard drive, or it can be a database entry held on servers thousands of miles away. If "information wants to be free" was an unofficial slogan for the first few decades of the information age (for an extended discussion see Wark 2006), cloud-based services bend the statement by proclaiming "information wants to be everywhere." As with information's longing to be free, it is debatable whether this desire for ubiquity is part of information's very ontology or whether it is simply something we wish upon our information. The cloud-based music services mentioned above certainly seem convinced that users are ready to move from ownership to access, so long as that access includes almost all the music they could imagine wherever they happen to be. Music in the cloud is an attempt to make the music commodity available everywhere. Your music. Anytime. Anywhere.

As the music commodity becomes increasingly pervasive across a wide range of services and devices, what is at stake for how users experience music and for the music commodity itself? The digital music commodity hastens the spread of what Anahid Kassabian calls "ubiquitous listening" (Kassabian 2001, 16). Ubiquitous listening is a mode of listening that acknowledges that most listening happens "alongside or simultaneous with other activities" (Kassabian 2001, 15). Music is omnipresent, both in terms of how much music users can listen to and the number of devices, places, and contexts in which they can encounter music. Yet there is a "sourcelessness" to these sounds as music seems to come from "everywhere and nowhere" at the same time (Kassabian 2001, 16). Malls, offices, and other public places are obvious examples of where music is projected but its source obscured, but even private listening experiences can seem sourceless. As users turn on their music players and go about other activities, the sound functions as a soundtrack to other activities rather than a specific activity of its own. The digital music commodity, which is highly mobile and easily integrated into a variety of services and devices, is an ideal format for ubiquity, and cloud-based music services rely on precisely this kind of logic. The cloud makes music accessible everywhere via the Internet, yet it is nowhere on a user's hard drive or computer. The exact details of where the music and its associated metadata are stored are secondary to the context of the overall service.

With music so thoroughly interwoven into everyday activities, it is possible the digital music commodity contributes to a lack of the specificity of musical experiences. Listeners may listen to more music then ever, though it is unclear whether they recognize listening as a distinct activity. Kassabian recalls the example of one of her students who turned on the radio to begin writing an assignment on a particular program only to find himself washing the dishes several minutes later (Kassabian 2001, 12). He forgot the radio was on, or rather, he internalized the radio and started doing chores, an activity he normally undertook alongside the radio. Omnipresent music creates a fabric that accompanies the patterns of our everyday actions. As listeners take in multiple media simultaneously instead of in sequence (Kassabian 2001, 15), the act of listening melts into other practices (Adorno 1934; DeNora 2000; Kassabian 2001). Users may very well use their music players to listen to music, but they also use them to make phone calls, to write essays, to take pictures, and to email, network, and connect. Music becomes merely one of many multimedia options.

Like the push toward multimedia near the end of the twentieth century, the cloud metaphor thus expresses a particular vision of computing and for the delivery of music commodities. Clouds, on bright summer days, are big white fluffy concoctions. For the most part they conjure positive images. They reflect "a whiteboard vision of heaven on earth," so the Internet as cloud is a kind of "holy condensation of bits" (Scanlon and Wieners 1999). Clouds are also ubiquitous and highly dispersed. They are free to look at and widely available. It is no wonder the metaphor is popular for explaining our relationship with data in the information economy. The cloud is an idealized portrait of what we expect from our information: it should always be there, wherever we are. This is particularly appealing for a commodity like music, something that users see and treat as a "technology of the self" (DeNora 2000, 46–47). If music is the soundtrack to our lives, then it seems like the ideal candidate for technologies that make it available in more places, at different times, through a variety of devices, interfaces, and ways.

But the cloud metaphor conceals as much as it reveals. Like actual clouds, the data cloud just seems to exist. Users take its makeup and infrastructure for granted, since the cloud seems as if it is anywhere users have access to the Internet. Underneath the idea of an ethereal and distributed network of connections and traffic, however, lies the cold hard physicality of warehouses, servers, generators, and climate controlled devices. This is the stuff of the cloud. "There's not really anything white or fluffy about it" (data center manager qtd. in Vanderbilt 2009). In 2009 there were more than seven thousand data centers in the United States alone, and as more centers proliferate, they continue to raise a host of geographical, economic, and political issues. These centers store hundreds of thousands of servers and require a huge amount of energy resources to function (keeping the servers cool, keeping them free of dust and moisture, keeping them on at all times). As a result, they tend to be located in regions that are dry or cool or that offer cheaper access to electricity. Given how booming the business for data centers is, though, many cities and states have started using either tax or energy incentives to encourage investment in their region (Jaeger et al. 2009; Miller 2013). The drive to cloud computing is reconfiguring economic and natural resource policies (both nationally and internationally), yet we continue to have a curious incuriosity about the stuff of the cloud (Jaeger et al. 2009).

Similarly, while cloud-based music services sell users on the ubiquity, mobility, and constant access the cloud provides, the metaphor obscures many of the drawbacks inherent in the services themselves and in their impact on music. Streaming, subscription, and other cloud-based services enter their users into service agreements that basically rent music out for a fee or dole it out under certain conditions. Music in the cloud allows other entities remote control over a user's library and makes music contingent on the service in question and a complement used to prop up other commodities. Cloud services allow for some legitimately novel and improved musical experiences, but as music moves from the status of a good that users maintain and curate on their personal computers to a service they turn on and off via multiple devices, they find a new mediator in their relationship with music. While music has always relied on the technologies of its production, distribution, and consumption, music in the cloud is a highly technologized vision that requires numerous preconditions for playback. It is a specific snapshot of music as a cultural commodity, one that views music as indelibly networked to particular providers and technologies.

CLOUD TUNES

One of the most critical differences between cloud computing and the model of personal computing most users have become accustomed to over the last two and a half decades is that the software programs and other infrastructural elements for their data no longer reside on their personal machines. They exist out there, in the cloud. This raises obvious comparisons to radio, cable television, movie rentals, or other commodity arrangements that rely on broadcasting, subscription, or rental rather than outright ownership. In the cloud, cultural commodities are stored elsewhere, managed by service providers, accessed rather than owned, dependent on the device used to access them, and so forth. At first glance, streaming services like Pandora, Spotify, and GrooveShark simply seem to offer a more interactive radio experience via the Internet. They are an updated and customizable means of accessing music broadcasts. But while the act of listening to music in the cloud is likely similar to previous media commodity arrangements, the comparison is incomplete.

Cloud-based music services make different requirements of their users, and they impose particular conditions on the music itself. Radio, for example, does not require one to enter personal data to listen to it, as is often the case when signing up for services like Pandora or Rhapsody. Radio also remains relatively indifferent to the content and technologies involved. With any number of radio devices, users are free to surf a variety of channels. Streaming and subscription services, in contrast, often depend on a particular combination of technologies, and they make it difficult or inconvenient to switch to other services. Different services offer different libraries depending on their contracts with the record labels, and it is difficult to combine music from different services or export data from one service to another. Since their very customizability and interactivity depend on the collection of personal data, cloud-based services embed users into their service more thoroughly than traditional radio. Users are of course free to switch to other services, but there is a cost for doing so; libraries, playlists, and preferences will all have to be rebuilt with the new service. Even social networks like Myspace or other basic streaming services that offer the ability to participate with the service without signing up for an account still limit the amount of interaction with the service or control over organization and playback that users can have without an account. Cloud-based services may feel familiar to radio, movie rentals, and the like, but they represent a significant shift away from the dominant mode of music consumption for the better part of the last century.

As with the jockeying over new online retail models, the shift to a digital music commodity in the cloud is a question about control. Historically, the record labels have been leery of cloud-based digital delivery services. Although MyPlay.com seemed to have some form of industrial support, the record labels never really warmed to more popular streaming/cloud pioneers like AudioNet or music locker services like MP3.com's Beam-It (Alderman 2001; Rothenberg 1999). Beam-It, like MyPlay.com, was supposed to allow users to "space shift" the music they already owned. After users loaded CDs into their computers, Beam-It kept track of which CDs users owned. They could then access and play their music from My.MP3. com on any browser. Unlike MyPlay.com, though, users did not have to upload individual copies of the songs they wanted in their locker. Instead, My.MP3.com pulled the songs from a huge database of CDs the company had purchased or, when needed, uploaded songs directly from the users to include in their database. In the eyes of the RIAA and the labels—and the court that eventually found in favor of the labels—MP3.com was not licensed to rebroadcast or distribute music in this manner. Although users could make backup copies of their music, there was no legal precedent for a company providing that service for users (Alderman 2001). The lawsuit resulted in the closure of Beam-It and crippling losses to MP3.com. Michael

Robertson, MP3.com's owner, continues to believe in Beam-It's model, though his latest attempt—a locker service called MP3 Tunes—also faced legal troubles (Stone 2010). Other similar media storage services, such as MegaUpload and RapidShare have faced similar opposition.

Much of the resistance on the part of the labels, and some artists, comes from a disbelief that they will be able to generate the kinds of profits they had in the CD era.[3] With subscription, storage, and streaming models priced anywhere from free to $15 a month, many labels and artists are not convinced that the volume of new traffic the services generate will make up for the fact that consumers aren't paying $15 per CD. Locker services are even more in question, as the labels argue that storing songs in a locker constitutes a need for a repurchase of that song. Google and Amazon, in fact, originally launched their music streaming services without the full consent of the major labels, and without official licensing deals for their catalogues thanks to these kinds of arguments (Singel 2011).

This conflict of interests speaks to the unevenness of transectorial innovation. When computing technologies begin to drive the music industries as much as the labels do, innovations in the former are often at odds with the business models of the latter. But the tension also revolves around the kind of commodity the digital music commodity is. If a user owns a local copy of a file, is the copy they store via a locker service simply a digital copy of something they already own? Or is it a new commodity that should be repurchased or reexploited under a new business model? Take, also, the example of streaming. Most services use either progressive streaming, which downloads a copy of the file in small chunks to the user's hard drive, or true streaming, which plays a file directly from a remote server and leaves no local copy. Although this seems like a mere technicality, the lack of a copy of the original file on a user's computer makes their library entirely dependent on a subscription to the service and a connection to the Internet. Users may not experience this as a serious limitation, but it effectively transforms recorded music from a durable and copyable good into "single use products (streams) that perish as they are consumed" (Anderson 2011, 160).

These seemingly trivial industrial use-case scenarios raise larger legal, economic, and ontological questions about the nature of digital goods and the classification of copies as commodities. Although we live undeniably in a "culture of the copy" (Schwartz 1996; Lessig 2004), with machines and technologies that allow for easy, rapid, and mass duplication of cultural content, we also live in a culture of the commodity that relies on scarcity and restricted flows of goods and services. This is why, as Hillel Schwartz so succinctly notes, "An object uncopied is under perpetual siege, valued less for itself than for the struggle to prevent its being copied" (1996, 212). The battles over the legality of copies in locker services or the technicalities of progressive versus true streaming are merely the opening words in a much longer and more difficult conversation about the nature and value of objects that can be provided in multiple digital forms.

Given the cybernetic character of the digital commodity, however, there is certainly no shortage of opportunities for the major labels and tech companies to extend their control over the flow and presentation of music, even if they cannot entirely control the flow of the digital objects themselves. If music in the cloud is an attempt to make the music commodity available everywhere, then many of the cloud-based services sanctioned by the music industries are attempts to ensure that every instance of music playback is somehow commodifiable, by introducing new (and ongoing) fees and new points of purchase for music. Music in the cloud represents the ultimate iteration of the "celestial jukebox," where the labels and other producers seek to exert organized technocratic control (Burkart and McCourt 2006). Major record labels and tech companies have developed CRM technology that acts like "sophisticated spyware" and DRM technology that "personalises network power" by creating trusted systems that enforce particular behaviors (Burkart and McCourt 2006, 357). Ostensibly positioned as a space where users have access to an infinite amount of music from an infinite amount of places, the celestial jukebox turns the music commodity from a cultural object into an efficient tool for data collection.

The celestial jukebox puts "new and enduring constraints on music's viability as a cultural practice protected from pure market functionality" (Burkart and McCourt 2006, 359). If left to develop unchecked, the celestial jukebox is a threat to music's very status as a sociocultural good: "In the audio-visual enclosures created by intellectual property law, contract law, and computer software, music collectors face a loss of property, control and usability, legal rights of first sale, consumer product protections, and other customary rights and privileges. It remains largely unclear who and what are in charge of the manner in which music reaches the music fan who has signed up for cultural services" (Burkart 2008, 250). Music in the cloud is one particular (and potential) manifestation of the idea of the celestial jukebox. And while it may seem convenient to keep all our music, email, and other documents on someone else's server, data in the cloud become at least partly the property of the companies that manage the service. The information is entirely dependent on the unregulated whims of the record labels and technology companies who manage it.

Music as a service provided via the cloud becomes what Zittrain (2008) calls "contingent." Contingency arises when devices, programs, and goods are "rented rather than owned" and are therefore "subject to instantaneous revisions" (Zittrain 2008, 107). Tethered appliances lock consumers into certain services and patterns of consumption. Once a user has subscribed to a specific service or bought a file with a particular kind of DRM, the commodities themselves are regulated by the terms of service and by the terms of the technology. With goods as services there is a constant connection between the producer and the product, allowing for ongoing updates and changes to the product itself (Zittrain 2008, 107). While this sounds like progress—and with certain products it may ultimately be cheaper and more convenient— contingency shifts control over devices and their capabilities even further away from the consumer. The features that drew users to buy a device or subscribe to a service may or may not continue to be provided in each upgrade. Products we use one day could change the next since they can essentially be "quickly reprogrammed without our assent" (Zittrain 2008, 176).

The cases of the MSN and Yahoo! stores described in the last chapter are clear examples of the negative consequences of contingency. Amazon's "recall" of a few titles by George Orwell on its Kindle e-book reader is an even more extreme example.[4] Although Amazon acknowledged the move was likely the wrong one, the company's behavior underscores the transience and instability of digital products that are governed by contingent connections to the cloud. When companies treat cultural commodities as software, they gain greater and more sustained control over those goods and the devices used for their playback. Just as clouds are subject to the whims of the wind, data in the cloud are often far beyond the control of the users who have invested time, effort, and money into creating and maintaining them.

It is not just content that is contingent. The devices for music playback are as well. Many companies that manufacture digital music devices deliver regular software and firmware updates in ways that can significantly hamper a user's experience of the product. Apple's iPod Touch and iPhone, for example, are updated every few months with revisions to the operating system. Although some users are content to use the devices as is, there is an active community of users who have hacked their gadgets to extend the phones' capabilities—a process known as "jailbreaking." When Apple caught on to this user practice, it started using the software updates for a dual purpose. Apple's updates not only provided bug fixes and regular maintenance, but they also included code to "brick" hacked devices: to return the phones and music players to an unhacked state and, in many cases, render them completely inoperable (BBC News 2007). The device was contingent on remotely controlled software updates that allowed Apple to prescribe specific uses and to restrict others.

Cloud services themselves are also contingent. Personal music collections in the cloud are subject to the successes and failures of the company that is charged with storing them. Spotify, for example, ran into some early troubles with its service when a large number of user accounts were hacked and their personal details made available. The hacker was able to access passwords, email addresses, birth dates, gender, postal codes, billing receipt details, and other information provided by users during registration (B. Johnson 2009). Since signing up for many cloud-based services requires users to provide this kind of data, music in the cloud exposes users and their libraries to risks that differ from those associated with previous media. With CDs or tapes users worried about lost, stolen, or damaged commodities. With music in the cloud users need be concerned with the network of information they make available that might potentially be vulnerable to exploitation. While CDs and tapes only required one other device for playback (i.e., CD players or tape players), music in the cloud is contingent on a network of technologies, devices, and connections (Burkart 2010, 129). Users who store their music in the cloud are also dependent on having regular access to the Internet, cell phones, and other data streams.

Previous music formats didn't require signing in, logging on, or other forms of authentication just to play music. Many cloud-based services, in contrast, use personal data as a way to authenticate the connection between the various interfaces and devices. Music listeners are thus dependent on the proper functioning of various pieces of software, interfaces, and devices in concert. While it is undeniable that these interfaces and devices open up new encounters between users and their music, music as software is contingent on other software and technologies to decode or encode specific files and file formats. Contingency complicates the process of playing music by incorporating more data and technology into the process. As different formats and services proliferate, more technology stands in between users and their music. Given the rapid rate of obsolescence for digital formats and technologies, these relationships are even more vulnerable than they have been with previous formats and playback technologies.

Music's contingency in the cloud ultimately impinges on the rights of musicians and users. Music as a service creates pressures to "'clientelize' and juridify private and cultural life" (Burkart 2010, 39). Subscribers to many cloud-based music services must accept the terms of service before they begin using the service. In the process users give up some of the traditional rights associated with music, most notably the right of first sale, or the first-sale doctrine. While users were previously free to buy a legal copy of a CD and then sell that CD to a used music store, the licensing of music as software calls that ability into question. Cloud-based services also offer a worrying lack of consumer control over data and services, lack of meaningful consent to advertising, and often lock consumers in to specific services by centralizing user data and not making it readily exportable (PrivacyComissioner 2010). Whereas the loss of physical artifacts like CDs or tapes could be considered damaging and an invasion of privacy, their exploitation makes nowhere near the amount of data available as current cloud-based music services.

Legislators and policy makers have had a difficult time keeping up with the flurry of new digital services that have emerged, so many digital distributors and retailers set their own rules for their technology outside the purview of the kind of government regulation, monitoring, and oversight that governed previous forms of the music commodity. Users' rights with the digital music commodity are decided unilaterally by the producer/seller, and as a very condition of using the service in the first place, the user must accept them. The end user license agreement for the iTunes Store, for example, gives Apple the right to change the terms of use of their downloads without any previous notice or warning (Burkart 2010, 73). As was the case with Amazon's Orwellian removal—where the terms of service said little about the company's ability to erase copies of books already purchased by consumers—companies that deal in digital goods view users' rights as always subject to change.

The rights of musicians are also in peril, as was the case of singer/songwriter Billy Bragg's experience with Myspace. Purchased by News Corp. for $580 million in July 2005, Myspace was a social network that let users download or stream songs for free. It's earliest iterations could be considered a cloud-based service for musicians, since artists could offload the duties of designing a website and hosting music files to the site. In 2006 Bragg withdrew his music from the site, stating that Myspace's user agreement put troubling conditions on the rights to copy, reproduce, and publicly perform the material found on the site. Specifically, Bragg was directing his complaint at a particular clause of the "Terms of Use" document that claimed that musicians "hereby grant to Myspace.com, a non-exclusive, fully-paid and royalty-free, worldwide license ... to use, copy, modify, adapt, translate, publicly perform, publicly display, store, reproduce, transmit, and distribute" content on the site (Myspace.com 2006).

After Bragg's high-profile interjection, Myspace quickly rewrote the terms of service to clarify that users were simply granting Myspace a limited license for use of the material on the site. Still, Bragg continued to push

Myspace and sites like it, since they frequently encroached on the rights of musicians (often without explicitly asking them) by treating music as a mere tool with which to attract traffic to their projects (see, e.g., Bragg 2008). Other musicians have opposed newer cloud-based services on similar grounds. Their concerns range from rights to control how their music appears on these sites to minimal royalty payments and worries over whether or not having their music available on free or almost-free streaming services cannibalizes sales of other formats of their music (Geere 2011; Lindvall 2011).

Part of the reason the rights of musicians and users have been relegated to the background is because the music commodity itself is secondary on these sites. Ubiquitous music increasingly takes on the role of loss leader or "complement": a good that increases the value of another service that is outside a company's core offering (Carr 2007). Myspace and other such sites overlook the rights of musicians or users because their decisions are made based on wholly other problems. The intricacies of the music commodity are secondary, if only because music itself is just one part of an overall offering that includes social networking or other end goals. Apple's success in the digital retail market, as noted in the last chapter, relied on exactly this kind of strategy. Apple could afford to sell songs at a price well below its competitors because it was more concerned with selling devices than selling music. As a cheaply priced and widely accessible commodity (through file-sharing networks), music served as a powerful complement to Apple's iPods and other devices. Cloud-based music services further enhance music's status as a complement. Music is just another piece of data employed to draw traffic, increase social networking, or add value to the newest gadget. Music is subject, as Bragg discovered, to the needs of the systems within which it resides. If music is not the focus of a site or a service, it ceases to drive the conditions, interfaces, and features of the service. It acts instead as a marketing tool.

The move to music in the cloud also extends the scope and scale of labor that is expected from the digital music commodity's users. As with the CDDB and iTunes, user labor provides a key source of value for cloud-based services, whether that's in providing the content for the various sites, feedback on the music through ratings and play counts, or as discussion moderators or online reviewers. More than just a question of free labor, some of this activity may even be displacing previous kinds of community, fandom, and scene-building activities that make music such a powerful cultural resource (Burkart 2010, 80–81). Last.Fm has scrobbling software that tracks how many times a user plays a song. Spotify and iTunes Genius scan play habits and recommend new music purchases or listenings based on that behavior. Facebook's "like" button on band pages, Google's "+1" feature, and a series of other related technologies are all now common parts of the music consumption process, a process that relies heavily on tracking consumer behavior and putting the resulting data to work in service of selling digital music. Of course, fans were performing many of these activities long before music went digital. They were recommending music to their friends and peers; they were sharing songs and CDs with each other and logging their preferences. The difference with music in the cloud is the extent to which these activities can be tracked, packaged, and offered back to users as part of the service. The cybernetic nature of the digital music commodity surfaces again and is extended to networked technologies. Previously uncommodified leisure practices are now routinely embedded into the business models of the services themselves. In many ways users cannot participate in cloud music *without* working.

CLOUDS GATHERING

Beyond the questions of rights and labor, the cloud raises some aesthetic issues for collecting, displaying, and presenting music. Collecting music within the confines of an online music service provider puts the status of the collection in question (Burkart 2010, 128). Users of subscription and other cloud services enter into service agreements in which access to the catalogue is dependent on subscription to the service. Once the subscription stops, so does access to the collection itself in many cases. This is a key difference between many analog and digital subscription models. With newspapers and magazines, for example, the commodities received persist until the user discards them. Even if users cancel their subscription, they still have access to the media they received during the period their subscription was active. The end of their subscription means the end of the delivery of future commodities but does not disrupt their previous collection. Cloud-based music subscription services are more like movie rentals: the music belongs to the user for a limited period of time. Users are paying for access to a collection rather than to a particular set of sound files with which they can build their own collection.

Personal computing offers access to hardware and to the original storage media, whereas cloud computing sees music collectors handing over the materials of the digital music commodity and the methods of its collection to those who operate the cloud. Keeping music collections in the cloud means never really knowing where those files reside and never fully controlling their management or organization. With music as a digital file stored locally on personal computers, music collectors had access to, and reasonable control over, the files themselves, the folder structures that governed their organization, and the interfaces through which collecting and playback occurred. They could change the metadata to suit their needs, order the collection and customize its appearance to suit their preferences. This is what fuels the cultural ownership that users feel over their libraries. That is, even if users have downloaded digital files (infringing or non) without paying for them, these features still allow them to feel ownership over the commodities without necessarily having economic ownership over them. The move to online subscription services in the cloud surrenders these capacities to music service providers and erodes this cultural ownership. Locker services allow for the most amount of cultural ownership since the appearance of and access to goods remain largely under the user's control, but the very ephemerality (not to mention legality) of many of these services puts this ownership in jeopardy. Many MegaUpload users, for example, found their data removed from the site shortly after the FBI took it offline (Paul 2012).

Some cloud services can also have an effect on the internal structure of commodities. Amazon's music service or iTunes Match, for example, will upgrade users' files to a different bit rate, and often a different format, in order to store them in the cloud. Even if a user has a file that was originally downloaded as a low quality MP3 file from a peer-to-peer service or ripped from a CD at 128 or 192 kilobits per second (kbps), the iTunes Store converts this file to a higher bit rate (256 kbps) and stores it in the AAC format. While the up-conversion and increased availability of music libraries from different devices are clearly beneficial for many users, the lack of control over the files, their format, and the possibilities of associated metadata and playlists disappearing or not working have created challenges for others (Lanxon 2012). These kinds of initiatives suggest the re-tuning of music's interface has repercussions for both its sonic character and its micromaterials. Many users may not see the format of a file or its metadata as a prime concern, but when these decisions start to affect the sound quality and usability of a file, it is not just audiophiles for whom these limitations matter. At stake is a question of control over the makeup of a user's library and the very files within it.

This dwindling sense of control over one's own music library is at the heart of two recent PR stumbles for Apple. In 2014 Apple and U2 partnered to make the band's latest album, *Songs of Innocence*, available automatically to more than five hundred million iTunes users. Regardless of whether they wanted the album, all iTunes users had the album visible in their library and could optionally download it to their personal libraries. Despite

Apple and U2's attempts to position the initiative as a free gift to fans, there was significant consumer backlash against what consumers saw as an unwanted (or at least unasked for) intrusion into their personal libraries (Sherwin 2014). The end of 2014 also saw Apple accused of deleting music from competing services from users' iPods between the years of 2007 and 2009 when users upgraded to a new version of the software (Elder 2014). Although there is contradictory evidence available regarding the veracity of the latter accusation, both issues raise the question of how much power cloud-based music services have over the constitution of an individual's music library. These are as much curatorial questions as they are questions about privacy and autonomy in an era of networked digital goods.

The cloud brings with it other curatorial implications. Whereas traditional music collections can be thought of as (carefully/lazily) curated exhibits of the self, cloud-based services perform all the tasks of gathering, sorting, and presenting music for the user. Part of the appeal of a music collection, or any collection, is the traces left behind when the collector makes decisions—what to keep, what to get rid of, what to show, what to hide, how much to keep, where to keep them, etc.—about the nature of the library. This applies equally to fanatic collectors and everyday consumers. As cultural commodities circulate through a person's collection, either from the effort of direct acquisition and maintenance or from the entropy of sheer accumulation, they reveal something about the person doing the collecting. Even in the case of digital files downloaded via file sharing, there are still decisions to be made about the nature of the library, even if the scale and scope of collecting practices have substantially increased. Users still need to invest time and effort in their collections, be it searching for files, downloading them, tagging them, organizing them within folders, and all manner of maintenance, and this provides much of the source for the cultural ownership they feel over their libraries. With online subscription services in the cloud, many of these activities disappear or are provided for users by the service. With cloud-based streaming and subscription services, music collections are instant and preselected. They are not compiled and tended to over time. Instead, users are either part of a service or not. Digital collections in the cloud are digital in the purest sense. They are a one or a zero, an on/off switch rather than an individually selected expression of one's own personal relationship with music.

This leveling of the collection has its benefits. Cloud-based subscription services promise all their users access to the same sizable collection of music for a fraction of the price it would cost to acquire those commodities individually. This makes it increasingly easy for younger or newer users to familiarize themselves rapidly and comprehensively with a particular artist or genre. It is also likely that no two users will navigate the cloud the same way, since the incorporation of playlists and other customization features will allow users to carve out their own kind of "collection" in the cloud. But these added benefits suggest that context has usurped content. In the cloud, with everyone sharing access to similar music, how information gets presented and made available is more important than the character of the information itself (Wikström 2009, 175). Music in the cloud is as much about managing how and when users connect to the cloud as it is about controlling the revenues from a single commodity.

This is partly why newer cloud-based models, like those provided by Google, Amazon, and Apple's iCloud, have taken on features of musical lockers. They offer users storage space for their songs and entrust most of the management of the collection and its metadata to the user. This model of ownership shares similarities with out-sourced storage lockers, vaults, and safety deposit boxes, but as with online subscription services, it is far more nebulous than these familiar forms. Although these companies offer limited versions of their services for free, access is often device- or software-dependent. The music remains the user's possession, even if they decide to leave the service, but the data their collection has generated remains hidden and inaccessible.

Given the range of different methods and providers offering cloud-based music services, users are now faced with a series of trade-offs and choices about the ways different services make available different information about the music commodity they enable and the ways in which they integrate that information into the overall music experience. Using the cloud for music collection, be it through subscription models or locker services entails addressing a series of questions about the music format and its affordances. Questions such as "How and where is this music used/ needed?" (Bodker 2004, 18) will become as central as questions about what music to listen to. Each context will bring with it its own interfaces, its own formats, and its own rules and terms for accessing the music. Furthermore, many cloud-based services prevent users from moving all their music from one service to another. A collection that has been built through Spotify is incompatible with one made through Google or Rhapsody. Each service provides its own kind of digital lifestyle management by locking user data to the specific provider.

In the cloud the collection multiplies and fragments. Not only do users have the choice among different formats of music, but they also have to decide between the different environments in which they want to access their music. Some users create hierarchies of materiality, keeping their most valuable music on physical formats (i.e., vinyl or CD) and more ephemeral, spur-of-the-moment songs in more liquid formats, like MP3s (Bodker 2004, 15). Cloud users accumulate music under different circumstances and "face a choice of reproduction and storage media, a media matrix, with different possibilities and cultural connotations" (Bodker 2004, 14). Music's older commodity forms have not simply disappeared into the cloud; they co-exist, intermingling and influencing each other. Music collections now consist of a mix of different micromaterials, each with their own prescriptions and affordances. Some of these songs and albums are authorized commodities, purchased through digital retailers. Others will be disguised and conflicted commodities that are identical in almost every way to their authorized counterparts, except that they were not paid for or obtained through legitimate means. Others, of course, will be "free," since many musicians give away songs and albums without charging for them. Some will be located on a user's computer, some on a company's remote server. Others still will reside on both. The cloud will be one collection among several that users maintain.

Collections are also becoming significantly more public thanks to latest innovations in streaming and cloud services. For some listeners the display of music libraries, like the display of book collections (Striphas 2006) or other media collections, has always been an important part of the consumption process, marking notions of class, identity, and distinction. However, cloud-based services and networked sites amplify the possibilities for displaying tastes and collections more publicly. From early social networking sites, where users posted profiles stating their tastes in music or friended and followed bands in which they took an interest, to newer services, like Spotify, that integrate a user's listening habits into their Facebook news feed, collections in the cloud can be readily made visible to an audience of friends and followers. Along with other "public displays of connection" (Donath and boyd 2004), the presentation of music collections extends the possibilities for sharing and socializing around music that Napster foreshadowed through its interface. However, housed as they are within social networking sites that rely on a steady stream of user data for the tailoring of advertising content and the curation of site content more broadly, these shared collections do far more work on social networking sites than they did with services like Napster. Services like Spotify and iTunes Genius rely on such sharing of collection information to fuel the algorithms that recommend what music a user might want to buy or listen to next. Although I do not wish to conflate social networking sites with cloud-based music services, it is worth noting the role that music has played across a variety of social media sites (Suhr 2012) and that the reverse is also true: social networking sites have contributed to the music commodity's re-tuning by virtue of how they have used the digital music commodity's fluidity and mobility as a premise or locus for social interaction.

Just as music and its social audiences are splintering into niches and subgenres, the actual act of playing music is fracturing. Whereas genre may have been a key driver of different musical communities, now, cultures are forming around the technologies and formats of playback (Harvey 2013). Each service and format gathers its own community. Through the ways in which the various technologies present, sort, and make music available, each of these communities fosters its own discourse around music and the experience of it. Music adapts to the services and devices through which it is accessed, creating highly individualized experiences as different users access different music from different devices and interfaces. The trend Winamp inaugurated with its "skin" feature is carried to its extreme: skins are no longer restricted to the surface-software changes that users can make to their media players; they are entirely different configurations of format, device, and sound. Given the increasing technological and social interdependence of music and the devices of its production, distribution, and consumption, music is becoming as much a technical experience as a musical one.

For some music collectors, the trade-offs are far too great. The conditions set out by cloud-based services and the celestial jukebox are "incommensurable" with previous ways of collecting, using, and experiencing music: "Given their obsession with control over making choices about playing music, why would music collectors choose to become subscribers to a music service that extinguishes so many aspects of users' control over music collections?" (Burkart 2010, 134). Why would lovers of music put up with a completely contingent relationship with music? For some listeners this is clearly rhetorical. But it is actually the crux of the current crisis with the place of music in social life. The more entrenched music as software becomes, the more natural it becomes to think of music as a service. The more ubiquitous music appears, the more difficult it is to conceive of it as a separate and distinct experience outside of everyday activities.

If there is a crisis in the music industry, then, it is not with the declining sales of recorded music. In fact, data from recent IFPI reports seem to suggest that total music sales are actually on the rise—though they come in different formats than they did, say, ten years ago—and that increases in streaming, digital sales, touring, and other revenue streams are starting to make up for declines in the sales of physical CDs (Martens 2010). The crisis, if we have to use that word, is perhaps more accurately located in the changing relationship people have with their music or the changing role of music in the contemporary moment. Music as software introduces new technological relationships to the processes of discovering, buying, and listening. Music is now part of a network of technologies and the singularity of the music experience from previous formats is now blended into a multimediated computing experience. Rather than a commodity of its own, music expresses itself through a number of other commodities and a variety of online and offline services. Phones come with music, as do websites, video games, and new cars. CDs are routinely given away in newspapers and magazines as promotions. Social networking sites, search engines, and other such technologies use online digital music as a draw for their services. Music is ubiquitous: it is both everywhere and nowhere (Kassabian 2001).

This is not to suggest that music is somehow less relevant or meaningful. Rather, it is to point out that, thanks to the qualities of the digital music commodity, the specificity of the music experience is giving way to a state of being that almost always includes music. This new musicalized state may lead to a less concentrated focus on music as an experience unto itself, but the ubiquity of the cloud and the digital music commodity offers new encounters with music that depend on its pervasiveness. Music has long served as a "technology of the self" (DeNora 2000, 46–47) that helps listeners express their identities and negotiate their everyday activities. With music available anytime anywhere via the cloud, there are more ways than ever to integrate it meaningfully into everyday life. This gives both music and everyday practices new meaning. Although the cloud is hardly as ubiquitous as the metaphor makes it sound, and it complicates curation by not providing the constant and unhindered access it promises, the pervasiveness of the digital music commodity thanks to the cloud may ultimately contribute to the persistence and enduring relevance of music as a cultural form.

Conclusion

Exceptional Objects

This book has examined the re-tuning that the popular recorded music commodity has undergone as a result of the transition from CDs to digital files on computers and other digital and networked devices. Far from a simple process of radical disruption or industrial dominance through new technologies, this transition has created a highly mobile, transectorial, conflicted, and cybernetic commodity. Music's micromaterials and interfaces—from Winamp to cloud services—embed it with new sources of value for users and artists but also with new forms of control for those looking to manage and maintain their hold over the distribution and sale of music commodities. Digital music files bring novel sonic, visual, and tactile experiences that seem to challenge the logic of commodification, but even as they circulate informally and illegitimately, they serve as a source of value for the formal industries that depend on them. Music's commodity form is one of the primary means by which users and listeners experience popular music. Rather than devalued and dematerialized through digitization, the materials of music's formats matter now more than ever because they are more embedded and networked into the commodity itself than they ever have been. This has implications for the future of music but also for the future of other digital cultural goods. It is never a safe bet to finish a book on new media with predictions, so I'll refrain from doing so; however, I do want to think through how the developments I've outlined in the previous chapters reshape our understanding of digital objects. But first we have one last experiment in re-tuning to explore.

In a blog post entitled "We Will Only Propagate Exceptional Objects," Kevin Barnes, the eccentric front man for the indie rock band Of Montreal, lays out the details for the launch of the group's 2008 album *Skeletal Lamping:*

The concept behind the Skeletal Lamping Collection is this: ideally, every object that you bring into your home, should feel exceptional to you. . . . A CD has little value, as an object, and the conventional, right angle plagued CD packaging, we've been forced to endure forever, has nothing new to offer us either. That is why, instead of following the tired path of the past, we've decided, to release a table top floral beast, a lantern, a collection of wall decals, a stallion shaped print, a collection of pins, and a clothing and tote bag line as our album packaging instead. (Barnes 2008)

For those familiar with the band, the release strategy mirrors the unconventional songs found in Of Montreal's music. More important, the example of *Skeletal Lamping* provides an insightful bookend to Prince's *Crystal Ball*. The album is an experiment with music's commodity form. It is rooted in an appreciation for the role the commodity plays in musical experiences and in a desire to use new technologies to reconsider our relationship with music as a cultural commodity. Of Montreal wanted its music to be both useful (i.e., it must have use value) and singular (i.e., it must have exchange value). The CD commodity, at least for Barnes, had ceased being either. It no longer provided the appropriate aesthetic or functional experience for storing and playing music. Instead, the band embedded its music into a variety of meaningful objects. The paper lantern, the wall/table stickers, and the other goods all came with a code and a link to a digital download of the album. They were not music commodities, per se, but they were not regular tote bags or pins either. They were exceptional objects, hybrids of digital music and repurposed commodities.

Although a skeptic might dismiss the launch as a publicity stunt—an indie rock band's attempt at positioning itself apart from traditional industrial logics—*Skeletal Lamping* shows how drastically the music commodity has changed as a result of de-tuning that decoupled musical content from its packaging. Music in its digital form can arrive on computers or mobile phones, but it can equally appear, as Of Montreal shows, on a giant floral print in the shape of a horse. This matters because, as I have tried to make clear, user experiences of music are highly dependent on and mediated by music's commodity form. Music is indelibly linked to, and sometimes at odds with, the technologies and materials that carry and present it.

The launch of *Skeletal Lamping* also documents the distance the music commodity has traveled since it began its migration to a digital format. Initially, on computers the music commodity was decontextualized and stripped of many of the materials that previously contributed to its use and exchange value. A result of transectorial innovations across the music and computing industries in the 1980s and 1990s, music's move to the computer was characterized by a series of false starts and halfway technologies that sought to acclimatize users to the playback of music on computers. As part of a wider push toward multimedia machines, music as a digital file was not just a technical challenge; it was a cultural process. The rise of digital music was entwined with a vision of computing as an act of personal expression and self-actualization.

In its new environment on computers, the Internet, and on various portable devices, digital music underwent a re-tuning of its interface. Thanks to metadata and the interfaces of new software and hardware, music's paratexts were reimagined and reconstructed. Programs like Winamp were among the first attempts to make music technically and culturally understandable on computers. Through skeuomorphs and other design cues, they presented digital music as a combination of the familiar and the novel. Through visualizers, skins, equalizers, and playlists, Winamp provided a new visual representation of music that emphasized its modularity and flexibility. Winamp also helped address the criticisms of digital music's sonically inferior status and brought with it some of the troubling gender conventions associated with high-fidelity stereo equipment. Winamp's interface and features drew on hi-fi conventions to position digital music not as better sound but as sound that could be bettered. Gradually, thanks to Winamp and technologies like the CDDB and ID3 tags, music transitioned from unrecognizable track 01s and track 02s to highly usable and valuable music files. These technologies—by-products of hobbyists, start-ups, and everyday users—were central in organizing, sorting, and playing digital music. They described music to their users and, in doing so, prescribed some of the ways in which users could interact with their libraries. Metadata were keystone technologies for bringing order to music files; they linked digital files to other digital files, they shaped how users found and used music in their libraries, and they provided the means for surveillance and new forms of market research.

Music's de-tuning created a moment of instability that provided a chance to reconsider the codes and conventions of the music commodity. I have stressed, along with Timothy Taylor, that "the music commodity has to be understood as always in flux, always caught up in historical, cultural, and social forces; music does not sit around exuding commodity status—it has to be commodified" (T. D. Taylor 2007, 282–83). The move to computers was part of a transitory moment that called the status of the music commodity into question while simultaneously reinforcing its influence. As much as technologies like Winamp, the CDDB, or Napster represented a challenge to the value and worth of the music commodity, or even an outright refusal to acknowledge music's commodity status, they were also central in developing features that made digital music a sellable thing. The micromaterials of programs like Winamp, the CDDB, and Napster introduced new sources of value for music as a digital file. By creating the interfaces, metadata, and audiences for digital music, these technologies made the experience of music on computers coherent and distinct from previous forms of the music commodity.

The case of Napster most clearly illustrated the discourse of disruption and devaluation. But despite the challenges Napster presented for ideas of intellectual property and the circulation of cultural content, the site was also a business that made visible the possibilities of a market for digital music commodities. By gathering an audience and providing ways to trace the valuable networked patterns and practices that audience generated, Napster connected a disparate group of users interested in a range of musical and digital goods. Napster's commodity community showed the value that resided in reframing music as a cybernetic commodity, and a host of new media measurement companies have emerged and now excel at extracting this information from music's various platforms. As BigChampagne did with Napster's audience, these new infomediaries are showing just how useful unsanctioned user practices can be for the development of new products, trends, and consumer research methods. Although Napster, like Winamp, adopted computing and hacker discourses on the power of technology to undermine power, both technologies are evidence that music never really existed in some pure and uncommodified state of free circulation. Even if music online was "free" through file-sharing services, it was still made to behave like a commodity. The Internet may have opened up possibilities for music as a gift or for alternative forms of exchange, but it did not strip music of all the features that contributed to its commodity character.

Music's move to a new format also offered an opportunity for companies involved in its production and distribution to extend and amplify their control over it as a cultural commodity. The micromaterials of digital music allowed record labels and technology companies to embed digital rights management, proprietary file formats, and other types of control into the very core of the commodity. Far from a disruptive technology, record labels and other actors saw the digital music commodity as a moment of technological change through which they could extend economic and cultural advantages via code, law, and regulation. The rise of online retail stores in the late 1990s and early 2000s initiated a series of struggles for control over the conventions of digital music. Digital rights management technology played a particularly influential role in the rise of the digital music commodity, locking users into digital enclosures made up of networks of interdependent technologies. Even though retail outlets like the iTunes Music Store have stopped wrapping their music in DRM, the legacy of the technology lives on in a broader and subtler kind of digital lifestyle management. With iTunes Apple integrated the act of buying music with the acts of playing and organizing it and made each listen a potential sales opportunity. The store is highly integrated and networked with other technologies. These subtle forms of control over digital music helped rebuild the music commodity's value; through playlists, price, and the store's organizational features, iTunes offered files and an experience that it believed was better than free.

The iTunes Store's dominance through the better part of the early 2000s, though, gave way toward the end of the decade as new streaming and cloud services emerged. Tied up with the computing industries' push toward cloud services, music in the cloud again brought the question of value to the fore. Although cloud services offer access to vast music catalogues from multiple locations and devices, they also make users' relationships with music much more contingent on the network of technologies that provide the service. As music becomes a service rather than a good, practices are commodified instead of objects. Music in the cloud leaves users a step removed from their collections; their control over their music becomes subject to variable and ever-changing license agreements and unclear boundaries around accepted uses and property rights.

Skeletal Lamping also hints at the complicated status of labor with digital music. Entwined as it is with computers and other objects, the digital music commodity includes not only the work of creating music but also the effort of building and designing the hardware, software, and peripherals that package digital music. The production costs for the *Skeletal Lamping* music commodity are a fraction of what they would have been had the band produced CDs. However, there are still the album's various iterations to consider (the wall print, the tote bag, the pins, etc.). The peripheral objects that house the digital music commodity are not nearly as infinitely reproducible as the songs they hold. Hardly immaterial, music's micromaterials are still intimately tied to the effort and work of design, coding, and production. While much of this labor stems from the tireless work of young, energetic computer coders from Silicon Valley or, in the case of much computing hardware, the cheap labor of out-sourced factory workers outside North America, the work of production and manufacturing is only part of the equation.

As the cases here have shown, many of the most important features of the digital music commodity have come from the work of users and hobbyists. These "laborers" have consistently contributed to the development of new musical experiences. They have designed interfaces and skins for Winamp. They have created and maintained massive metadata databases like the CDDB or designed file structures like ID3 tags for embedding contextually relevant information about the music into digital files. The labor of Napster's commodity community presented the viability of a more widespread digital music retail market and proved how valuable cybernetic commodities could be for companies involved in data mining and surveillance. Even at the iTunes Music Store, a host of user-generated work (from iMixes to user ratings of songs and albums) is routinely incorporated into the overall digital music experience. In some cases, like iTunes' iMixes, this labor is freely given; in others, as with Napster's commodity community, it is freely taken by actors looking to exploit the data that labor provides. The digital music commodity is a cybernetic commodity. It creates multiple registers of value and profit (selling digital music, selling the data digital music generates, selling the devices for digital music, etc.) that make different demands on users. The digital music commodity does not just implicate users in its production, reproduction, and circulation; it is entirely dependent on user labor for its value, shape, and existence. The digital music commodity is inherently a user-generated commodity.

Skeletal Lamping reveals the contradictory and conflicted nature of the digital music commodity. On the one hand the album's launch details acknowledge that the music commodity is an increasingly mobile and shape-shifting one. The decoupling of musical content and certain aspects of its physical packaging has opened up a variety of possibilities for its repackaging (like the merchandise Of Montreal embedded with digital codes). Music as code is fluid and configurable. It is less bound to any one particular material expression. It gets re-tuned through interfaces like Winamp or iTunes. On the other hand *Skeletal Lamping* is keenly attuned to music's materialities and to the objectness of the music commodity, be it analog or digital. It admits that digital music becomes physical in a variety of ways, through a number of interfaces, technologies, and packages and that these manifestations matter. As much as programs like Winamp, iTunes, and Napster were lines of immaterial code, they were also crucial portals in concretizing music's commodity form. Take, for example, Winamp's visualizer or the way Napster's interface made the idea of the network visible. These were visions of how the digital music commodity could and should appear. Like Of Montreal, they recognized the packaging and interfaces that wrap and carry music deserve to be as exceptional as the music itself.

FORMATTING CULTURE

The music industry has been the canary in the coal mine of digitization; many of the changes and impacts of the digital transition were first visible in the case of music. Audio content on CDs was already digital, making it easier to copy and transfer than, for example, books or television. Digital music, once encoded and compressed, was also a significantly smaller file than, say, a thirty-minute television show, a two-hour movie, or a video game. Given these material conditions, digital music was better suited for transmission over the limited Internet connections of the early 1990s. Moreover, audio required fewer computer system resources than video or videogames, meaning that more users could reasonably take part in using their computer systems as audio playback machines, regardless of the quality of their devices. There were certainly plenty of sites devoted to sharing text files and images, but rarely was the entire commodity available (i.e., chapters from books, articles from newspapers, or images from magazines might have been accessible, but entire books, magazines, or newspapers in digital form were rarely in circulation). The music commodity, then, was one of the first to undergo its re-tuning, preceding its peers in providing a consistent (or at least recognizable) experience between its digital and non-digital forms. As other cultural commodities converge on computers and other portable devices, the codes and conventions that govern the formatting of culture are further called into question.

The pace of technological developments through the 1990s and early 2000s has led, in many places, to more capable computers, better Internet connections, and higher quality technologies for the compression and transmission of all kinds of digital files. As a result, the issues detailed here for the case of music have spilled over into other industries (Rich and Lee 2000; Sandoval 2009). Books, movies, magazines, newspapers, and television and the industries that produce and distribute these cultural goods are currently in the midst of their own re-tunings, working through the mechanics of how to present, organize, and sell their digital commodities. Thanks to technologies like BitTorrent and hubs like the Pirate Bay, movies, television shows, and video games are now just as popular candidates, if not more so, than music for file sharing. Entire books, comics, and other printed texts (cover and all) are available as PDFs or other digital formats on relatively easy to find locker sites like 4Shared. As with music in its early digital days, some niches and interests are better served than others, though best-selling material is often available in multiple languages and formats. Newspaper and magazine commodities are not as readily available in their entirety as some of these other cultural products on file-sharing networks, but they still face the challenge of how to package and sell a digital version of their commodity, given that much of the content is available freely online.

More research on the digitizations taking place across various media industries is emerging in the areas of film, radio, news, and books (Benson-Allott 2013; Dixon 2013; Hilmes 2013; Manovich 2013; B. Scott 2005; Striphas 2009; Tryon 2007). Although it still seems early to speculate on the effects of the various re-tunings that each of these commodities is currently undergoing, I hope that my efforts here to detail the music commodity's re-tuning are instructive and applicable for other cultural goods. Also, given their common base as software, it is possible to generalize about some key features in order to monitor them for better understanding the flow of digital culture.

Rematerialized Commodities

While Prince's *Crystal Ball* initiative seems laughable now, stuck as it was in its inability to fully deliver on its futuristic intents, the decade following the arrival of Winamp has seen analogous attempts to sell commodities digitally by trying to replicate previous models of music retail and distribution. Companies have tried to enforce scarcity on their cultural products that would provide the same, and in some cases more, control over their commodities. From digital rights management on movies and television shows to other kinds of technological locks and policies (such as e-book lending policies), there have been a range of attempts to enforce particular ways of using (or not using) digital cultural commodities. While digital rights management, at least in music, has become a less overt strategy, the digital lifestyle management strategies that companies like Apple pushed are migrating to other industries and products. Gaming platforms are working as digital enclosures through a chain of technologies, and new apps and software are made for contingent and tethered devices and platforms. Increasingly, decisions about our media will depend on the platform through which we intend to consume them. Netflix subscribers, for example, will have the benefits of on-demand relationships with their favorite television and movie content, though their media collections remain in a library that they do not own in any true sense of the word. Their experience of these cultural commodities will be shaped by the interfaces of the various devices through which they consume media (computers, tablets, phones, regular televisions, etc.), but they will also be subject to intermittent Internet connections, the vagaries of licensing deals, and the curatorial practices of the service itself. Although television will be more collectible now than it has been previously, it will also face some of the same playback challenges of the music commodity, such as the disaggregation into smaller clips that can be distributed through outlets like YouTube and the reaggregation of these smaller components into new forms of playlists or otherwise organized commodities.

Software has long been conditioned by the demands of its various platforms (Montfort and Bogost 2009); certain software suites, titles, and franchises operative on one platform are not operative on another. But as cultural commodities become yet another kind of software, the politics of the various platforms on which they are available take on an increasing importance. The content producers who make new forms of content explicitly designed for certain platforms, the device makers who control the retail spaces in which these cultural commodities are sold, and the very distribution technologies involved in delivering entertainment media all exert significant control over culture in its digital form. Some platforms will be open and generative; others will be closed and contingent. Users will face choices between user-friendly systems that hide or manage complexity, like Apple's, and ones that are more complex but also more conducive to experimentation and exploration, like the early versions of Winamp.

While much of today's software is increasingly cross-platform, thanks to things like Application Programming Interfaces that allow for interoperability of applications and platforms, traditional constraints on the cultural good itself (from copyrights to licenses to region-specific broadcast deals) still work against these new forms of presentation. The uneven success and rollout of Spotify in its various markets is a telling example of the ways in which new technologies and platforms bump up against traditional industrial logics. Spotify originally launched in Sweden in 2008 to initial success, but shortly after coming out of private beta in the United Kingdom, the service was hit with notices to remove a good deal of its content, which it had not properly licensed (Paine 2009). Its subsequent launch in many other countries and regions was delayed by similar licensing troubles. Spotify did not launch in the United States, for example, until 2011 and in Canada until 2014. Spotify is currently available in fifty-eight countries and covers most of North and South America, Europe, and Australia, but each market and region is served different catalogues of music. Despite the anytime-anywhere promises of cloud computing, much of music's circulation is still regulated by the vagaries of national borders and region-by-region rights management policies.

Considering the number of new media through which users can access and consume cultural content (music, film, and TV on Apple's iPods; books on Amazon's Kindles; newspapers in digital PDFs), the underlying protocols that govern this content, these devices, and their associated business models are a critical juncture where contests of power play out. The properties of new digital tools have opened up new ways of communicating and interacting among users, companies, and digital goods, but they've also allowed for new forms of surveillance and product management. This will become especially important as cultural commodities migrate into "app" format, single-task applications available for smartphones, computers, tablets, and other devices. Major music artists like Bjork and Sting have released expensive and expansive multimedia-loaded app-based albums. Hollywood producer Neal Edelstein *(The Ring)* has released a movie designed as (and to be consumed through) an app. TV shows and books are regularly consumed through apps and, increasingly, produced specifically as apps. The proliferation of app-based cultural commodities is an extension of the transectorial innovations that have taken place in music and computing over the past three decades.

Although none of these examples suggests that apps will be the future format for digital commodities, they do signal another stage of the re-tuning process. Given that many of these applications allow for different kinds of tactile manipulation with cultural products (swiping, pinching, zooming) and their digitally parsed pieces are designed to be remixed and remade through user interaction, the artifactual integrity of cultural commodities is again called into question. To be certain, the interactivity afforded with many of these commodities is limited and controlled by the constraints of the application, but apps represent another iteration of digital packaging for cultural commodities. They are a specific manifestation of software, a particular aesthetic and functional presentation of code that will represent yet another interface through which users access, sort, store, and experience digital cultural commodities.

Infomediaries and Cybernetic Commodities

Given that cultural commodities, as data, can be manipulated, sorted, and related in ways that greatly extend human capacities, new classes of service are emerging that truly treat cultural goods as software, as code upon which other code can be written or built. Although there was hope that the lower costs of production for digital commodities and the abundant avenues for their distribution would somehow disintermediate the media industries, there has been instead a proliferation and multiplication of newer intermediaries (iTunes, Netflix, Hulu, Facebook, Amazon) rather than a retraction. Just as Nielsen's SoundScan and Gracenote's CD Database provided the informational infrastructure for the last two decades in the music industries, newer companies like BigChampagne, The EchoNest, Music Xray, and others are vying to provide the data by which these industries make their everyday decisions.

This new category of intermediaries—what I have elsewhere called infomediaries (Morris 2015)—are playing an increasingly central role in the expansion of digital cultural commodities. They do not provide access to cultural content per se. Rather, they power the databases, relational connections, and measurement data that are fueling the next generation of digital media services. While most media industries have been driven primarily by the acquisition, management, and licensing of rights, infomediaries create an extra layer of informational commodities based on paratextual and micromaterial data. Rather than exploiting rights, they are designed to exploit the computational potential of digital commodities by collecting and compiling data about music, movies, television, or books that can be put in the service of creating novel ways to recommend, curate, and experience culture. Whereas early digital music services struggled to gain access to large enough catalogues of music to be successful, infomediaries bypass the thorny process of rights by creating their own databases of information about cultural commodities. End-point providers (Spotify, iTunes, Netflix, Amazon) will still need to manage media rights, but infomediaries distinguish themselves by managing the rights to valuable databases useful to a wide variety of stakeholders (digital media service providers, media publications, labels, studios and broadcasters, etc.). In music these data fuel recommendation services and other added-value technologies in Spotify, Rdio, and Pandora; and companies like Netflix and Amazon are already utilizing similar kinds of databases for other kinds of media.

There are all kinds of commercial applications for infomediary databases, from trend analysis to strategic planning to hit prediction. Infomediaries, however, will function as producers as they provide the tools and resources to help other developers make their creations possible. Given the importance their databases will play, they will serve as a potential site for the consolidation of power in the digital cultural industries. Just as the CDDB grew to control the information backbone of the early phase of digital music, so, too, will these infomediaries provide keystone information that will govern much of the way culture gets sorted, organized, and presented in its digital formats.

Curation and Algorithmic Commodities

If the early phase of digitization saw companies replicating traditional models of scarcity and ownership over their newly digital commodities, the next phase of digitization will see cultural goods blown up into millions of data points. Big Data will collide with Big Culture, and every song, book, TV show, or movie will be parsed into its component pieces. These pieces are being reassembled into databases designed to facilitate new modes of curation and recommendation for cultural content. While we tend to think of curation as a distinctly human capability, digital formats have made cultural commodities infinitely analyzable and quantifiable in ways that make them increasingly amenable to algorithmic exploitation. Whether or not we've hit what Uricchio (2011) calls an "algorithmic turn" is an open-ended question, but algorithms are an increasingly important part of the vocabulary for analyses of how users interact with data and cultural content. As "code with consequences" (Gillespie 2014), algorithms play an influential role in the social construction of knowledge. They enact power through logistics, through organization, through what they include and exclude in their equations and outputs, and through the ways their results are presented, and widely understood, as computational objectivity: "This is undoubtedly an expression of power, not of someone having power over someone else, but of the software making choices and connections in complex and unpredictable ways in order to shape the everyday experiences of the user" (Beer 2009, 997). Given that the relative complexity of algorithms makes them difficult objects (subjects?) of study, though, it is tempting to mystify algorithms to the extent that they become the point where analysis stops: "Why is this result showing up? Why am I being recommended this song or this movie? It must be the algorithm." However, algorithms should not be the end of a sentence but the start of a series of questions about the various "ways of knowing" that we've delegated to digital devices and about why algorithms are increasingly trusted as sources for the discovery of cultural content. The algorithms and databases that underpin today's digital music services (Last.fm, iTunes Genius, Pandora, Spotify, etc.) are unspecified blends of machine technology and human practice, and each proposes novel techniques for personalizing audio experiences.

Keeping in mind Mark Katz's (2004) notion of phonographic effects—where musicians, during the advent of recording technology, altered their style of play to be better captured by microphones—it will be interesting to trace whether any discernible "algorithmic effects" are emerging in various spheres of cultural production. Will creative producers develop certain styles, sounds, or visual techniques that cater to these new algorithmic uses of culture (the musical variant of search engine optimization)? Will they resort to particular information-generation techniques because they are easier or more likely to be picked up by algorithms? In an article reviewing several streaming and recommendation services (Spotify, Pandora, etc.), music critic Sasha Frere-Jones (2010) flashed back to the influence that the Roland TR-808 drum machine had on the sound of hip-hop and dance music. He argues that whoever programmed the sounds and the timing of the machine likely had a greater impact on the shape of these genres than did the hundreds of famous artists who ended up using it on their albums. He goes on to say, "Similarly, the anonymous programmers who write the algorithms that control the series of songs in these streaming services may end up having a huge effect on the way that people think of musical narrative—what follows what, and who sounds best with whom" (Frere-Jones 2010). Frere-Jones points precisely to the key logistical role infomediaries play in the presentation and discovery of cultural content. With digital cultural commodities able to be parsed into countless components (frames, beats, phonemes, GPS coordinates, velocity, word count, shot length, etc.), the authority of algorithms and the infomediary databases that underpin them will exert pressures on creative producers to make their cultural content amenable to algorithmic analysis and discovery.

Labor and Conflicted Commodities

A final site in which to monitor the progression of digitization in various media industries will be cultural labor. The various chapters in this book have called attention to the complexity of the labor processes involved in the production of cultural commodities. Not only is there the highly global and distributed labor involved in the production of the devices and technologies used for consumption of entertainment media, but the process of cultural production itself is also highly segmented into its component stages (recording, production, distribution, marketing, etc.). The act of creating and distributing cultural goods is such a decidedly complex task that pinpointing whose labor contributes to what kind of value is a futile task. Further, the cases here have tried to underscore the influence and importance of users during the process of commodification, as they contribute their time, skill, and data to creating media products that can ultimately be used and understood as sellable objects.

Just as the CDDB's informational database was a co-creation between its users and the company, or just as Napster's software became valuable only once its cybernetic potential was realized, cultural production more generally now relies on all kinds of co-creative efforts between users and producers. Artists are increasingly becoming "cultural entrepreneurs" (M. Scott 2012) or taking part in what might be called cultural entrepreneurship: they are using new technologies to manage their own cultural production, often calling on fans and friends to participate in the funding, packaging, and distribution of their cultural content. While the terms *work* or *labor* may still apply, they may not fully capture the complexity of the relationships between users and artists in the production process. They do, however, point to the fact that in the commodity, the work of both users and producers meet.

The flip side to this co-creative labor, however, places a greater burden on artists to take control of aspects of their career that they previously delegated to other actors in the cultural industries (labels, studios, managers, etc.). While some will feel comfortable entering into productive collaborations with fans and followers, others will be overwhelmed, or at least overburdened, with having to build and maintain these productive networks for co-creation.

Of course, much innovation will continue to occur in legal gray zones. For every locked technology or platform that arrives, users and hobbyists find technological solutions to route around restrictions. The Cydia store, an alternative "app store" for users who have jailbroken their iPhones, is an entire marketplace of primarily unsanctioned software products. File-sharing networks continue to play an important role in the distribution of all kinds of media, and numerous independently run and user-curated websites exist for the unsanctioned repurposing, remixing, and extending of industrially sanctioned commodities (fan fiction, mods, etc.). While many of these spaces may seem like replacements for traditional commodities or threats to existing business models, they will continue to exist in that tension that Napster exemplified: the combination of antimarket sentiments and practices that still provide industrially useful feedback, information, and cybernetic commodities. Digital commodities will remain conflicted and co-created commodities, available freely and for a price, both tools of subversion and means for greater control and surveillance.

THE PROMISE OF DIGITAL COMMODITIES

As much as Of Montreal's blog post was a press release about the band's upcoming album, it was also part manifesto. Echoing the hopes of the multimedia revolution, Barnes wanted to use a moment of technological change to open up possibilities for a range of music-commodity experiments. He wanted to propagate exceptional objects: "Now, we find ourselves in the middle of an exciting epoch: A time, when new technology has shattered the conventional business model and has set a paradigm shift in motion. For some people in the music biz, this is terrifying. For us, it is a fucking miracle! While the kings are in a stupor, we are going to take full advantage of the changing guard" (Barnes 2008). Underneath the rhetoric of kings and miracles Barnes is pointing to what is exciting about the transition to a digital music commodity and to digital media commodities more generally. It is a moment that puts on display the codes and conventions that have governed the circulation of culture and allows them to be interrogated. Even if such transitory moments are not necessarily blank slates, they open up fissures through which new relationships with media and its technologies are audible and visible.

Barnes's optimism is mirrored in the many musicians, labels, and producers who hold out hope that digital music might reorganize the traditional balance of power in the music industries. The Future of Music Coalition (FMC)—an organization that serves as a voice for musicians in matters of US technology and cultural policy decisions—sums up this possibility in its manifesto: "Recent advances in digital music technology are loosening the stranglehold of major label, major media, and chain-store monopolies. Digital download and online streaming technology offers musicians a chance to distribute their music with minimal manufacturing and distribution costs, with immediate access to an international audience" (FMC 2000). For the FMC digital music offers two primary opportunities: (1) economic advantages and (2) the possibilities for structural change. The economics of digital music production create significant cost-savings. Traditionally, artists see anywhere from 10 to 14 percent of sale of a $16 or $17 CD, the rest going to label and retail overhead, marketing, and other costs (Byrne 2007; Thomson and Zisk 2003; Krasilovsky and Shemel 2000).[1] Digitization eliminates a number of these costs entirely, and it greatly reduces some others. There are still studio fees, marketing and advertising campaigns, time and effort for discovering new talent, and administration fees, but "manufacturing and distribution costs for digital goods are approaching zero" (Byrne 2007). New costs may emerge (bandwidth costs, fees to manage the software and hardware infrastructure, etc.), but these pale in comparison to the costs for reproducing, shipping, and retailing a physical product. Aside from economic benefits, digital music also portends structural changes. Artists increasingly have access to a wide variety of tools that allow them to produce, distribute, and market their own music and circumvent the traditional paths of circulation. Digital technologies, in theory, also put artists directly (or at least more directly) in contact with their fans. Cutting out the intermediaries makes it cheaper to produce and market music, and it potentially affords artists more intimate and meaningful relationships with their fans (FMC 2000, 2010). Although the particulars differ for various industries, there are similar cost savings to be realized in television, movies, books, and software.

Unfortunately, these particular promises have yet to materialize. Instead of fewer intermediaries between artists and consumers, there are simply different ones (and in some cases more of them). Most online stores continue to yield a similarly small percentage of return to artists, despite the savings brought by digitization. Instead of better compensation, numerous artists and reports have noted that musicians actually stand to make less money through iTunes and newer streaming services than through traditional retail channels. Digital models like iTunes, Spotify, and other cloud services are strikingly similar to their analog predecessors, if not worse (Byrne 2007; Thomson and Zisk 2003; Bailey and Bakos 1997). In fact, as these services mature, many artists and industry critics have started focusing more closely on the royalties these sites pay out and have made public statements on the matter. The *New York Times* detailed the case of cellist Zoe Keating, whose math figured she was receiving an average of less than half a penny (0.42 cent) per stream on Pandora (Sisario 2013). The Future of Music Coalition estimates iTunes Radio royalties at even less (0.1 cent) per song plus a 15 percent cut of advertising revenue (M. Davis 2013). Similar outcry over Spotify royalty rates from musicians led Spotify to publish figures for its payout structure (Hogan 2013; Dredge 2013; Sherwin 2013). Although Spotify pays a percentage based on total plays rather than a per-stream rate, this still only amounts to between 0.6 cent and 0.84 cent per play. The micropayments are split among labels, publishers, and other entities, leaving artists with a fraction of this original fraction. For these reasons artists like Thom Yorke and Taylor Swift have removed material from streaming services and publicly criticized the damage these tech companies are doing to the value of music (Dredge 2013; Sherwin 2013).

It is far from clear whether these cloud and streaming services represent a sustainable model for artists, established or emerging, but the specific royalty rates are less important here than the debate itself. Beyond the question of compensation, as I suggested in chapter 5, the move to the cloud may even further limit the rights of users and musicians compared to previous music formats. Although music as a digital file offers the potential to disrupt the traditional ways of doing business, it also offers new forms of control and power (surveillance, data mining, etc.), and raises new challenges for dividing up a dwindling amount of profits among an increasingly spread-out number of transectorial players.

This is not to suggest that digital media commodities are without promise. The migration of music on CDs to music as digital files has opened up a wealth of opportunities for artists looking to communicate their art. *Skeletal Lamping* is just one of a number of recent experiments with the form and circulation of the digital music commodity. Radiohead's launch of *In Rainbows* via download from its website on a pay-what-you-wish basis is another (Byrne and Yorke 2007; Ryzic 2007). Other artists like Brooklyn-based mashup artist Girl Talk or UK rockers the Charlatans have followed suit, offering a similar deal for users (Gibson 2007; Pandey 2008). Trent Reznor of Nine Inch Nails seeded one of his recent albums on file-sharing services and encouraged users to download it for free. He also developed a live action "video" game with album-related clues that drove users to his concerts, his website, and his music (Rose 2007). Ambient pop singer Imogen Heap decided to offer up early studio mixes of her songs and kept in correspondence with users via video blogs and social networking sites to obtain their feedback on the music and the packaging that went along with her album *Ellipse* (Fusilli 2009). Singer-songwriter Amanda Palmer has explored numerous ways of incorporating user feedback, creative contributions, and funding into her production and touring process, going as far as fan-funding her tour and crowd-sourcing fans from each city to play in her backup band the night the show was in their city.

Undeniably, the success of these initiatives is largely because of the pre-existing popularity of the acts in question—popularity that comes from years of traditional marketing and promotion provided by the industrial system these artists are now trying to circumvent. As I noted in chapter 4, Radiohead's experiment is as much an example of how to splinter and commodify to an ever-greater extent the various components of recorded music as it is a forward-looking use of digital music's affordances. I have also argued elsewhere that Imogen Heap's co-production efforts cannot be understood outside her attempts to create a set of ancillary commodities that her fans might purchase beyond her music (Morris 2013a). I refer to these high-profile initiatives not because they are inherently a challenge to the commodification of digital music but because they are the visible surface of a much larger set of experiments taking place. Countless independent and emerging artists are trying different models of making and circulating the digital music commodity. There are bands asking users to pay what they want on sites like Bandcamp. There are artists giving away digital songs with the purchase of an accompanying physical artifact. Websites like Kickstarter encourage users to invest in bands, like stocks, and the funding helps seed the production of new music. Other music retail sites are toying with variable pricing based on the popularity of songs on the site: as a song gets more popular, its price increases, adding a kind of monetary value to the process of discovery. At one time, Swedish file-sharing site the Pirate Bay was developing a business model that saw users pay a certain price for access to music, a fee that varied depending on how much computer storage space and resources the user contributed to the Pirate Bay's commercially available cloud service (Urquhart 2009). These kinds of innovations are rife at all registers of the music industries; in the words of one journalist, business plans are the new punk (Van Buskirk 2007b).

Again, these models are not feasible moves for all artists. Many of them are short-term trends or one-off opportunities. Some of the sites mentioned above, in fact, have already failed because of poor economic performance or lack of users. These initiatives also have more structural issues: Amanda Palmer's crowd-source backup band idea was called into question when it was discovered she wasn't planning on paying the fans who appeared and played onstage with her; Imogen Heap's co-productions place a significant labor burden on artists that takes their focus off of music and displaces it to managing and incentivizing a network of fans; Thom Yorke has even reconsidered the damage Radiohead's pay-what-you-want model may have done to perceptions of value around the music commodity (Adams 2013). Moreover, marketers for established record label artists are quite handily finding ways to incorporate fan and user labor into their campaigns and album-production process, ranging across the spectrum from honest and transparent co-creation to more opaque forms of cooptation of user labor and sentiments.

Ultimately, I highlight these practices not because they should serve as a template for future artists to follow but because they are a signal for a much larger set of experiments that are taking place at many levels of many cultural industries. Irrespective of these various strategies and their varying successes, it is important to recognize how these initiatives demonstrate the flexibility and multiplicity of digital media commodities. Regardless of what these specific examples hold for the economics of music or the structure of the music industries, the promise of digital music lies in its recombinatory possibilities. The digital music commodity opens music up to multiple modes of presentation. Songs can come out in batches of twos or threes, they can be priced at ten cents or ten dollars. They can have a variable price or no price at all. There are few rules about length. There are few standards of organization and presentation. The digital music commodity can be sold in a store or directly by artists. It can be a service or a good or a gift. iTunes, Spotify, and many other digital retailers tame these possibilities in the name of user-friendliness. The music industry is anxious to solve the digital dilemma and is looking for what Patrik Wikström informally calls "the new business model that will save us all" (2010). They are hoping for technology, like iTunes or Spotify, that can return value to music and galvanize enough users to define the model for making and marketing music for the next several years. But in their attempts to achieve a consistent and convenient process, these digital retailers standardize and rob the digital music commodity of much of its force. The promise of digital music does not reside in one particular way of selling or distributing. In fact, the search for a standardized business model runs counter to the very nature and potential of digital music.

Importantly, the examples I have provided do not make music, or any other cultural good, any less a commodity. Even though they make music available for free or charge users with the task of assigning a price, the essence of the music commodity does not disappear. Price is only one part of a commodity, and it is often, as the cases here have revealed, its least interesting attribute. What these examples share, however, is a desire to make users and listeners question what kind of a commodity music is and what value it holds for them. The above experiments with the codes and conventions of music's commodity form encourage both artists and users to reevaluate what the music commodity is worth when it inhabits a digital form. As one of Radiohead's managers notes about the *In Rainbows* initiative: "The industry reacted like the end was nigh. '[Radiohead have] devalued music, giving it away for nothing.' Which wasn't true: We asked people to value it, which is very different semantics to me" (qtd. in Byrne and Yorke 2007). Free music does not mean music without value, nor does it mean music that is not a commodity. In this case free, or the possibility of free, forces a kind of questioning of the relationships between users and the objects that circulate around them.

If commodities have social lives, users are and have always been part of the commodification process. The digital music commodity makes this abundantly clear. We have seen experiments that force users to think critically about the commodification process and about the value of music in its digital form. They ask us to reconsider our relationship with music: How much is music worth? What do we use it for? Where do we want to access it, and what should it look and sound and feel like when we do? This kind of critical engagement is the moment afforded to us by the digital music commodity.

The promise of digital music, then, is precisely that it turns our attention toward the process of commodification. Despite claims of digital music's immateriality, the very material aspects of the digital music experience examined here offer a greater, not lesser, moment to reconsider our relationship with commodities. Digital music, like countless other technologies, may never live up to all its promises. It may never fully disrupt the structure of the music industry or reduce the number of intermediaries standing between artists and their listeners. As much as digital music promises greater diversity, interactivity, and control over music selection, it also brings digital enclosures, proprietary technologies, surveillance, and data mining. But digital music's less grandiose promise—to turn our attention back to the meaning and form of the music commodity and to reengage with the role of music in our lives—is already being realized.

For all the fears about file sharing and the devaluation of music and other media as commercial products, music will not likely escape its commodity form. In many ways, as my research here suggests, we do not want it to. The commodity form helps us make sense of the objects around us and eases the transition to new practices and technologies. Music, like other cultural commodities, has a kind of double meaning. There is the meaning that comes from how a particular artist or song affects any given individual. But there is also meaning tied to the ways in which the music commodity appears and how it is acquired. Standing in line waiting for hours to get tickets to a show, rushing to a music store on Tuesday morning to hear the newest releases, or hooking up a microphone to a computer to digitize a song are just some of the stories that form around the music commodity. These experiences are an integral part of music's effects and affects. The examples provided here show how the digital music commodity has encouraged artists to present their creative process as part of their product. Through their production and marketing techniques they are trying to present a particular mode and method of being musicians and of forming relationships with their fans. Beyond the actual music, these artists' willingness to open up various aspects of creation, marketing, pricing, or distribution to users is as much a part of the significance of the commodities in question as any of the individual songs the artists are promoting. Are these merely marketing stunts? Are they novelty acts designed to use new platforms and technologies to draw attention? Or are they genuine attempts to rethink music's potential given its new status as a digital commodity? Regardless of the response, they have prompted users to reconsider their own relationship with the artist in question and the music commodity more generally.

The materials that make up the music commodity and define the contexts of its circulation mediate how users encounter and interact with the music it contains. This has long been true for music, but it is amplified as a result of digitization. Experiments like *Skeletal Lamping* or *In Rainbows* hold promise because they turn our attention to this moment, when the commodity form and music meet. Consider the following review of *In Rainbows:*

> Like many music lovers of a certain age, I have a lot of warm memories
> tied up with release days. I miss the simple ritual of making time to
> buy a record. I also miss listening to something special for the first
> time and imagining, against reason, the rest of the world holed up in
> their respective bedrooms, having the same experience. Before last
> Wednesday [when Radiohead released *In Rainbows* for download
> online], I can't remember the last time I had that feeling. I also can't
> remember the last time I woke up voluntarily at 6 a.m. either, but like
> hundreds of thousands of other people around the world, there I was,
> sat at my computer, headphones on, groggy, but awake, and hitting
> play. (Pytlik 2007)

Nostalgia for the release days of old gives way to a realization that new kinds of social experiences with music are possible with the digital music commodity. Not only had Radiohead's experiment successfully recaptured, at least for Pytlik, the pleasures of anticipation and acquisition that came with the CD commodity; it revealed the distinct experience the digital music commodity engenders. Although the stories we tell about digital music may not involve ritual visits to record stores or waiting for physical records to hit physical shelves, they will involve watching music play through the interfaces of software like Winamp, sorting and organizing music in countless ways thanks to embedded metadata, or seeing music circulate through a connected network of users like Napster. In these and other ways the digital music commodity offers us its own moments of meaning-making; the stories we will tell about digital music will reflect the myriad of ways it can be embedded into different aspects of our everyday lives. *Skeletal Lamping* acknowledges that music has a social life that extends long beyond its commodity phase and far beyond its original intended uses. The tote bags, wall prints, and floral patterns that Of Montreal was peddling will persist and circulate in ways that are completely separate from, yet always rooted in, the music they housed. The band's experiment, along with countless others taking place across the music industries, reveals that there is still a desire for making exceptional objects and for finding creative ways of propagating them. Despite the potential limitations digital music poses, artists, hobbyists, and users are using digital music to call into question the codes and conventions of its commodity form. In doing so, they make visible the promise of digital music: to turn our attention to the commodification of culture and to force a reconsideration of the role music plays in the contemporary moment.

Notes

INTRODUCTION

1. As Lisa Gitelman (2006, 1) and other new media scholars have argued, "looking into the novelty years, transitional states, and identity crises of different media stands to tell us much, both about the course of media history and about the broad conditions by which media and communication are and have been shaped" (see also Marvin 1988).

2. See, e.g., Adorno (1938), Appadurai (1986), Attali (1985), Baudrillard (1981), Benjamin (1969), Dyer-Witheford (1999), Frith (1996), Haug (1987), Lukács (1971), Marx (1867), Smith (1776), Taussig (1993), Willis (1991).

3. See, e.g., Plato's *Phaedrus;* Benjamin's (1969) notion that "aura" withers in light of mechanical reproduction; Adorno's (1938, 38) worries that rationalized reproduction creates a standardized commodity shorn of its "ethereal and sublime" characteristics; and Attali's (1985) claim that mass repetition through technological reproduction destroys the force of music and serves as a means of social control.

4. Matthew Kirschenbaum defines *born digital* as "first generation electronic objects": objects that enjoy "no material existence outside of the electronic environment of a computational file system" (2002, 20).

5. Though there is little empirical work on feelings of ownership, the attachment many users feel toward their music collections is well documented (see, e.g., Bull 2005; and Bull 2007). The users described in Bull's work are heavily invested in their digital music collections, though that investment is only sometimes the result of a financial transaction.

6. Where possible, I have used older versions of the software. Through ported programs, change logs, and sites like Really Rare Wares (http://www.rjamorim.com/rrw/) or the Graphical User Interface gallery (http://www.guidebookgallery.org/), I track the changes that occur to the programs and their interfaces as they develop.

7. For the cases of Winamp, the CDDB, iTunes, and Napster, the Wayback Machine offered access to the companies' websites during the early stages of

their emergence (approximately 1997 to 2002). Screenshots taken at monthly intervals (or whenever the sites were updated) provided an archive of images and text to complement the descriptive analyses detailed above. The Wayback Machine was also useful in following the evolution of ID3.com and the CDDB as well as some of the companies involved in its commercialization. The iTunes Store does not have its own "website" since the store is integrated into the software. However, I still made use of the Wayback Machine to analyze software on which iTunes is based (SoundJam MP) and to follow the development of iTunes on Apple's main website (Apple.com).

CHAPTER 1. MUSIC AS A DIGITAL FILE

1. As Turner (2013) argues, the term *multimedia* actually dates back to the 1930s and 1940s and to a strange mix of academics and Bauhaus artists who were advocating for alternatives to mass media that included multi-image, multisound sourced environments in an attempt to create a new kind of democratic American citizen.

2. The MP3, for example, compresses data such that an MP3 file is about 1/12 the size of the same file on a CD.

3. New technologies rarely emerge in isolation and are almost always the result of a network of ideas, practices, and people. Winamp is no exception. The program's origins involve contributions and ideas from other programmers like Dmitry Boldyrev and Tomislav Uzelac, as well as claims of copyright infringement and fraud regarding the ownership of the program's central code (Frankel et. al. 1999, 9; Haring 2000: 101) .

4. Although Gnutella's official existence was brief, thousands of users grabbed the program before AOL took it offline. Since it was an open-source program, imitation versions started sprouting up. The following generation of peer-to-peer software, like LimeWire, SoulSeek, and other similar applications, was based on its code.

5. Sterne notes that what critics are really arguing about when they complain of missing frequencies and sonic data is not fidelity but *definition*, the "sound recording's 'acuity and precision in rendering of detail'" or "the audible range of frequencies . . . the recording produces" (Sterne 2006a, 342 [drawing on Chion 1994, 98]).

6. In larger software production firms managers and executives may be more responsible for determining functionality than designers. Nullsoft's operations, however, at least during its early stages, were small enough that the designers, in many cases, were also the managers and executives. The act of design was also the act of management. Even when AOL acquired the company, Frankel and the Nullsoft designers still drove the features included, despite management's desires (as the earlier explanation of Gnutella indicates).

7. See Helmore (2013) for multiple variations of this argument; "the death of the album" is a historically consistent enough phrase to warrant its own Wikipedia entry.

8. For further discussion of playlists see chapter 4, about the rise of online retail outlets and their novel ways of repackaging discrete musical commodities into other album-like groupings.

CHAPTER 2. MAKING TECHNOLOGY BEHAVE

1. Although I call this a "minor" technical feat, it is by no means a minor social one. Like the Domain Name System that translates the Internet's various numerical IP addresses into easy-to-recall website names, the CDDB and ID3 tags perform invaluable functions for sorting and categorizing music, especially for nontechnical users.

2. Machine Readable Cataloguing (MARC) structures how catalogue cards are prepared to produce searchable call numbers for library users. Flickr, YouTube, and many other large Internet-based databases feature "tags": small nonhierarchical keywords that users create. These user-centric schemes are responsive to change, easier to use, and often more participatory and accessible than professional standards like MARC. They are incredibly customizable but can suffer from a lack of universality and accuracy.

3. Graham Toal was also instrumental in the founding of the CDDB. He provided server space for the database and suggested advertising as a means to generate revenue for the site (Van Buskirk 2006).

4. There were also specific hardware cues that could be read by programs like AutoRun, which was software that told the computer what kind of disc was inserted and then performed an appropriate action (such as playing it or opening it). However, AutoRun relied on the structure of the disc itself in making its decisions, so it is not as much a case of metadata as some of the other forms listed here.

5. The Yellow Book for CD-ROMs (1988), Orange Book for recordable and rewriteable CD-R and CD-RW discs (1992), and the Green Book for interactive multimedia discs (CD-I).

6. Rundgren's *No World Order* was reportedly the first commercial CD-I ever released. Rundgren also gave himself the pseudonym TR-I—Todd Rundgren-Interactive—from 1993 to 1995. For Rundgren, "interactive" was not just a type of CD; it was a way of life.

7. ID3v1 actually placed the tag at the end of the file, which took longer to process and caused difficulties during streaming.

CHAPTER 3. THIS BUSINESS OF NAPSTER

1. Scholarly research on the site has focused on its implications for music distribution, online communities, and intellectual property. As a collision of corporations, technologies, and consumers, Napster's disruptive capabilities were noted, even if limited by the larger framework of a tightly controlled music industry (McCourt and Burkart 2003). There was great interest in the kinds of music communities forming around the site (Beuscart 2005; Poblocki 2001), as well as in the discursive identities of users (Woodworth 2004) and the

music industries (Logie 2006; Spitz and Hunter 2005) constructed around file-sharing practices and the types of (gift) exchanges taking place (Giesler and Pohlmann 2003; Leyshon 2003). There was, and continues to be, debate over the impact of Napster and file sharing more generally on the sales of recorded music, with some research suggesting direct economic harm is evident (Liebowitz 2006), some concluding file sharing results in more music purchased (Oberholzer-Gee and Strumpf 2007), and still others reaching more ambiguous conclusions that place Napster and its effects in a more complex and competitive media entertainment ecosystem (Grassmuck 2010; Marshall 2004; Zentner 2006). The response to Napster from hackers, technology activists, and artists also galvanized a wider set of debates around intellectual property and copyright for digital goods (Barbrook 1998; Boon 2010; Dyer-Witheford 1999; Fisher 2004; Gillespie 2007; Lessig 2004; McLeod 2005; Vaidhyanathan 2003). These debates led to alternate visions of property (e.g., copyleft, Lessig's creative commons, and various open-source projects) while the legal details of the trial and defense created lasting discourses about noninfringing uses of P2P (Ku 2002).

2. Accounting for multiple logins and duplicate usernames, a more modest count of thirty to forty million users is likely more accurate (Robinson and Halle, 2002, 378)

3. The term *virtual community* is particularly prevalent in scholarship on the Internet and the early years of the Web, much of it extolling the virtues of the open and free communication that can come with the crafting, presentation, and mingling of virtual selves and identities enabled through computer-mediated networked interaction (Licklider and Taylor 1968; Rheingold 1994; Smith and Kollock 1999; Turkle 1984, 1995; Wellman, 1999). There was, at the time, optimism that in these virtual spaces and communities—most of which were text-based multiuser environments—users could leave behind the physical traces of their bodies, lives, and identities to explore alternative and more fluid ideas of identity. Later research on virtual communities has made clear these online environments were not nearly as separate from offline nonvirtual spaces as it was initially hoped (Dibbell1993; Nakamura 2002; Terranova 2004; White 2006), but the kinds of interactions taking place in many of these virtual communities still make them profoundly rich sites for thinking through notions of community and communication (Baym 2010).

4. Hardly exclusive to Napster, anticonsumerist ideas and images are frequently put in the service of promoting further consumption (T. Frank 1997; Heath 2005).

5. Although viral marketing through computers likely dates back to the first spam messages sent over the Internet in 1983, Napster, Winamp, and many of the other music/media software programs released during this period made use of viral marketing strategies relying on users to encourage other users to take up the product since they had little budget for more traditional forms of advertising.

6. Menn is highly critical of the influential and, in his view, highly detrimental role John Fanning played in Napster's history. Menn argues that John

was a bad businessman who took advantage of his nephew (by giving Shawn only a 30 percent share in the company), scared away would-be investors, and set Napster up for an imminent showdown with the RIAA.

7. The minimum advertised price program was a plan to help local music retailers compete with the heavily discounted prices advertised by electronics and Big Box superstores. But the US Federal Trade Commission (FTC) found in May 2000 that record labels were instead using the strategy to discourage discounting of CD prices and artificially inflating prices. The FTC claimed this cost consumers collectively $480 million between 1996 and 1999 (see Kot 2000; McCourt and Burkart 2003).

8. For specifics on how Napster's P2P indexing and search functions worked, see Parameswaran, Susarla, and Whinston (2001).

9. In the literature on human computer interaction (HCI), comparisons are often made to software as a kind of sorcery or magic. Chun criticizes this from a media/software studies point of view, but other deconstructions also exist within the field of HCI (see, e.g., Hoare 1984; Oberschelp 1998).

10. Chris Anderson's *Free: The Future of a Radical Price* (2009) is perhaps the most explicit call to media industry executives to realize the value that lies in free and abundant exchange of cultural goods. The use of *radical* in the subtitle diverges strongly from the use of the term in literature about Napster's disruptive potential; *radical,* it seems, can represent both the destruction of traditional business models and the extension of them.

CHAPTER 4. CLICK TO BUY

1. SightSound settled its five-year lawsuit against CDNow and N2K out of court. According to the agreement, Bertelsmann conceded the patents were valid but admitted no infringement on its part (Chang 2004).

2. Business method and software patents are difficult to distinguish, since business method patents often involve software. The USPTO (2009) notes that a business method patent "encompasses machines and their corresponding methods for performing data processing or calculation operations, where the machine or method is utilized in the 1) practice, administration, or management of an enterprise, or 2) processing of financial data, or 3) determination of the charge for goods or services." The USPTO does not have a separate category for software patents, and the odd status of software as part product, part algorithm complicates its patentability. For a longer discussion see Morris (2013b).

3. Although there were other similar sites, these three were certainly the largest and longest lived.

4. It should be noted, however, that, technically, users were still paying for computers, software, Internet connections, and other related costs.

5. Also, given that DRM only applied to people who were paying for digital files, DRM had a twisted logic that penalized users for doing the "right" thing. Embedding DRM in files that customers purchased was like a teacher lecturing

the five students who showed up to class about how attendance needs to be better. DRM is a way of punishing the people that support your business by limiting their use rights while giving nonpaying customers even more incentive to continue pursuing noncommercial alternatives.

6. It is unclear how much Apple ever wanted to include DRM in its store in the first place and to what extent the record labels pressured Apple to implement a secure file format (Jobs 2003).

7. Rather than starting from scratch, Apple purchased technology and intellectual property from a software company called Casady & Greene, publishers of the first popular Mac-based music player, SoundJam MP (Clark 2003).

8. This one-click functionality required an account to be set up and linked to a credit card. Apple licensed its "one-click" technology from Amazon. The deal was somewhat controversial. Many in the tech community opposed to the idea of business method patents criticized Amazon for patenting something as simple as a click-to-buy button, whose only real innovation was a mildly novel use of "cookie" technology (for more see Morris 2013b). Apple's deal with Amazon in a sense legitimized Amazon's claim to the patent and drew the ire of those already united against Amazon's attempt to patent the very means of digital purchase.

9. There is little public documentation that details the process by which Apple selects its featured artists (other than some of the vague wording in the contract for applying to sell material in the store discussed in the preceding paragraph). The choice of who gets featured likely involves a mix of media partnerships, paid placements, and internal curation. Like search engine optimization, there is also a subindustry of consultants who advise musicians and labels on how to make their albums more likely to be featured on the store (including catchy cover images and well-worded album write-ups).

10. Of course, iTunes was not the only retailer treating music as a side interest. Big-box discount stores like Target, Wal-Mart, and the like had been steadily lowering the price of music during the 2000s, with constant sales and discounts. Digitization is often blamed for the devaluation of music, but big-box retailers had done just as much as any digital outlet to rob music of its former exchange value.

11. As Dan Kois (2004) points out in his hilariously titled article, "Beyoncé, Your Mix Tape Sucks," celebrity mixes range from tasteful to absurd. Kois is particularly incensed by the fact that more than half of the fourteen songs on Beyoncé's mix are by the pop diva herself, her relatives, or her former bands. Kois notes that celebrity playlists are rarely put together for any kind of musical value. Rather, they are simply another venue for celebrities to spread their brand.

CHAPTER 5. MUSIC IN THE CLOUD

1. This is not the case with GrooveShark, where users can choose the song or the album they wish to stream, though as of this writing the site's legal status is in question.

2. Last.Fm is currently owned by CBS, so its reliance on broadcast strategies is not surprising.

3. It should be noted that CD-era profits were highly inflated because of the high number of consumers that were essentially replacing older formats with CDs and policies exerted by major record labels on retailers that basically mandated the shift away from vinyl toward CDs by not buying back unsold vinyl albums (McLeod 2005).

4. After discovering that it did not have all the rights necessary to sell electronic versions of books like *1984* and *Animal Farm*, Amazon remotely erased copies that users had already purchased through their Kindles. Consumers were understandably annoyed, not realizing that Amazon had the right, the authority, or even the ability to delete something consumers believed they owned. One student who had been using his Kindle to make notes and annotations on his digital copy of *1984* lost not only the product but also the product of his labor (Stone 2009).

CONCLUSION

1. This number can vary greatly depending on the particulars of the artist's contract, and on the kinds of upfront costs the label adds into the deal.

Works Cited

Abbate, Janet. *Inventing the Internet*. Cambridge, MA: MIT Press, 1999.

Acland, Charles R. "The Last Days of Videotape." *Flow TV* 11, no. 2 (2009): http://flowtv.org/2009/11/the-last-days-of-videotapecharles-r-acland-concordia-university/.

Adams, Tim. "Thom Yorke: 'If I Can't Enjoy This Now, When Do I Start?'" *Guardian*, Feb. 23, 2013. www.theguardian.com/music/2013/feb/23/thom-yorke-radiohead-interview/print.

Adorno, Theodor W. "Music in the Background." 1934. In *Essays on Music*, edited by Richard Leppert, 506–512. Berkeley: University of California Press, 2002.

———. "On the Fetish-Character in Music and the Regression of Listening." 1938. In Adorno 2001, 29–60.

———. "The Form of the Phonograph Record." *October* 55, no. 4 (1990): 55–61.

———. *The Culture Industry: Selected Essays on Mass Culture*. Edited by J.M. Bernstein. London: Routledge, 2001.

Alderman, John. *Sonic Boom: Napster, MP3, and the New Pioneers of Music*. Cambridge, MA: Perseus, 2001.

Allen, Matthew. "Web 2.0 as an Argument against Convergence." *First Monday* 13, no. 3 (2008): http://firstmonday.org/htbin/cgiwrap/bin/ojs/index.php/fm/article/view/2139/1946.

Amorim, Roberto. "Xingsound MP2 Player." Really Rare Wares, Feb. 14, 2007. http://web.archive.org/web/20070214091726/http://www.rjamorim.com/rrw/xingsound.html.

Anderson, Benedict. *Imagined Communities: Reflections on the Origin and Spread of Nationalism*. London: Verso, 1991.

Anderson, Chris. *The Long Tail: Why the Future of Business Is Selling Less of More*. New York: Hyperion, 2006.

———. *Free: The Future of a Radical Price*. New York: Hyperion, 2009.

Anderson, Jay. "Stream Capture: Returning Control of Digital Music to the Users." *Harvard Journal of Law & Technology* 25, no. 1 (2011): 160–77.

Anderson, Tim J. *Popular Music in a Digital Music Economy: Problems and Practices for an Emerging Service Industry.* New York: Routledge, 2014.

Andersson, Jonas. *Online File Sharing: Innovations in Media Consumption.* New York: Routledge, 2014.

Andrejevic, Mark. "The Kinder, Gentler Gaze of Big Brother: Reality TV in the Era of Digital Capitalism." *New Media & Society* 4, no. 2 (2002): 251–70.

———. *iSpy: Surveillance and Power in the Interactive Era.* Lawrence: University Press of Kansas, 2007.

Angell, David, and Brent Heslop. "Multimedia without the Hype." *PC Magazine,* June 29, 1993, 71.

Ankerson, Megan Sapnar. "Dot-Com Design: Cultural Production of the Commercial Web in the Internet Bubble (1993–2003)." PhD diss., University of Wisconsin, Madison, 2010.

Ante, Spencer. "Inside Napster." Business Week Online, August 13, 2000a. www.businessweek.com/stories/2000–08–13/inside-napster.

———. "Napster's Shawn Fanning: The Teen Who Woke Up Web Music." Business Week Online, April 12, 2000b. https://web.archive.org/web/20080124130214/http://www.businessweek.com/ebiz/0004/em0412.htm.

Appadurai, Arjun. "Introduction: Commodities and the Politics of Value." In *The Social Life of Things: Commodities in Cultural Perspective,* edited by Arjun Appadurai, 3–64. Cambridge: Cambridge University Press, 1986.

Apple. "iTunes Music Store Hits Five Million Downloads." Apple.com, Press Release, June 23, 2003a. www.apple.com/pr/library/2003/06/23iTunes-Music-Store-Hits-Five-Million-Downloads.html.

———. "iTunes Music Store Sells over One Million Songs in First Week." Apple.com, Press Release, May 5, 2003b. www.apple.com/pr/library/2003/05/05iTunes-Music-Store-Sells-Over-One-Million-Songs-in-First-Week.html.

———. "iTunes Celebrates Its First Anniversary; over 70 Million Songs Purchased." Apple.com, Press Release, April 28, 2004. www.apple.com/pr/library/2004/04/28iTunes-Celebrates-Its-First-Anniversary-Over-70-Million-Songs-Purchased.html.

———. "iTunes Canadian Downloading Agreement." Internal document, 1–46, 2005.

———. "Changes Coming to the iTunes Store." Apple.com, Press Release, Jan. 6, 2009. www.apple.com/pr/library/2009/01/06itunes.html.

Arvidsson, Adam, and Elanor Colleoni. "Value in Informational Capitalism and on the Internet." *Information Society* 28, no. 3 (2012): 135–50.

Attali, Jacques. *Noise: The Political Economy of Music.* Minneapolis: University of Minnesota Press, 1985.

Atwood, Brett. "Winamp." *Billboard,* August 23, 1997, 93.

Auletta, Ken. "Searching for Trouble: Why Google Is on Its Guard." *New Yorker,* Oct. 12, 2009, 46–56.

Bailey, Joseph P., and Yannis Bakos. "An Exploratory Study of the Emerging Role of Electronic Intermediaries." *International Journal of Electronic Commerce* 1, no. 3 (1997): 1–14.

Bakos, Yannis. "The Emerging Role of Electronic Marketplaces on the Internet." *Communications of the ACM* 41, no. 8 (1997): 35–42.

———. "The Emerging Landscape for Retail E-commerce." *Journal of Economic Perspectives* 15, no. 1 (2001): 69–80.

Banerjee, Scott. "New Ideas, New Outlets." *Billboard,* Nov. 6, 2004, 47–48.

Bangeman, Eric. "Apple Passes Wal-Mart, Now #1 Music Retailer in U.S." Ars Technica, April 2, 2008. http://arstechnica.com/news.ars/post/20080402 -apple-passes-wal-mart-now-1-music-retailer-in-us.html.

———. "Record Exec Confirms Jobs' Comment about 'Greedy' Industry." Ars Technica, Sept. 25, 2005. http://arstechnica.com/old/content/2005/09/5348.ars.

Barbrook, Richard. "The Californian Ideology." *Science as Culture* 26, no. 6 (1996): 44–72.

———. "The Hi-Tech Gift Economy." *First Monday* 3, no. 12 (1998): http:// firstmonday.org/htbin/cgiwrap/bin/ojs/index.php/fm/article/view/631 /552.

———. "The Napsterisation of Everything." *Science as Culture* 2, no. 11 (2002): 277–85.

Barnes, Kevin. "We Will Only Propagate Exceptional Objects." Of Montreal, Sept. 27, 2008. www.ofmontreal.net/2008/09/27/we-will-only-propagate -exceptional-objects/.

Batson, Paula. "Leading Online Music Service Myplay.Com Now Offers the Infinite Locker." PR Newswire, May 30, 2000. www.thefreelibrary.com /Leading+Online+Music+Service+myplay.com+Now+Offers+the +Infinite...-a062446275.

Baudrillard, Jean. *For a Critique of the Political Economy of the Sign.* St. Louis, MO: Telos, 1981.

Baym, Nancy K. *Personal Connections in the Digital Age.* Cambridge: Polity, 2010.

———. "Data Not Seen: The Uses and Shortcomings of Social Media Metrics." *First Monday* 18, no. 10 (2013): http://firstmonday.org/ojs/index.php/fm /article/view/4873/3752.

BBC. "iTunes User Sues Apple over iPod." BBC News, Jan. 6, 2005. http://news .bbc.co.uk/2/hi/technology/4151009.stm.

———. "Apple iPhone Warning Proves True." BBC News, Sept. 28, 2007. http://news.bbc.co.uk/2/hi/7017660.stm.

———. "Retailer Best Buy to Buy Napster." BBC News, Sept. 15, 2008. http:// news.bbc.co.uk/go/pr/fr/-/2/hi/technology/7617248.stm.

———. "Napster—10 Years of Turmoil." BBC News, June 26, 2009. http:// news.bbc.co.uk/2/hi/technology/8120320.stm.

Beer, David. "Power through the Algorithm? Participatory Web Cultures and the Technological Unconscious." *New Media & Society* 11, no. 6 (2009): 985–1002.

————. "Mobile Music, Coded Objects and Everyday Spaces." *Mobilities* 5, no. 4 (2010): 469–84.

Behar, Michael. "It's Playback Time! And MP3 Is Only the Beginning." *Wired*, August 1999, 124–25. http://archive.wired.com/wired/archive/7.08/dl_opener.html.

Benjamin, Walter. "Unpacking My Library: A Talk about Book Collecting." In *The Object Reader*, edited by Fiona Candlin and Raiford Guins, 257–62. New York: Routledge, 2009.

————. "The Work of Art in the Age of Mechanical Reproduction." In *Illuminations*, 217–52. New York: Schocken, 1969.

Benson-Allott, Caetlin. *Killer Tapes and Shattered Screens: Video Spectatorship from VHS to File Sharing*. Berkeley: University of California Press, 2013.

Bermejo, Fernando. *The Internet Audience: Constitution and Measurement*. New York: Peter Lang, 2007.

————. "Audience Manufacture in Historical Perspective: From Broadcasting to Google." *New Media & Society* 11, no. 1–2 (2009): 133–54.

Berry, David M. *Copy, Rip, Burn: The Politics of Copyleft and Open Source*. London: Pluto, 2008.

————. *The Philosophy of Software: Code and Mediation in the Digital Age*. New York: Palgrave Macmillan, 2011.

————, ed. *Life in Code and Software: Mediated Life in a Complex Computational Ecology*. London: Open Humanities Press, 2012. www.livingbooksaboutlife.org/books/Life_in_Code_and_Software/Introduction.

Beuscart, Jean-Samuel. "Napster Users between Community and Clientele: The Formation and Regulation of a Sociotechnical Group." *Sociologie du travail* 47 (2005): S1–S16.

BigChampagne. "Big Champagne: Company Overview." *Business Week*, March 4, 2010.

Bijker, Wiebe E., and John Law. *Shaping Technology/Building Society: Studies in Sociotechnical Change*. Cambridge, MA: MIT Press, 1992.

Bodker, Henrik. "The Changing Materiality of Music." *Papers from the Centre for Internet Research* (2004): 1–25.

Bolin, Göran. "The Labour of Media Use." *Information, Communication & Society* 15, no. 6 (2012): 796–814.

Bolter, J. David, and Richard A. Grusin. *Remediation: Understanding New Media*. Cambridge, MA: MIT Press, 1999.

Boon, Marcus. *In Praise of Copying*. Cambridge, MA: Harvard University Press, 2010.

Borland, John. "Programmers Prepare New, Free MP3 Format." CNET News, June 16, 2000. http://news.cnet.com/2100–1023–242030.html.

————. "Napster Buyout Blocked; Fire Sale Likely." CNET News, Sept. 3, 2002a. http://news.cnet.com/Napster-buyout-blocked-fire-sale-likely/2100–1027_3–956382.html.

————. "Roxio Closes Napster Asset Buy." CNET News, Nov. 27, 2002b. http://news.cnet.com/2100–1023–975627.html.

Bourdieu, Pierre. *Language and Symbolic Power.* Translated by John B. Thompson. Cambridge: Polity, 1991.

Bowman, John. "Free Your iPod." CBC News, Feb. 9, 2006. www.cbc.ca/news2/background/tech/ipod.html.

Bragg, Billy. "The Royalty Scam." *New York Times,* March 22, 2008.

Braman, Sandra, and Stephanie Roberts. "Advantage ISP: Terms of Service as Media Law." *New Media & Society* 5, no. 3 (2003): 422–48.

Breen, Christopher. "Roll Your Own Audio CDs." *MacUser,* June 1, 1996, 117.

Bremser, Wayne. "Jazz in 2500? iTunes versus Preservation." Harlem.org, Feb. 28, 2004. www.harlem.org/itunes/.

Bronson, Po. "Rebootlegger." *Wired,* July 1998. http://archive.wired.com/wired/archive/6.07/newmedia.html.

Brown, Ian. "Queuing Up for the First Coming of 'the Jesus Phone.'" *Globe and Mail,* June 29, 2007. www.theglobeandmail.com/globe-debate/queuing-up-for-the-first-coming-of-the-jesus-phone/article723961/?page=all.

Brown, Janelle. "The Napster Parasites." Salon.com, Feb. 9, 2001. http://archive.salon.com/tech/feature/2001/02/09/napster_parasites/.

Brown, Stan. "Taming iTunes and iPod for Classical Music (and Non-classical Too)." July 6, 2008. http://oakroadsystems.com/genl/itunes.htm.

Bruno, Antony. "Q&A: Former RIAA CEO Rosen Talks Napster." Billboard.biz, June 1, 2009. www.billboard.com/biz/articles/news/1269832/billboardbiz-qa-former-riaa-ceo-rosen-talks-napster.

Bruns, Axel. "Towards Produsage: Futures for User-Led Content Production." Paper presented at Cultural Attitudes towards Communication and Technology, Tartu, Estonia, June 28–July 1, 2006.

Brynjolfsson, Erik, and Michael D. Smith. "Frictionless Commerce? A Comparison of Internet and Conventional Retailers." *Management Science* 46, no. 4 (2000): 563–85.

Bull, Michael. "No Dead Air! The iPod and the Culture of Mobile Listening." *Leisure Studies* 24, no. 4 (2005): 343–55.

———. *Sound Moves: iPod Culture and Urban Experience.* New York: Routledge, 2007.

Burkart, Patrick. "Loose Integration in the Popular Music Industry." *Popular Music and Society* 28, no. 4 (2005): 489–500.

———. "Trends in Digital Music Archiving." *Information Society* 24, no. 4 (2008): 246–50.

———. "On the Digital Music Wars: Where Are We Now?" *Flow TV* 9, no. 7 (2009): http://flowtv.org/?p=2453#.

———. *Music and Cyberliberties.* Middletown, CT: Wesleyan University Press, 2010.

Burkart, Patrick, and Tom McCourt. *Digital Music Wars: Ownership and Control of the Celestial Jukebox.* Lanham, MD: Rowman and Littlefield, 2006.

Buzzard, Karen. *Tracking the Audience: The Ratings Industry from Analog to Digital.* New York: Routledge, 2012.

Byrne, David. "David Byrne's Survival Strategies for Emerging Artists—and Megastars." *Wired,* Dec. 18, 2007. http://archive.wired.com/entertainment /music/magazine/16-01/ff_byrne?currentPage=all.

Byrne, David, and Thom Yorke. "David Byrne and Thom Yorke on the Real Value of Music." *Wired,* Dec. 18, 2007. http://archive.wired.com/entertainment /music/magazine/16-01/ff_yorke?currentPage=all.

Campbell, D. Grant. "The Birth of the New Web: A Foucauldian Reading of the Semantic Web." *Cataloging & Classification Quarterly* 43, no. 3/4 (2007): 9–20.

Capuzzi, Joan. "CDNow Reinvents the Music Store to the Tune of $3 Million in Sales a Year." *Business Philadelphia,* Jan. 1 1996.

Carlsson, Anders. "The Forgotten Pioneers of Creative Hacking and Social Networking—Introducing the Demoscene." Paper presented at Re:Live— Media Art Histories 2009, Melbourne, Australia, 2009.

Carr, Nicholas. "The Strategic Value of Complements." In *Digital Renderings,* May 6, 2007. www.nicholasgcarr.com/digital_renderings/archives/the _strategic_value.shtml.

———. "Cloud Computing, circa 1965." In *Rough Type,* Nov. 28, 2009. www .roughtype.com/archives/2009/11/cloud_computing_1.php.

Carroll, John Millar. *Human-Computer Interaction in the New Millennium.* New York: ACM Press, 2002.

CBC. "French Bill Threatens iPod, iTunes Exclusivity." CBC News, March 18, 2006. www.cbc.ca/news/arts/french-bill-threatens-ipod-itunes-exclusivity -1.575984.

"CD Text Specifications Announced by Licensors Philips and Sony." *Audio Week,* June 10, 1996. https://global-factiva-com.ezproxy.library.wisc.edu /ha/default.aspx#./!?&_suid=14278612742420387089942814 78226.

CDDB. "Fans Choose Reeves Gabrels on the Net; CDDB Empowers Users to Opt-in for MP3 Only Album." Business Wire, Nov. 4, 1999a. www.mi2n .com/press.php3?press_nb=3112.

———. "New CDDB(2) Service and Software Development Kit Announced." PR Newswire, July 19, 1999b. www.thefreelibrary.com/New+CDDB %282%29+Service+and+Software+Development+Kit+Announced.-a055184939.

———. "New Media Pioneers Ann Greenberg and Ty Roberts Join CDDB. com." Business Wire, 1999c. www.gracenote.com/company_info/press /1999/1999040700/.

Ceruzzi, Paul E. *A History of Modern Computing.* Cambridge, MA: MIT Press, 1998.

Chalmers, Rachel. "Open CD Database Launched after Escient Gets Tough." *Computergram International,* March 10 1999. www.thefreelibrary.com /Open+CD+Database+Launched+After+Escient+Gets+Tough.-a054071297.

Chanan, Michael. *Repeated Takes: A Short History of Recording and Its Effects on Music.* London: Verso, 1995.

Chang, Samantha. "CDNow: This Week in Brief." *Billboard,* March 6, 2004, 10.

Cherry, Steven. "Selling Music for a Song." *IEEE Spectrum,* Dec. 2004, 56.

Chion, Michel. *Audio-Vision: Sound on Screen*. Translated by Claudia Gorbman. New York: Columbia University Press, 1994.

Christensen, Clayton M. *The Innovator's Dilemma: When New Technologies Cause Great Firms to Fail*. Boston: Harvard Business School Press, 1997.

Chun, Wendy Hui Kyong. "On Software, or the Persistence of Visual Knowledge." *Grey Room* 18 (Winter 2004): 26–51.

———. "On 'Sourcery,' or Code as Fetish." *Configurations* 16, no. 3 (2008): 299–324.

———. *Programmed Visions: Software and Memory*. Cambridge, MA: MIT Press, 2011.

Clark, Don. "Gambits & Gadgets in the World of Technology." *Wall Street Journal*, July 3, 2003.

Cloonan, Martin. "Mastering Tickets." Live Music Exchange Blog, Feb. 24, 2012. http://livemusicexchange.org/blog/mastering-tickets/.

Cohen, Jonathan. "Radiohead Remix Promo Drives Single Up U.S. Chart." Reuters/Billboard, April 14, 2008. www.reuters.com/article/entertainmentNews /idUSN1435208020080414.

Coté, Mark, and Jennifer Pybus. "Learning to Immaterial Labour 2.0: MySpace and Social Networks." *Ephemera* 7, no. 1 (2007): 88–106. www .ephemerajournal.org/sites/default/files/7–1cote-pybus.pdf.

Coyle, Karen. "Understanding Metadata and Its Purposes." *Journal of Academic Librarianship* 31, no. 2 (2005): 160–63.

Cramer, Florian, and Matthew Fuller. "Interface." In *Software Studies: A Lexicon*, edited by Matthew Fuller, 149–53. Cambridge, MA: MIT Press, 2008.

Culbertson, Katie. "Carmel Company Ready to Mine High-Tech Entertainment Market." *Indianapolis Business Journal*, Nov. 10, 1997, 53.

Dansby, Andrew. "Big Brother Is from Houston." *Houston Chronicle*, April 25, 2008.

Davis, John Siebert. "Going Analog: Vinylphiles and the Consumption of the 'Obsolete' Vinyl Record." In *Residual Media*, edited by Charles R. Acland, 222–38. Minneapolis: University of Minnesota Press, 2007.

Davis, Michelle. "How Does iTunes Radio Pay Artists?" Future of Music Coalition. http://futureofmusic.org/blog/2013/10/17/how-does-itunes -radio-pay-artists.

Dean, Jodi. "Communicative Capitalism: Circulation and the Foreclosure of Politics." *Cultural Politics* 1, no. 1 (2005): 51–74.

Dean, Katie. "The House That Music Fans Built." Wired.com, July 7, 2004. http://archive.wired.com/entertainment/music/news/2004/07/64033 ?currentPage=all.

Debord, Guy. *The Society of the Spectacle*. New York: Zone, 1995.

Dellis. "Old-Timers." Winamp User Forum. March 11, 2001. http://forums .winamp.com/showthread.php?t=44250.

Dempsey, Lorcan, and Rachel Heery. "Metadata: A Current View of Practice and Issues." *Journal of Documentation* 54, no. 2 (1998): 145–72.

DeNora, Tia. *Music in Everyday Life.* Cambridge: Cambridge University Press, 2000.

Dibbell, Julian. "A Rape in Cyberspace." *Village Voice,* Dec. 23, 1993. www.villagevoice.com/2005–10–18/specials/a-rape-in-cyberspace/.

Dixon, Wheeler W. *Streaming: Movies, Media, and Instant Access.* Lexington: University Press of Kentucky, 2013.

Dodge, Martin, and Rob Kitchin. "Software, Objects, and Home Space." *Environment and Planning A* 41, no. 6 (2009): 1344–65.

Donath, Judith, and danah boyd. "Public Displays of Connection." *BT Technology Journal* 22, no. 4 (2004): 71–82.

Dowd, Timothy. "From 78s to MP3s: The Embedded Impact of Technology in the Market for Prerecorded Music." In *The Business of Culture: Perspectives on Entertainment and Media,* edited by Joseph Lampel, Jamal Shamsie, and Theresa K. Lant. Mahwah, NJ: Lawrence Erlbaum, 2006.

Dredge, Stuart. "Thom Yorke Calls Spotify 'the Last Desperate Fart of a Dying Corpse.'" Guardian.com, Oct. 7, 2013. www.theguardian.com/technology/2013/oct/07/spotify-thom-yorke-dying-corpse/print.

Drew, Rob. "Mixed Blessings: The Commercial Mix and the Future of Music Aggregation." *Popular Music and Society* 28, no. 4 (2005): 533–51.

———. "New Technologies and the Business of Music: Lessons from the 1980s Home Taping Hearings." *Popular Music and Society* 73, no. 3 (2014): 253–72.

Drummond, Mike. "Music Industry Arms for Combat: IBM, Record Labels Team in Online Distribution Experiment." *San Diego Union-Tribune,* Sept. 19, 1999.

Dube, Ric. "After Three Years and a Wild Media Ride, IUMA's Fate Remains Tied to Its Utopian Vision." *Webnoize,* no. 1 (Jan. 1997): http://web.archive.org/web/19970627115250/www.webnoize.com/specialreports/97–1/iuma/iuma-1.htm.

Dyer-Witheford, Nick. *Cyber-Marx: Cycles and Circuits of Struggle in High-Technology Capitalism.* Urbana: University of Illinois Press, 1999.

———. "E-Capital and the Many-Headed Hydra." In *Critical Perspectives on the Internet,* edited by Greg Elmer, 129–64. Oxford: Rowman and Littlefield, 2002.

Dyer-Witheford, Nick, and Greig de Peuter. *Games of Empire: Global Capitalism and Video Games.* Minneapolis: University of Minnesota Press, 2005.

Economist. "Clash of the Clouds; Cloud Computing." *Economist,* Oct. 15, 2009. www.economist.com/node/14637206.

———. "Cloudy with a Chance of Rain." Economist.com, March 5, 2010. www.economist.com/node/15640793.

———. "Cloud Computing: A Market for Computing Power." *Economist,* Feb. 19, 2011, 74.

Eisenberg, Evan. *The Recording Angel: Music, Records, and Culture from Aristotle to Zappa.* 2nd ed. New Haven, CT: Yale University Press, 2005.

Elberse, Anita. "Should You Invest in the Long Tail?" *Harvard Business Review,* July-August 2008, 88–96.

Elder, Jeff. "Apple Deleted Rivals' Songs from Users' iPods." Digits, *Wall Street Journal*, Dec. 3, 2014. http://blogs.wsj.com/digits/2014/12/03/apple-deleted-rivals-songs-from-users-ipods/.

Ernesto. "Show Doing Well on BitTorrent? We'll Buy It, Says Media Giant." Torrent Freak. http://torrentfreak.com/show-doing-well-on-bittorrent-well-buy-it-121010/.

Ettema, J., and C. Whitney. "The Money Arrow: An Introduction to Audiencemaking." In *Audiencemaking: How the Media Create the Audience*, edited by J. Ettema and C. Whitney, 1–18. Thousand Oaks, CA: Sage, 1994.

Evangelista, Benny. "Assessing Napster—10 Years Later." *San Francisco Chronicle*, June 1, 2009.

Evens, Aden. *Sound Ideas: Music, Machines, and Experience.* Minneapolis: University of Minnesota Press, 2005.

Feeley, Jim, and Suzanne Stefanac. "Desktop CD-ROM Publishing." *Macworld*, March 1, 1995, 6.

Fisher, William W. *Promises to Keep: Technology, Law, and the Future of Entertainment.* Stanford, CA: Stanford University Press, 2004.

FMC. "The Future of Digital Infrastructure for the Creative Economy." Future of Music Coalition, Feb. 16, 2010. http://futureofmusic.org/article/article/future-digital-infrastructure-creative-economy.

———. "The Future of Music Manifesto." Future of Music Coalition, June 1, 2000. http://futureofmusic.org/article/article/future-music-manifesto.

Frank, Steven J. "The Death of Business-Method Patents." *IEEE Spectrum*, March 2009, 32–35.

Frank, Thomas. *The Conquest of Cool: Business Culture, Counterculture, and the Rise of Hip Consumerism.* Chicago: University of Chicago Press, 1997.

Frankel, Justin, Dave Greely, and Ben Sawyer. *MP3 Power! With Winamp.* Cincinnati, OH: Muska and Lipman, 1999.

Frere-Jones, Sasha. "You, the D.J.: Online Music Moves to the Cloud." *New Yorker*, June 14, 2010, 138–39.

Friedman, Ted. *Electric Dreams: Computers in American Culture.* New York: New York University Press, 2005.

Frith, Simon. *Performing Rites: Evaluating Popular Music.* Oxford: Oxford University Press, 1996.

Fry, Christine. "The Community as a Commodity: The Age Graded Case." *Human Organization* 36, no. 2 (1977): 115–23.

Fry, Jason. "Three Veterans Advise the Next Tech Wave: It's All about Business." *Wall Street Journal*, Dec. 31, 2001, B1.

Fuchs, Christian. "Labor in Informational Capitalism and on the Internet." *Information Society* 26, no. 3 (2010): 179–96.

Fuller, Matthew. *Software Studies: A Lexicon.* Leonardo Books. Cambridge, MA: MIT Press, 2008.

Fusilli, Jim. "A Heap of Surprises: 'Ellipse' Is Modern Pop Full of Invention." *Wall Street Journal*, August 28, 2009.

Galloway, Alexander R. *Protocol: How Control Exists after Decentralization.* Cambridge, MA: MIT Press, 2004.

———. *The Interface Effect.* Cambridge: Polity, 2012.

Garfinkel, Simson, and David Cox. "Finding and Archiving the Internet Footprint." Paper presented at the First Digital Lives Research Conference: Personal Digital Archives for the 21st Century, London, Feb. 9–11, 2009.

Garland, Eric. Email, 2009a.

———. "The 'In Rainbows' Experiment: Did It Work?" NPR, Nov. 16, 2009b. www.npr.org/blogs/monitormix/2009/11/the_in_rainbows_experiment _did.html.

Garnham, Nicholas. "Contribution to a Political Economy of Mass-Communication [1986]." In *Media and Cultural Studies: Keyworks,* edited by M.G. Durham and D.M. Kellner, 225–52. Oxford: Blackwell, 2001.

Garofalo, Reebee. "From Music Publishing to MP3: Music and Industry in the Twentieth Century." *American Music* 17, no. 3 (1999): 318–53.

Geere, Duncan. "200+ Labels Withdraw Their Music from Spotify: Are Its Fortunes Unravelling?" Wired.com, Nov. 18, 2011. www.wired.com /epicenter/2011/11/200-labels-withdraw-their-music-from-spotify-are-its -fortunes-unravelling/all/1.

Gessler, Nicholas. "Skeuomorphs and Cultural Algorithms." Paper presented at Evolutionary Programming VII: Proceedings of the 7th International Conference on Evolutionary Programming, Berlin, 1998.

Gibson, Owen. "Radiohead's Bid to Revive Music Industry: Pay What You Like to Download Albums." *Guardian,* Oct. 2, 2007.

Giesler, Markus, and Mali Pohlmann. "The Social Form of Napster: Cultivating the Paradox of Consumer Emancipation." *Advances in Consumer Research* 30 (2003): 94–100.

Gillen, Marilyn A. "The Enter-Active File: Selling Online." *Billboard,* August 19, 1995, 66.

Gillespie, Tarleton. *Wired Shut: Copyright and the Shape of Digital Culture.* Cambridge, MA: MIT Press, 2007.

———. "The Relevance of Algorithms." In *Media Technologies: Essays on Communication, Materiality, and Society,* edited by Tarleton Gillespie, Pablo Boczkowski, and Kristen Foot, 167–93. Cambridge, MA: MIT Press, 2014.

Gitelman, Lisa. *Always Already New: Media, History, and the Data of Culture.* Cambridge, MA: MIT Press, 2006.

Glaister, Dan. "Slave to the Rhythm." *Guardian,* March 13, 1998, 17.

Gomery, Douglas. *The Coming of Sound: A History.* New York: Routledge, 2005.

Gopinath, Sumanth S. *The Ringtone Dialectic: Economy and Cultural Form.* Cambridge, MA: MIT Press, 2013.

Gopinath, Sumanth, and Jason Stanyek, eds. *Anytime, Anywhere? An Introduction to the Devices, Markets and Theories of Mobile Music.* Vol. 1. New York: Oxford University Press, 2014a.

————. *The Oxford Handbook of Mobile Music Studies.* Vol. 1. New York: Oxford University Press, 2014b.

Gracenote. "Geddy Lee Uses Cutting Edge Technology to Offer Exclusive Online Interview through New Album." PR Newswire, 2000. www.prnewswire.com /news-releases/geddy-lee-uses-cutting-edge-technology-to-offer-exclusive -online-interview-through-new-album-75696227.html.

————. "Gracenote Alleges Roxio Breached Contract, Infringed Its Patents, Violated the Digital Millennium Copyright Act, and Improperly Used Its Trademarks." PR Newswire, 2001a. www.prnewswire.com/news-releases /gracenote-files-lawsuit-against-roxio-inc-71741682.html.

————. "Gracenote Announces Music Management Solution for Peer-to-Peer Networks." PR Newswire, 2001b. www.prnewswire.com/news-releases /gracenote-announces-music-management-solution-for-peer-to-peer -networks-74068427.html.

————. "Gracenote (TM) Launches Digital Music Tracking Service." PR Newswire, 2001c. www.prnewswire.com/news-releases/gracenotetm -launches-digital-music-tracking-service-72037887.html.

————. "Gracenote Creates New Standard for Classical Music Display on Digital Devices." Business Wire, 2007. www.businesswire.com/news /home/20070108005809/en/Gracenote-Creates-Standard-Classical-Music -Display-Digital#.VRm1WDvF_3U.

————. "Gracenote Celebrates 10 Year Anniversary." Gracenote.com, Press Release, July 15, 2008. www.gracenote.com/company_info/press/071508–2/.

————. "Gracenote Reaches Global Media Database Milestone." Sept. 9, 2010. www.sony.com/SCA/company-news/press-releases/gracenote/2010 /gracenote-reaches-global-media-database-milestone-.shtml.

Gracyk, Theodore. *Rhythm and Noise: An Aesthetics of Rock.* Durham, NC: Duke University Press, 1996.

Grassmuck, Volker. "Academic Studies on the Effect of File-Sharing on the Recorded Music Industry: A Literature Review." Social Science Research Network (SSRN), May 14, 2010. http://dx.doi.org/10.2139/ssrn.1749579.

Gray, Jonathan. *Show Sold Separately: Promos, Spoilers, and Other Media Paratexts.* New York: New York University Press, 2010.

Green, Dave. "Demo or Die!" *Wired,* July 1995. http://archive.wired.com /wired/archive/3.07/democoders.html.

Greenberg, Jane. "Metadata and the World Wide Web." In *Encyclopedia of Library and Information Science,* edited by Miriam Drake, 1876–88. New York: Marcel Dekker, 2003a.

————. "Metadata Generation: Processes, People and Tools." *Bulletin of the American Society for Information Science and Technology* 29, no. 2 (Dec. /Jan. 2003b): 16–19.

Greenburg, Zack O'Malley. "Why Wu-Tang Will Release Just One Copy of Its Secret Album." *Forbes,* March 26, 2014 www.forbes.com/sites /zackomalleygreenburg/2014/02/12/golden-oldies-how-to-become-a -music-publishing-mogul/.

Greenfeld, Karl Taro, Joshua Quittner, Bill Syken, Chris Taylor, and Nathaniel Wice. "Disabling the System." *Time Canada,* Sept. 13, 1999, 14.

Gruberman, Ken, and Ken McQuillin. "Multimedia and Audio." *MacUser,* Feb. 1, 1991, S38.

Grunin, Lori. "Utility Coaxes CD-Audio out of Your ROM Drive." *PC Magazine,* Jan. 29, 1991, 432.

Guberman, Daniel. "Post-Fidelity: A New Age of Music Consumption and Technological Innovation." *Journal of Popular Music Studies* 23, no. 4 (2011): 431–54.

Gunster, Shane. *Capitalizing on Culture: Critical Theory for Cultural Studies.* Toronto: University of Toronto Press, 2004.

Hair, Arthur R. "Method for Transmitting a Desired Digital Video or Audio Signal." US Patent 5,191,573, filed Sept. 18, 1990, and issued March 2, 1993. www.google.com/patents/US5191573?dq=5191573.

———. "System for Transmitting Desired Digital Video or Audio Signals." US Patent 5,675,734, filed Feb. 27, 1996, and issued June 13, 1988. www.google.com/patents/US5675734?dq=5675734.

Hall, Bronwyn H. "Business and Financial Method Patents, Innovation, and Policy." *Scottish Journal of Political Economy* 56, no. 4 (2009): 443–73.

Hansell, Saul. "The iTunes Store: Profit Machine." *New York Times,* August 11, 2008. http://bits.blogs.nytimes.com/2008/08/11/steve-jobs-tries-to-downplay-the-itunes-stores-profit/.

Hansen, Evan, and Eliot Van Buskirk. "MP3's Loss, Open Source's Gain." *Wired,* Feb. 23, 2007. https://web.archive.org/web/20080504030122/http://www.wired.com/entertainment/music/news/2007/02/72785?currentPage=all.

Haring, Bruce. *Beyond the Charts: MP3 and the Digital Music Revolution.* Los Angeles: JM Northern Media, 2000.

Harmon, Amy. "Piracy, or Innovation? It's Hollywood vs. High Tech." *New York Times,* March 14, 2002, C1.

Harris, Ron. "MyPlay.com Helps Store Music Files." *Associated Press Writer,* Oct. 13, 1999.

Hartley, Matt. "Thank You, Napster." *Globe and Mail,* May 19, 2009. www.theglobeandmail.com/technology/digital-culture/thank-you-napster/article1371912/.

Harvey, Eric. "Digital Dilemmas and Promotional Possibilities: Circulating Music in the Late Age of the MP3." PhD diss., Indiana University, 2013. ProQuest (UMI 3601803).

Haug, Wolfgang Fritz. *Commodity Aesthetics, Ideology and Culture.* New York: International General, 1987.

Hayes, Brian. "Cloud Computing." *Communications of the ACM* 51, no. 7 (July 2008): 9–11.

Hayles, N. Katherine. *How We Became Posthuman: Virtual Bodies in Cybernetics, Literature, and Informatics.* Chicago: University of Chicago Press, 1999.

Hearn, Alison. "Structuring Feeling: Web 2.0, Online Ranking and Rating, and the Digital 'Reputation' Economy." *Ephemera* 10, no. 3/4 (2010): 421–38. www.ephemerajournal.org/contribution/structuring-feeling-web-20-online -ranking-and-rating-and-digital-%E2%80%98reputation%E2%80%99 -economy.

Heath, Joseph. *The Rebel Sell: Why the Culture Can't Be Jammed.* Chichester, UK: Capstone, 2005.

Helmore, Edward. "Is the Album Dead? Katy Perry, Miley Cyrus, and Elton John Hit by Dramatic US Sales Slump." *Guardian*, Nov. 2, 2013. www .theguardian.com/music/2013/nov/02/is-music-album-dead-us-worst -ever-sales-figures.

Hemos. "Escient (CDDB Company) Trying to Monopolize Market?" Slashdot, March 8, 1999. http://slashdot.org/story/99/03/08/0945228/escient-cddb -company-trying-to-monopolize-market.

Hesmondhalgh, David. "User-Generated Content, Free Labour and the Cultural Industries." *Ephemera* 10, no. 3/4 (2010): 267–84. www.ephemerajournal.org /contribution/user-generated-content-free-labour-and-cultural-industries.

Heylin, Clinton. *Bootleg: The Secret History of the Other Recording Industry.* New York: St. Martin's, 1994.

Hilmes, Michele. "The New Materiality of Radio: Sound on Screens." In *Radio's New Wave: Global Sound in the Digital Era,* edited by Jason Loviglio and Michele Hilmes, 43–61. New York: Routledge, 2013.

Hoare, C.A.R. "Programming: Sorcery or Science?" *Software, IEEE* 1, no. 2 (1984): 5–16.

Hodgson, Jessica. "Recorded Music Sales Declines Set to Continue." Dow Jones International News, March 27, 2007. https://global-factiva-com.ezproxy .library.wisc.edu/ha/default.aspx#./!?&_suid=142775205689006323924404 56897.

Hogan, Marc. "Spotify Reveals How Much, or How Little, It Pays Per Stream." Spin.com, Dec. 3, 2013. www.spin.com/articles/spotify-details-royalty -payouts-cents/.

Horrigan, John. "Use of Cloud Computing Applications and Services." Pew Research Center's Internet and American Life Project, Sept. 12, 2008. www .pewinternet.org/2008/09/12/use-of-cloud-computing-applications-and -services/.

"How Downloaders Are Tracked: Music Industry Discloses Techniques to Stop File-Sharing." MSNBC.com, August 27, 2003. www.nbcnews.com /id/3078421/ns/technology_and_science-games/t/how-downloaders-are -tracked.

Howe, Jeff. "Big Champagne Is Watching You." *Wired*, Oct. 2003. http:// archive.wired.com/wired/archive/11.10/fileshare.html.

Howells, Jan. "Napster Teams up with Bootlegger." Newswire, 2000. www .v3.co.uk/v3-uk/news/1947782/napster-teams-bootlegger.

Howison, James, and Abby Goodrum. "Why Can't I Manage Academic Papers Like MP3s? The Evolution and Intent of Metadata Standards." Paper presented at the Proceedings of the Colleges, Code and Intellectual Property Conference, College Park, MD, June 10–11, 2004.

Huhn, Mary. "Metallica Bows to iTunes; Beatles, Led Zeppelin, Radiohead Still Holding Out." NYPost.com, August 2, 2006. www.foxnews.com/story /0,2933,206566,00.html.

Hunt, Robert M. "You Can Patent That? Are Patents on Computer Programs and Business Methods Good for the New Economy?" *Business Review,* First Quarter 2001, 5–15.

Hyde, Lewis. *The Gift: Imagination and the Erotic Life of Property.* New York: Random House, 1983.

IFPI. "IFPI Digital Music Report 2013." London: International Federation of the Phonographic Industry, 2013a.

———. "Recording Industry in Numbers." London: International Federation of the Phonographic Industry, 2013b.

———. "IFPI Digital Music Report 2014." London: International Federation of the Phonographic Industry, 2014.

Ishida, Yoshinobu, Madayuki Ishida, Kenji Gotoh, Tohru Yoshihara, Keiji Nakamura, Kunihiko Nakagawa, and Junji Yanabe. "On the Development of Mini Disc Players." *IEEE Transactions on Consumer Electronics* 39, no. 3 (1993): 364–71.

Jaeger, Paul T., Jimmy Lin, Justin M. Grimes, and Shannon N. Simmons. "Where Is the Cloud? Geography, Economics, Environment, and Jurisdiction in Cloud Computing." *First Monday* 14, no. 5 (2009): http://firstmonday .org/htbin/cgiwrap/bin/ojs/index.php/fm/article/view/2456/2171.

Jakobsson, Peter, and Fredrik Stiernstedt. "Pirates of Silicon Valley: State of Exception and Dispossession in Web 2.0." *First Monday* 15, no. 7 (2010): http://firstmonday.org/ojs/index.php/fm/article/view/2799.

———. "Reinforcing Property by Strengthening the Commons: A New Media Policy Paradigm?" *Triple C: Cognition, Communication, Cooperation* 10, no. 1 (2012): 49–55.

Jenkins, Henry. *Convergence Culture: Where Old and New Media Collide.* New York: New York University Press, 2006.

Jobs, Steve. *Apple Music Special Event: Introducing iTunes.* San Francisco, 2003. Video. www.youtube.com/watch?v=B2n86TROxzY.

Johnson, Bobbie. "Cloud Computing Is a Trap, Warns Gnu Founder Richard Stallman." *Guardian,* Sept. 29, 2008. www.theguardian.com/technology /2008/sep/29/cloud.computing.richard.stallman.

———. "Hackers Break into Spotify." *Guardian,* March 4, 2009. www .theguardian.com/technology/2009/mar/04/online-music-spotify-hacked.

Johnson, Steven. *Interface Culture: How New Technology Transforms the Way We Create and Communicate.* San Francisco: HarperEdge, 1997.

Jones, Christopher. "Open-Source 'Napster' Shut Down." Wired News, March 15, 2000. https://web.archive.org/web/20071019223411/http://www .wired.com/science/discoveries/news/2000/03/34978.

Jones, Steve. "Music That Moves: Popular Music, Distribution, and Network Technologies." *Cultural Studies* 16, no. 2 (2002): 213–32.

Jones, Steve, and Amanda Lenhart. "Music Downloading and Listening: Findings from the Pew Internet and American Life Project." *Popular Music and Society* 27, no. 2 (2004): 185–99.

JupiterMediaMetrix. "Jupiter Media Metrix Reports Multi-country Napster Usage Statistics for February 2001." PR Newswire, March 2001. www .prnewswire.com/news-releases/jupiter-media-metrix-reports-multi-country -napster-usage-statistics-for-february-2001–82340537.html.

Kahney, Leander. *The Cult of Mac.* San Francisco: No Starch Press, 2004.

Kan, Ti. "Take the CD Player to the *n*th Dimension." XMCD, 2004. www.amb .org/xmcd/.

Kaptanis, Arthur. "Should Last a Lifetime Sampling the Latest in Sound." *Globe and Mail,* March 5, 1983, E11.

Karaganis, Joe, ed. *Media Piracy in Emerging Economies.* New York: Social Science Research Council, 2011.

Kassabian, Anahid. "Ubiquitous Listening and Networked Subjectivity." *Echo: A Music-Centered Journal* 3, no. 2 (2001): www.echo.ucla.edu/Volume3 -issue2/kassabian/.

———. *Ubiquitous Listening: Affect, Attention, and Distributed Subjectivity.* Berkeley: University of California Press, 2013.

Katz, Mark. *Capturing Sound: How Technology Has Changed Music.* Berkeley: University of California Press, 2004.

Keightley, Keir. "Low Television, High Fidelity: Taste and the Gendering of Home Entertainment Technologies." *Journal of Broadcasting & Electronic Media* 47, no. 2 (2003): 236–59.

———. "Long Play: Adult-Oriented Popular Music and the Temporal Logics of the Post-War Sound Recording Industry in the USA." *Media, Culture & Society* 26, no. 3 (2004): 375–91.

Kedrosky, Paul. "The Jesus Phone." *Wall Street Journal,* June 29, 2007, A15.

Kelty, Christopher M. *Two Bits: The Cultural Significance of Free Software.* Durham, NC: Duke University Press, 2008.

King, Brad. "EMI Gets Down with Downloads." Wired.com, July 17, 2000a. www.wired.com/techbiz/media/news/2000/07/37561.

———. "Offspring Pirates Napster Gear." Wired.com, June 2, 2000b. www .wired.com/culture/lifestyle/news/2000/06/36733.

Kirkpatrick, David D., and Andrew Ross Sorkin. "Bertelsmann in Deal to Buy Music Start-Up." *New York Times,* May 30, 2001. www.nytimes.com/2001 /05/30/business/bertelsmann-in-deal-to-buy-music-start-up.html.

Kirschenbaum, Matthew G. "Editing the Interface: Textual Studies and First Generation Electronic Objects." *Text* 14 (2002): 15–51.

Kitchin, Rob, and Martin Dodge. *Code/Space: Software and Everyday Life.* Cambridge, MA: MIT Press, 2011.

Klein, Naomi. *No Logo: Taking Aim at the Brand Bullies.* Toronto: Knopf Canada, 2000.

Knopper, Steve. *Appetite for Self-Destruction: The Spectacular Crash of the Record Industry in the Digital Age.* New York: Free Press, 2009.

Kois, Dan. "Beyoncé, Your Mix Tape Sucks: The Perils of iTunes Celebrity Playlists." Slate.com, May 26, 2004. www.slate.com/id/2101245/.

Kopytoff, Igor. "The Cultural Biography of Things: Commoditization as Process." In *The Social Life of Things: Commodities in Cultural Perspective,* edited by Arjun Appadurai, 64–92. New York: Cambridge University Press, 1986.

Kot, Greg. "Who Stole Metallica's Money? Record Companies Are the Culprits, Not Napster Users." *Chicago Tribune,* May 17, 2000.

———. *Ripped: How the Wired Generation Revolutionized Music.* New York: Scribner, 2009.

Kozinets, Robert V. "Can Consumers Escape the Market? Emancipatory Illuminations from Burning Man." *Journal of Consumer Research* 29, no. 1 (June 2002): 20–38.

Krasilovsky, M., and S. Shemel. *This Business of Music.* New York: Billboard Books, 2000.

Kreps, Daniel. "Radiohead Launch 'Nude' Remix Contest." *Rolling Stone,* April 1, 2008. www.rollingstone.com/rockdaily/index.php/2008/04/01/radiohead -launch-nude-remix-contest/.

Krigel, Beth Lipton. "Music Initiative Raises Questions." CNET News, Dec. 16, 1998. http://news.cnet.com/Music-initiative-raises-questions/2100–1023 _3–219163.html?tag=mncol.

Ku, Raymond Shih Ray. "The Creative Destruction of Copyright: Napster and the New Economics of Digital Technology." *University of Chicago Law Review* 69, no. 1 (2002): 263–324.

Kushner, David. "The World's Most Dangerous Geek." RollingStone.com, Jan. 13, 2004. www.rollingstone.com/news/story/5938320/the_worlds _most_dangerous_geek.

Lacher, Kathleen T., and Richard Mizerski. "An Exploratory Study of the Responses and Relationships Involved in the Evaluation of and in the Intention to Purchase New Rock Music." *Journal of Consumer Research* 21, no. 2 (1994): 366–80.

Lamy, Jonathan, Cara Duckworth, and Liz Kennedy. "Worldwide Recording Industry Announces Precedent-Setting Initiative to Address New Digital Music Opportunities." RIAA, Press Release, Dec. 15, 1998. https://web.archive .org/web/20071013221904/http://riaa.com/newsitem.php?news_year_filter= 1998&resultpage=&id=2F25E12D-6941–25B3-E47E-8B80246720EF.

Lange, David. "Taking Music Risks." David Lange Blog, Oct. 16, 2009. http:// mcvaymediarocks.blogspot.com/2009/10/taking-music-risks.html.

Lanxon, Nate. "How to Reset iTunes Match (without Losing Metadata or Playlists)." Wired.co.uk. www.wired.co.uk/news/archive/2012–01/12/how -to-reset-itunes-match.

Lash, Jolie. "Napster Tells Offspring to Cease and Desist." RollingStone.com, June 2, 2000a. www.rollingstone.com/news/story/5922622/napster_tells _offspring_to_cease_and_desist.

————. "The Offspring Bootleg Napster." RollingStone.com, June 1, 2000b. www.rollingstone.com/news/story/5925432/the_offspring_bootleg_napster.

Latour, Bruno. "Mixing Humans and Nonhumans Together: The Sociology of a Door-Closer." *Social Problems* 35, no. 1 (1988): 298–310.

Lazar, Jonathan, Jinjuan Feng, and Harry Hochheiser. *Research Methods in Human-Computer Interaction*. West Sussex: John Wiley and Sons, 2010.

Lazzarato, Maurizio. "Immaterial Labour." In *Radical Thought in Italy*, edited by Paolo Virno and Michael Hardt, 133–47. Minneapolis: University of Minnesota Press, 1996.

Lee, Benjamin, and Edward LiPuma. "Cultures of Circulation: The Imaginations of Modernity." *Public Culture* 14, no. 1 (2002): 191–213.

Leeds, Jeff. "Apple, Digital Music's Angel, Earns Record Industry's Scorn." *New York Times*, August 27, 2005.

Legrand, Emmanuel. "Sony Presses on with SACD (Super Audio CD)." *Billboard*, Sept. 11, 1999, 1.

————. "SACD Trying to Fit In: Format Still Not Fully Established at Retail." *Billboard*, Sept. 25, 2004, 6.

Lemos, Robert. "Access Denied: Companies Fight over CD Listings, Leaving the Public Behind." CNET News, May 24, 2001. https://web.archive.org/web/20071225124659/http://www.news.com/2009–1023–258109.html.

————. "Sightsound.Com to Music Sites: Pay Up!" ZDNet News, Jan. 28, 1999. www.zdnet.com/article/sightsound-com-to-music-sites-pay-up/.

Leonhard, Gerd. *Music 2.0: Essays by Gerd Leonhard*. N.p.: Gerd Leonhard, 2008. http://gerdleonhard.typepad.com/files/music2obook_hires-1.pdf.

Lessig, Lawrence. *Code and Other Laws of Cyberspace*. New York: Basic Books, 1999.

————. *Free Culture: How Big Media Uses Technology and the Law to Lock Down Culture and Control Creativity*. New York: Penguin, 2004.

Levitin, Daniel J. *This Is Your Brain on Music: The Science of a Human Obsession*. New York: Dutton, 2006.

Levy, Stephen. "The iPod Revolution." *Los Angeles Times*, Oct. 22, 2006.

Leyshon, Andrew. "Scary Monsters: Free Software, Peer-to-Peer Networks, and the Spectre of the Gift." *Environment and Planning D: Society and Space* 21, no. 5 (2003): 533–58.

Licklider, J. C. R., and R. W. Taylor. "The Computer as a Communication Device." *Science and Technology* 76 (April 1968): 21–31.

Liebowitz, Stan. "File Sharing: Creative Destruction or Just Plain Destruction?" *Journal of Law and Economics* 49, no. 1 (2006): 1–28.

Lindvall, Helienne. "Behind the Music: Why Won't Grooveshark Remove My Music?" Guardian.com, Dec. 12, 2011. www.theguardian.com/music/musicblog/2011/dec/12/grooveshark-music-site.

Lobato, Ramon. *Shadow Economies of Cinema: Mapping Informal Film Distribution*. London: Palgrave Macmillan/BFI, 2012.

Logie, John. *Peers, Pirates, and Persuasion: Rhetoric in the Peer-to-Peer Debates*. West Lafayette, IN: Parlor, 2006.

Love, Courtney. "Courtney Love Does the Math." Salon.com. www.salon
.com/2000/06/14/love_7/.

Lukács, Georg. "Reification and the Consciousness of the Proletariat." In
History and Class Consciousness: Studies in Marxist Dialectics. Cambridge,
MA: MIT Press, 1971.

MacUser. "Winning Hearts and Minds (and Wallets)." *MacUser,* Jan. 1, 1989, 223.

Maher, Jimmy. *The Future Was Here: The Commodore Amiga.* Cambridge,
MA: MIT Press, 2012.

Mancini, Rob. "Update: Offspring, Napster Reach T-Shirt Accord." MTV.com,
June 5, 2000. www.mtv.com/news/articles/1432578/20000605/offspring
.jhtml.

Manes, Stephen. "Seek and Ye Shall Find—but How?" *PC Magazine,* Jan. 31,
1989, 85.

Mann, Charles C. "The Heavenly Jukebox." *Atlantic,* Sept. 2000, 39–59.

———. "The Year the Music Dies." *Wired,* Feb. 2003. http://archive.wired
.com/wired/archive/11.02/dirge.html.

Manning, Peter. *Electronic and Computer Music.* Oxford: Oxford University
Press, 2004.

Manovich, Lev. *The Language of New Media.* Cambridge, MA: MIT Press, 2001.

———. *Software Takes Command: Extending the Language of New Media.*
New York: Bloomsbury, 2013.

Marriott, Michel. "A Music-Sharing Service That Gets Along with Record
Companies." *New York Times,* Feb. 1, 2001.

Marshall, Lee. "The Effects of Piracy upon the Music Industry: A Case Study of
Bootlegging." *Media, Culture & Society* 26, no. 2 (2004): 163–81.

Martens, Todd. "Overall Music Sales Hit an All-Time High in 2009." Pop &
Hiss: *L.A. Times* Music Blog, Jan. 6, 2010. http://latimesblogs.latimes.com
/music_blog/2010/01/overall-music-purchases-hit-an-alltime-high-in-
2009.html.

Marvin, Carolyn. *When Old Technologies Were New: Thinking about Electric
Communication in the Late Nineteenth Century.* New York: Oxford
University Press, 1988.

Marx, Karl. *Capital.* 1867. Edited by David McLellan. Oxford: Oxford
University Press, 1995.

———. "Capital. Volume 1, Part 1." In *The Marx-Engels Reader,* edited by
C. Tucker Robert, 302–29. New York: Norton, 1978.

Marzorati, Gerald. "How the Album Got Played Out." *New York Times,* Feb. 22,
1998. www.nytimes.com/1998/02/22/magazine/how-the-album-got-
played-out.html.

Mathes, Adam. "Folksonomies—Cooperative Classification and Communication
through Shared Metadata." Dec. 2004. www.adammathes.com/academic
/computer-mediated-communication/folksonomies.html

Mathews, Anna Wilde. "Applause, Applause: What Do Audiences Want?
Entertainment Companies Are Looking for Answers on the Web." *Wall
Street Journal,* Oct. 29, 2001.

Mauss, Marcel. *The Gift: Forms and Functions of Exchange in Archaic Societies.* New York: Norton, 1967.

McCourt, Tom. "Collecting Music in the Digital Realm." *Popular Music and Society* 28, no. 2 (2005): 249–52.

McCourt, Tom, and Patrick Burkart. "When Creators, Corporations and Consumers Collide: Napster and the Development of On-Line Music Distribution." *Media, Culture & Society* 25, no. 3 (2003): 333–50.

McCourt, Tom, and Eric W. Rothenbuhler. "Soundscan and the Consolidation of Control." *Media, Culture & Society* 19, no. 2 (1997): 201–18.

McLeod, Kembrew. "MP3s Are Killing Home Taping: The Rise of Internet Distribution and Its Challenge to the Major Label Music Monopoly." *Popular Music and Society* 28, no. 4 (2005): 521–31.

Meehan, Eileen. "Ratings and the Institutional Approach: A Third Answer to the Commodity Question." *Critical Studies in Mass Communication* 1, no. 2 (1984): 216–25.

———. "Gendering the Commodity Audience: Critical Media Research, Feminism, and Political Economy." In *Sex & Money,* edited by Eileen Meehan and Ellen Riordan, 209–22. Minneapolis: University of Minnesota Press, 2001.

Menn, Joseph. *All the Rave: The Rise and Fall of Shawn Fanning's Napster.* New York: Crown Business, 2003.

Miege, Bernard. "The Cultural Commodity." *Media, Culture & Society* 1, no. 3 (1979): 297–311.

Miller, Rich. "The Billion Dollar Data Centers." Data Center Knowledge, April 29, 2013. www.datacenterknowledge.com/archives/2013/04/29/the -billion-dollar-data-centers/.

Minidisc.org. "MZ-1 Operating Instructions." Minidisc.org, 2009. www .minidisc.org/mz1_manual/cover.html.

Minter, Jeff. "Llamasoft: Home of the Virtual Light Machine and the Minotaur Project Games." 2005. http://minotaurproject.co.uk/vlm.php.

Mitchell, Jared. "Can't Stop the Music." *Globe and Mail,* May 15, 1987, P76.

Mohamed, Arif. "A History of Cloud Computing." *Computer Weekly,* March 27, 2009. www.computerweekly.com/feature/A-history-of-cloud -computing.

Montfort, Nick, and Ian Bogost. *Racing the Beam: The Atari Video Computer System.* Cambridge, MA: MIT Press, 2009.

Moore, Thurston, ed. *Mix Tape: The Art of Cassette Culture.* New York: Universe, 2004.

Morris, Jeremy Wade. "Artists as Entrepreneurs, Fans as Workers." *Popular Music and Society* 37, no. 3 (2013a): 273–90.

———. "Non-practical Entities: Business Method Patents and the Digitization of Culture." *Critical Studies in Media Communication* 31, no. 3 (2013b): 212–29.

———. "Curation by Code: Infomediaries and the Data Mining of Taste." *European Journal of Cultural Studies* 18 (, 18, nos. 4 and 5 (2015).

Morrow, Guy. "Radiohead's Managerial Creativity." *Convergence: The International Journal of Research into New Media Technologies* 15, no. 2 (2009): 161–76.

Mosco, Vincent. *The Political Economy of Communication: Rethinking and Renewal.* Thousand Oaks, CA: Sage, 1996.

"Multimedia Business Analyst." *Business Conference and Management Reports,* 1995.

Murdock, Graham. "Blindspots about Western Marxism: A Reply to Dallas Smythe." *Canadian Journal of Political and Social Theory* 2, no. 2 (1978): 109–19.

Murphy, Jamie, Noor Hazarina Hashim, and Peter O'Connor. "Take Me Back: Validating the Wayback Machine." *Journal of Computer-Mediated Communication* 13, no. 1 (2007): 60–75.

Myspace.com. "MySpace.com Terms of Use Agreement." Myspace, March 17, 2006. https://web.archive.org/web/20060326194533/http://viewmorepics.myspace.com/misc/terms.html?z=1.

Nakamura, Lisa. *Cybertypes: Race, Ethnicity, and Identity on the Internet.* New York: Routledge, 2002.

Napoli, Philip M. "The Audience Product and the New Media Environment: Implications for the Economics of Media Industries." *International Journal on Media Management* 3, no. 2 (2001): 66–73.

———. *Audience Evolution: New Technologies and the Transformation of Media Audiences.* New York: Columbia University Press, 2011.

Napster. "It's Here: Napster V2.0 Is Now Available." Napster.com, Oct. 8, 1999, Internet Archive screengrab. http://web.archive.org/web/19991008215720/http://napster.com/.

———. "Napster/Bertelsmann Q&A." Napster.com, Nov. 9, 2000a, Internet Archive screengrab. http://web.archive.org/web/20001109035400/http://www.napster.com/index.html.

———. "Support Napster!" Napster.com, August 15, 2000b, Internet Archive screengrab. http://web.archive.org/web/20000815053013/http://www.napster.com/.

———. "Terms of Use." Napster.com, Feb. 29, 2000c, Internet Archive screengrab. http://web.archive.org/web/20000229161718/www.napster.com/terms.html.

———. "Napster Is Continuing to Comply." Napster.com, May 3, 2001a, Internet Archive screengrab. http://web.archive.org/web/20010503152752/http://www.napster.com/.

———. "News Flash!" Napster.com, March 22, 2001b, Internet Archive screengrab. http://web.archive.org/web/20010322195829/http://www.napster.com/index.html.

———. "Preview the New Napster." Napster.com, June 2, 2001c, Internet Archive screengrab. http://web.archive.org/web/20010602055307/http://www.napster.com/.

Negus, Keith. *Producing Pop: Culture and Conflict in the Popular Music Industry.* London: Edward Arnold, 1992.

Ness, Laura. "Xing Technology Ships Xingsound Mpeg Audio Compression Software." Business Wire, Oct. 12, 1993. https://global-factiva-com.ezproxy .library.wisc.edu/ha/default.aspx#./!?&_suid=142778034125207716975531 07515.

Newman, Michael. "Patented Attack: Sightsound.com Claims It's Owed a Fee Every Time Music or Videos Are Downloaded from the Web." *Pittsburgh Post-Gazette*, Feb. 7, 1999, F1.

Nguyen, Kim. "Five Major Music Companies and IBM Successfully Complete Electronic Music Distribution Trial." Press Release, Feb. 2, 2000. www-03 .ibm.com/press/us/en/pressrelease/1889.wss.

Nilsson, Martin. "History of ID3 Tags." ID3.org, Dec. 17, 2006a. www.id3.org /History.

———. "ID3 Frames." ID3.org, Dec. 17, 2006b. www.id3.org/Frames.

———. "ID3 Contributors." ID3.org, Jan. 4, 2007. www.id3.org/Contributors.

Nowak, Florence. "Challenging Opportunities: When Indian Regional Music Gets Online." *First Monday* 19, no. 10 (2014): http://firstmonday.org/ojs /index.php/fm/article/view/5547/4126.

NPD. "iTunes Continues to Dominate Music Retailing, but Nearly 60 Percent of iTunes Music Buyers Also Use Pandora." NPD Group, Research Report Press Release, Sept. 18, 2012. www.npd.com/wps/portal/npd/us/news /press-releases/itunes-continues-to-dominate-music-retailing-but-nearly -60-percent-of-itunes-music-buyers-also-use-pandora/.

O'Malley, Chris. "Carmel, Ind.-Based Escient Buys Internet-Based Music Database Firm." *Indianapolis Star and News*, August 13, 1998.

O'Reilly, Tim. "What Is Web 2.0: Design Patterns and Business Models for the Next Generation of Software." O'Reilly Group, Sept. 30, 2005. http://oreilly .com/web2/archive/what-is-web-20.html.

Oberholzer-Gee, Felix, and Koleman Strumpf. "The Effect of File Sharing on Record Sales: An Empirical Analysis." *Journal of Political Economy* 115, no. 1 (2007): 1–42.

Oberschelp, W. "The Sorcerer and the Apprentice: Human-Computer Interaction Today." *AI & Society* 12, no. 1–2 (1998): 97–104.

Olsen, Stefanie. "Will Instant Messaging Become Instant Spamming?" CNET News, Oct. 26, 2001. http://news.cnet.com/2100–1023–252765.html.

OneJ1Way. "Napster? Charging? What? No Way!" Winamp User Forum, Jan. 30, 2001. http://forums.winamp.com/showthread.php?t=40691&highli ght=Napster+Sell.

Orlowski, Andrew. "Your 99c Belong to the RIAA—Steve Jobs." *Register*, Nov. 7, 2003. www.theregister.co.uk/2003/11/07/your_99c_belong/.

Oudshoorn, Nelly, and T. J. Pinch. *How Users Matter: The Co-construction of Users and Technologies*. Cambridge, MA: MIT Press, 2003.

Paine, Andre. "Spotify Hit by Licensing Restrictions." Billboard.com, Jan. 29, 2009. www.billboard.com/biz/articles/news/global/1275407/spotify-hit-by -licensing-restrictions.

Palenchar, Joseph. "Waveform Analysis to Boost Appeal of CDDB Database." *TWICE: This Week in Consumer Electronics,* June 17, 2002, 38.

Pandey, Swati. "Sales Secondary in the Business Model." *Los Angeles Times,* July 5, 2008.

Parameswaran, Manoj, Anjana Susarla, and Andrew B. Whinston. "P2P Networking: An Information-Sharing Alternative." *Computer* 34, no. 7 (2001): 31–38.

Paul, Ian. "What MegaUpload's Demise Teaches about Cloud Storage." *PCWorld,* Jan. 20, 2012. www.pcworld.com/article/248461/what_megauploads_demise _teaches_about_cloud_storage.html.

Petzinger, Thomas. "Two Entrepreneurs Try to Turn Net Patent into a Blockbuster." *Wall Street Journal,* May 7, 1999.

Petzold, Charles. "Putting Sound on PCs: An Introduction to Waveform Audio." *PC Magazine,* Nov. 12, 1991.

Piatier, André. "Transectorial Innovations and the Transformation of Firms." *Information Society* 5, no. 4 (1987/88): 205–31.

Pinch, Trevor, and Frank Trocco. "The Social Construction of the Early Electronic Music Synthesizer." In *Music and Technology in the Twentieth Century,* edited by Hans-Joachim Braun, 67–83. Baltimore: Johns Hopkins University Press, 2002.

Platoni, Kara. "Pandora's Box: Can a Company's Musicological Data Mining Breathe New Life into the Music Industry?" *East Bay Express,* Jan. 11, 2006.

Pletz, John. "Escient Set to Light the Afterburners." *Indianapolis Business Journal,* Nov. 30, 1998.

Poblocki, Kacper. "The Napster Network Community." *First Monday* 6, no. 11 (2001): http://firstmonday.org/ojs/index.php/fm/article/view/899/808.

Pohlmann, Ken C. *The Compact Disc Handbook.* Madison, WI: A-R Editions, 1992.

Poster, Mark. *The Mode of Information: Poststructuralism and Social Context.* Chicago: University of Chicago Press, 1990.

Potts, Daniel. "ID3 Tags Demystified." *Australian PC World,* Oct. 1, 2002, 140.

Powers, Devon. "Lost in the Shuffle: Technology, History, and the Idea of Musical Randomness." *Critical Studies in Media Communication* 31, no. 3 (2014): 244–64.

Preece, Jenny, Yvonne Rogers, Helen Sharp, David Benyon, Simon Holland, and Tom Carey. *Human-Computer Interaction.* Essex: Addison-Wesley Longman, 1994.

Pride, Dominic. "U.K. Bands Attack Convention Thru Internet." *Billboard,* August 6, 1994, 3.

Prince. "*Crystal Ball* Announcement." Oct. 16, 1997, Internet Archive screen-grab. http://web.archive.org/web/19980130101812/love4oneanother.com /future.htm#cbsite.

Privacy Commissioner. "Reaching for the Cloud(S): Privacy Issues Related to Cloud Computing." Ottawa: Office of the Privacy Commissioner of Canada, 2010. www.priv.gc.ca/information/pub/cc_201003_e.cfm

Pytlik, Mark. "Radiohead in Rainbows: 9.3." Pitchfork Media, Oct. 15, 2007. http://pitchfork.com/reviews/albums/10785-in-rainbows/.

Rawsthorn, Alice. "IBM Lays Groundwork for Digital System." *Financial Times,* August 11, 1998.

Razlagova, Elena. "The Past and Future of Music Listening: Between Freeform DJs and Recommendation Algorithms." In *Radio's New Wave: Global Sound in the Digital Era,* edited by Jason Loviglio and Michele Hilmes, 62–76. New York: Routledge, 2013.

Reece, Doug. "CuteMX/Napster: The Next Big Thing in MP3?" MP3.com, Nov. 3, 1999. Internet Archive screengrab. http://web.archive.org /web/20000817083047/http://www.mp3.com/news/421.html.

Reiss, Randy, and Chris Nelson. "Fans Expose Crack in the Artist's *Crystal Ball.*" VH1.com. www.vh1.com/artists/news/150038/03251998/prince.jhtml.

Reppel, Alexander E., Isabelle Szmigin, and Thorsten Gruber. "The iPod Phenomenon: Identifying a Market Leader's Secrets through Qualitative Marketing Research." *Journal of Product and Brand Management* 15, no. 4 (2006): 239–49.

Rheingold, Howard. *The Virtual Community: Homesteading on the Electronic Frontier.* New York: HarperPerennial, 1994.

Rhody, Jason. "Game Fiction: Playing the Interface in Prince of Persia: The Sands of Time and Asheron's Call." Paper presented at the DiGRA 2005 conference Changing Views—Worlds in Play, Vancouver, BC, June 16–20, 2005. www.digra.org/wp-content/uploads/digital-library/06276.06108.pdf.

Rich, Laura, and Hane Lee. "Analysis: Napsterization: Music Was Just the Beginning." CNN.com, July 19, 2000. http://archives.cnn.com/2000/TECH /computing/07/19/movies.v.napster.idg/.

Robinson, Laura, and David Halle. "Digitization, the Internet, and the Arts: Ebay, Napster, Sag, and E-Books." *Qualitative Sociology* 25, no. 3 (2002): 359–83.

Rogers, Yvonne, Helen Sharp, and Jenny Preece. *Interaction Design: Beyond Human-Computer Interaction.* West Sussex: John Wiley and Sons, 2011.

Rose, Frank. "Secret Websites, Coded Messages: The New World of Immersive Games." *Wired,* Dec. 20, 2007. http://archive.wired.com/entertainment /music/magazine/16–01/ff_args.

Rosen, Nick. "Internet Gives a Break to Budding Pop Stars." *Sunday Times (London),* August 7, 1994.

Rothenberg, Randall. "Rob Glaser, Moving Target." *Wired,* August 1999. http://archive.wired.com/wired/archive/7.08/glaser.html.

Rothenbuhler, Eric W. "The Compact Disc and Its Culture: Notes on Melancholia." In *Cultural Technologies: The Shaping of Culture in Media and Society,* edited by Göran Bolin, 36–50. New York: Routledge, 2012.

Rothenbuhler, Eric W., and John Durham Peters. "Defining Phonography: An Experiment in Theory." *Musical Quarterly* 81, no. 2 (1997): 242–64.

Ryzic, Melena. "Radiohead Fans, Guided by Conscience." *New York Times,* Oct. 4, 2007.

Saffo, Paul. "Multimedia: Seeing Is Deceiving." *Personal Computing,* August 1, 1989, 2.

Sandman2012. "Winamp Equalizer." Winamp User Forum. May 28, 2002. http://forums.winamp.com/showthread.php?t=89148&highlight=Equalizer.

Sandoval, Greg. "Q&A: A Front-Row Seat for Media's Meltdown." CNET News, Oct. 27, 2009. http://news.cnet.com/8301–31001_3–10383572–261 .html.

Scanlon, Jessie Holliday, and Brad Wieners. "The Internet Cloud." Computerworld, July 16, 1999. www.computerworld.com.au/article/104942/guest_column _internet_cloud/.

Schiller, Dan. *How to Think about Information.* Urbana: University of Illinois Press, 2007.

Schmidt, Eric, and Danny Sullivan. "Conversation with Eric Schmidt Hosted by Danny Sullivan." Search Engine Strategies Conference, San Jose, CA, August 9, 2006. www.google.com/press/podium/ses2006.html.

Schwartz, Evan I. "Multimedia Is Here, and It's Amazing." *Businessweek,* Dec. 15, 1991, 130–31. www.bloomberg.com/bw/stories/1991–12–15 /multimedia-is-here-and-its-amazing.

Schwartz, Hillel. *The Culture of the Copy: Striking Likenesses, Unreasonable Facsimiles.* New York: Zone, 1996.

Scott, B. "A Contemporary History of Digital Journalism." *Television & New Media* 6, no. 1 (2005): 89–126.

Scott, Michael. "Cultural Entrepreneurs, Cultural Entrepreneurship: Music Producers Mobilising and Converting Bourdieu's Alternative Capitals." *Poetics* 40, no. 3 (2012): 237–55.

Segal, David. "Pop Notes." *Washington Post,* June 7, 2000, C5.

Shao, Maria, Richard Brandt, Neil Gross, and John Verity. "It's a PC, It's a TV— It's Multimedia." *Business Week,* Oct. 9, 1989, 152–66.

Sherburne, Philip. "Digital Djing App That Pulls You In." *Grooves* 10, no. 1 (2003): 46–47.

Sherwin, Adam. "Free U2 Album: How the Most Generous Giveaway in Music History Turned PR Disaster." *Independent,* Sept. 19, 2014. www.independent .co.uk/arts-entertainment/music/features/free-u2-album-how-the-most -generous-giveaway-in-music-history-turned-into-a-pr-disaster-9745028 .html.

———. "Spotify Answers Thom Yorke Attacks by Revealing '$0.006 per Play' Royalties Figure." *Independent,* Dec. 3, 2013. www.independent.co.uk/life -style/gadgets-and-tech/spotify-answers-thom-yorke-attacks-by-revealing -0006-per-play-royalties-figure-8980274.html.

Shugold, Mark. "Classical Music in Small Bytes: The Promise and Problems of Online Downloads." *Andante,* Oct. 16, 2005.

SightSound. "It's Launch Time ... SightSound Technologies was First to Electronically Sell a Music Download via the Internet." SightSound Technologies. Screengrab, Sept. 27, 1995. www.sightsound.com/?page_id=489.

Singel, Ryan. "Amazon, Dropbox, Google and You Win in Cloud-Music Copyright Decision." Wired.com, August 22, 2011. www.wired.com /epicenter/2011/08/cloudmusic-is-not-a-crime/.

Singer, Michelle. "Roll over Beethoven: iTunes' New Standard." AP/CBS News, Jan. 9, 2007. www.cbsnews.com/stories/2007/01/09/ces/main2339906 .shtml.

Sisario, Ben. "As Music Streaming Grows, Royalties Slow to a Trickle." *New York Times*, Jan. 28, 2013. www.nytimes.com/2013/01/29/business/media /streaming-shakes-up-music-industrys-model-for-royalties.html.

Smith, Adam. *The Wealth of Nations*. 1776. London: J. M. Dent and Sons, 1977.

Smith, Gene. *Tagging: People-Powered Metadata for the Social Web*. Berkeley, CA: New Riders, 2008.

Smith, Marc A., and Peter Kollock, eds. *Communities in Cyberspace*. New York: Routledge, 1999.

Smith, Tony. "IBM's Project Madison: The Music Industry's Manhattan Project?" *Register*, Feb. 9, 1999. www.theregister.co.uk/1999/02/09/ibms _project_madison_the_music/

Smythe, Dallas W. "On the Audience Commodity and Its Work." In *Media and Cultural Studies: Keyworks*, edited by M. G. Durham and Douglas Kellner, 253–79. Oxford: Blackwell, 1981.

Somogyi, Stephan. "Burn, Baby, Burn." *Macworld*, Sept. 1, 1998, 91.

"Sony Corp of America to Acquire Gracenote." *Wall Street Journal*, April 23, 2008. www.wsj.com/articles/SB120896517919638433.

"Sony, Philips Agree on CD Text Function." Reuters, June 5, 1996. https:// global-factiva-com.ezproxy.library.wisc.edu/ha/default.aspx#./!?&_suid= 1427810499648037147426861333832.

Sorrel, Charlie. "So Long, and Thanks for All the Cash: Yahoo Shuts Down Music Store and DRM Servers." Wired.com, July 25, 2008. www.wired.com /gadgetlab/2008/07/so-long-and-tha/.

Spitz, David, and Starling D. Hunter. "Contested Codes: The Social Construction of Napster." *Information Society* 21 (2005): 169–80.

Spotify. "Spotify Hits 10 Million Global Subscribers." May 21, 2014. https://press .spotify.com/us/2014/05/21/spotify-hits-10-million-global-subscribers/.

Stahl, Matt, and Leslie M. Meier. "The Firm Foundation of Organizational Flexibility: The 360 Contract in the Digitalizing Music Industry." *Canadian Journal of Communication* 37, no. 3 (2012): 441–58.

Stern, Monika. "Mi Wantem Musik Blong Mi Hemi Blong Evriwan" [I want my music to be for everyone]: Digital Developments, Copyright, and Music Circulation in Port Vila, Vanuatu." *First Monday* 19, no. 10 (2014): http:// firstmonday.org/ojs/index.php/fm/article/view/5551/4130.

Sterne, Jonathan. "The Death and Life of Digital Audio." *Interdisciplinary Science Reviews* 31, no. 4 (2006a): 338–48.

———. "The MP3 as Cultural Artifact." *New Media & Society* 8, no. 5 (2006b): 825–42.

————. "Out with the Trash: On the Future of New Media." In *Residual Media,* edited by Charles R. Acland, 16–31. Minneapolis: University of Minnesota Press, 2007.

————. *MP3: The Meaning of a Format.* Durham, NC: Duke University Press, 2012.

Steuer, Eric. "The Infinite Album." *Wired,* Sept. 2006, 172–75. http://archive .wired.com/wired/archive/14.09/beck.html.

Stone, Brad. "Amazon Erases Orwell Books." *New York Times,* July 17, 2009.

————. "A Dream for Music, but Labels' Nightmare." *New York Times,* March 12, 2010.

Strauss, Neil. "A Prolific Recording Artist Tries to Remake the Music Business through the Internet." *New York Times,* August 4, 1997.

Straw, Will. "Music as Commodity and Material Culture." *Repercussions* 7–8 (Spring-Fall 2002): 147–72.

————. "In Memoriam: The Music CD and Its Ends." *Design and Culture* 1, no. 1 (2009): 79–92.

Streeter, Thomas. *The Net Effect: Romanticism, Capitalism, and the Internet.* New York: NYU Press, 2010.

Striphas, Ted. "Disowning Commodities: Ebooks, Capitalism, and Intellectual Property Law." *Television & New Media* 7, no. 3 (2006): 231–60.

————. *The Late Age of Print: Everyday Book Culture from Consumerism to Control.* New York: Columbia University Press, 2009.

————. "The Abuses of Literacy: Amazon Kindle and the Right to Read." *Communication and Critical/Cultural Studies* 7, no. 3 (2010): 297–317.

Styvén, Maria. "The Intangibility of Music in the Internet Age." *Popular Music and Society* 30, no. 1 (2007): 53–74.

Suhr, H. Cecilia. *Social Media and Music: The Digital Field of Cultural Production.* New York: Peter Lang, 2012.

Sullivan, Jennifer. "Napster: Music Is for Sharing." Wired.com, Nov. 1, 1999a. www.wired.com/print/science/discoveries/news/1999/11/32151.

————. "RIAA Suing Upstart Startup." Wired.com, Nov. 15, 1999b. www .wired.com/techbiz/media/news/1999/11/32559.

Swartz, A. "Musicbrainz: A Semantic Web Service." *Intelligent Systems, IEEE* 17, no. 1 (2002): 76–77.

Takahashi, Corey. "Capitol Plans to Be First Major Label to Sell Pop Song On-Line, Then in Stores." *Wall Street Journal,* Sept. 5, 1997.

Taussig, Michael T. *Mimesis and Alterity: A Particular History of the Senses.* New York: Routledge, 1993.

Taylor, Bryan C., Christof Demont-Heinrich, Kirsten J. Broadfoot, Jefferson Dodge, and Cuowei Jiana. "New Media and the Circuit of Cyber Culture: Conceptualizing Napster." *Journal of Broadcasting and Electronic Media* 46, no. 4 (2002): 607–29.

Taylor, Chris. "Best Inventions 2003: The 99¢ Solution." *Time,* Nov. 16, 2003, 66–69.

Taylor, Timothy Dean. "The Commodification of Music at the Dawn of the Era of 'Mechanical Music.'" *Ethnomusicology* 51, no. 2 (2007): 281–305.

Tedesco, Richard. "AOL Stakes out Net Music Turf." *Broadcasting & Cable,* June 7, 1999, 44.

Tench, Megan. "Napster Fans Say They're Taking Moral High Ground." *Toronto Star,* March 11, 2001, F2.

Terranova, Tiziana. *Network Culture: Politics for the Information Age.* Ann Arbor, MI: Pluto, 2004.

Théberge, Paul. *Any Sound You Can Imagine: Making Music/Consuming Technology.* Hanover, NH: Wesleyan University Press, 1997.

Thibaud, Jean Paul. "The Sonic Composition of the City." In *The Auditory Culture Reader,* edited by Michael Bull and Les Back, 329–42. Oxford: Berg, 2003.

Thomson, Kristin, and Brian Zisk. "iTunes and Digital Downloads: An Analysis." Future of Music Coalition, June 15, 2003. www.futureofmusic .org/article/article/itunes-and-digital-downloads-analysis.

Trachtenberg, Jeffrey A. "How Philips Flubbed Its U.S. Introduction of Electronic Product." *Wall Street Journal,* June 28, 1996a.

———. "Sony, Unfazed by Flops, Rolls out Minidisc for Third Time in U.S." *Wall Street Journal,* July 24, 1996b.

Traiman, Steve. "DVD Audio: The Next Chapter." *Billboard,* August 28, 1999, 84.

Tryon, Chuck. "New Media Studies and the New Internet Cinema." *University of Michigan Library* 5, no. 1 (2007): 1–15.

Tsioulcas, Anastasia. "Classical Retail's New Composition." *Billboard,* May 12, 2007, 36.

Tsurushima, Katsuaki, Tadao Yoshida, Kazuhiko Fujiie, Kenzo Akagiri, and David H. Kawakami. "Minidisc: Disc-Based Digital Recording for Portable Audio Applications." In *Collected Papers on Digital Audio Bit-Rate Reduction,* edited by N. Gilchrist and C. Grewin, 190–96. New York: Audio Engineering Society, 1996.

Turkle, Sherry. *The Second Self: Computers and the Human Spirit.* New York: Simon and Schuster, 1984.

———. *Life on the Screen: Identity in the Age of the Internet.* New York: Simon and Schuster, 1995.

Turner, Fred. "Where the Counterculture Met the New Economy: The Well and the Origins of Virtual Community." *Technology and Culture* 46 (2005): 485–512.

———. *From Counterculture to Cyberculture: Stewart Brand, the Whole Earth Network, and the Rise of Digital Utopianism.* Chicago: University of Chicago Press, 2006.

———. *The Democratic Surround: Multimedia and American Liberalism from World War II to the Psychedelic Sixties.* Chicago: University of Chicago Press, 2013.

Turow, Joseph. *Niche Envy: Marketing Discrimination in the Digital Age.* Cambridge, MA: MIT Press, 2006.

————. *The Daily You: How the New Advertising Industry Is Defining Your Identity and Your World.* New Haven, CT: Yale University Press, 2011.

Uricchio, William. "The Algorithmic Turn: Photosynth, Augmented Reality, and the Changing Implications of the Image." *Visual Studies* 26, no. 1 (2011): 25–35.

Urquhart, James. "Can Pirate Bay's New Cloud Business Model Succeed?" CNET News, July 18, 2009. www.cnet.com/news/can-pirate-bays-new-cloud-business-model-succeed/.

USPTO. "USPTO White Paper—Automated Business Methods—Section III Class 705." July 4, 2009. www.uspto.gov/patents/resources/methods/afmdpm/class705.jsp.

Vaidhyanathan, Siva. *Copyrights and Copywrongs: The Rise of Intellectual Property and How It Threatens Creativity.* New York: New York University Press, 2003.

Valence, Nikos. "Patents Pending." *CFO, The Magazine for Senior Financial Executives,* Sept. 22, 2000, 83.

Van Buskirk, Eliot. "Listening Post: Gracenote Defends Its Evolution." Wired News, Nov. 13, 2006. http://archive.wired.com/entertainment/music/commentary/listeningpost/2006/11/72105?currentPage=all .

————. "Radiohead Blows Off iTunes, Sells Full Albums in MP3 Format." Wired.com, Sept. 17, 2007a. https://web.archive.org/web/20090522112752/http://www.wired.com/listening_post/2007/09/radiohead-blows/

————. "Radiohead Makes Business Plans the New Punk Rock." Wired.com, Dec. 12, 2007b. www.wired.com/entertainment/music/commentary/listeningpost/2007/12/listeningpost_1210.

————. "Radiohead's *In Rainbows* Outsold Previous Albums Despite Giveaway." Wired.com, Oct. 16, 2008a. http://blog.wired.com/music/2008/10/radioheads-in-r.html.

————. "Yahoo: We'll Reimburse Users for Terminated Music." Wired.com, July 28, 2008b. https://web.archive.org/web/20090819231539/http://www.wired.com/listening_post/2008/07/yahoo-to-reimbu/.

————. "Ten Years after Napster, Music Industry Still Faces the (Free) Music." Wired.com, Oct. 26, 2009. www.wired.com/epicenter/2009/10/ten-years-after-napster-music-industry-still-faces-the-free-music/.

Vanderbilt, Tom. "Data Center Overload." *New York Times,* June 14, 2009.

van Dijck, José. "Facebook as a Tool for Producing Sociality and Connectivity." *Television & New Media* 13, no. 2 (2011): 160–76.

————. "Users like You? Theorizing Agency in User-Generated Content." *Media, Culture & Society* 31, no. 1 (2009): 41–58.

Varanini, Giancarlo. "Q&A: Napster Creator Shawn Fanning." ZDNet News, March 3, 2003. www.zdnet.com/news/q-a-napster-creator-shawn-fanning/96066.

Vellucci, Sherry L. "Metadata for Music." *Fontes Artis Musicae* 46, no. 3/4 (1999): 205–17.

Venkatesh, Alladi. "Computers and Other Interactive Technologies for the Home." *Communications of the ACM* 39, no. 12 (1996): 47–54.

Venkatesh, Alladi, and Nicholas Vitalari. "A Post-Adoption Analysis of Computing in the Home." *Journal of Economic Psychology* 8 (1987): 161–80.

Wallach, Jeremy. "The Poetics of Electrosonic Presence: Recorded Music and the Materiality of Sound." *Journal of Popular Music Studies* 15, no. 1 (2003): 34–64.

Wark, McKenzie. "Information Wants to Be Free (but Is Everywhere in Chains)." *Cultural Studies* 20, no. 2–3 (2006): 165–83.

Wellman, Barry. *Networks in the Global Village: Life in Contemporary Communities.* Boulder, CO: Westview Press, 1999.

White, Michele. *The Body and the Screen: Theories of Internet Spectatorship.* Cambridge, MA: MIT Press, 2006.

Whitehead, Jonathan. "Second Declaration of Jonathan Whitehead." Recording Industry Association of America (Plaintiff) v. Verizon Internet Services (Defendant), Court Declaration, August 26, 2003. www.docstoc.com /docs/165845649/Declaration-of-Jonathan-Whitehead-in-Support.

Wickre, Karen. "Get Music at Net.now." *Computer Life,* March 1, 1995, 60.

Wikström, Patrik. *The Music Industry: Music in the Cloud.* Cambridge: Polity, 2009.

———. "Music Firms Can No Longer Afford to Stonewall Online Innovators." *Reluctantly Virtual,* March, 15 2010. https://musicinthecloud.wordpress .com/2010/03/15/music-firms-can-no-longer-afford-to-stonewall-online -innovators/

Williamson, John, and Martin Cloonan. "Rethinking the Music Industry." *Popular Music* 26, no. 2 (2007): 305–22.

Willis, Susan. *A Primer for Daily Life.* London: Routledge, 1991.

Wilson, Kim. "Escient TuneBase 2000i Music Server." Audio Visual Revolution, Feb. 1, 2000. www.avrev.com/home-theater-feature-articles/best-of-top -100-lists/avrev.coms-best-of-2000-list.html.

Winamp. "Advertising Information." Winamp.com, Dec. 12, 1998, Internet Archive screengrab. http://web.archive.org/web/19990218062248/www .winamp.com/ads/.

———. "Winamp Change Log: What's New in Winamp 2.11." Software changelog, 1997–99. https://web.archive.org/web/19990422173945/http:// winamp.com/winamp/newfeatures.html.

Woodworth, Griffin Mead. "Hackers, Users, and Suits: Napster and Representations of Identity." *Popular Music and Society* 27, no. 2 (2004): 161–84.

Xiph. "What's in a Name?" Xiph.org, 2009. http://xiph.org/xiphname.

Zentner, Alejandro. "Measuring the Effect of File Sharing on Music Purchases." *Journal of Law and Economics* 49, no. 1 (2006): 63–90.

———. "Online Sales, Internet Use, File Sharing, and the Decline of Retail Music Specialty Stores." *Information Economics and Policy* 20, no. 3 (2008): 288–300.

"Ziggy on CD-ROM." Media Monitor, July 15, 1994. https://global-factiva
  .com.ezproxy.library.wisc.edu/ha/default.aspx#./!?&_suid=1427860700336
  010656818374991417.
Zittrain, Jonathan. *The Future of the Internet and How to Stop It.* New Haven,
  CT: Yale University Press, 2008.

Index

Page numbers followed by 'f' indicate figures and by 'n' indicate notes.

a2b, 40
AAC (Advanced Audio Coding), 3, 40, 141–42, 144, 186
Acland, Charles, 135–36
AC Nielsen, 99
A.D.D. Marketing, 125–26
Advanced Audio Coding (AAC), 3, 40, 141–42, 144, 186
advertising. *See* marketing
Aerosmith, xvi*f*, 131
aesthetics, 55, 185
album art, 91
AlbumDirect (Project Madison) (IBM), xvii*f*, 137–38
albums, 64
algorithmic commodities, 203–4
algorithmic effects, 203–4
Altec-Lansing, 53
Amazon, 144, 153, 221n4; Cloud Drive, 172–74, 188; as infomediary, 202; iTunes Match, 186; Kindle, 144, 181, 221n4; music streaming services, 179; one-click technology, 220n8
Amazon.com, 135, 137
Amiga, 36
anarcho-communism, 103–4
Anderson, Chris, 153, 156
Anderson, Tim J., 151, 153

Andersson, Jonas, 128–29
Andrejevic, Mark, 119
anticonsumerism, 218n4
"anytime, anywhere" music, 167
AOL, 32, 45–46, 62, 216n4
Appadurai, Arjun, 9–10
Apple, 25, 36, 92, 129, 132; community building, 159; "Definitive 80s" playlist, 160; FairPlay, 141–45; feature artists, 220n9; file formats, 220n6; iCloud, 174, 188; iMixes, 159–60, 162, 197; iPad, 164; iPhone, 9, 164, 181–82; iPod, xvii*f*, 129, 142, 146, 163–64, 184, 187; iPod Touch, 164, 181–82; iTunes. *See* iTunes; marketing campaigns, 145; "99¢ solution," 151–52, 155–56, 164; one-click technology, 220n8; playlists, 160; pricing, 151–56; questionable practices, 186–87; "Rip, Mix, Burn" campaign, 141
Apple Store, 147
Application Programming Interfaces, 200
applications (apps), 201
Argentina, 98
art: album art, 91; computer art, 54–55
artists: Bauhaus artists, 216n1; as cultural entrepreneurs, 205; feature

artists, 220n9. *See also specific artists*
Atari, 36, 55
AT&T, 40
Atwood, Brett, 43
audience, institutionally effective, 101
audience participation, 100–101; audience measurement, 119–28; customer-relations management (CRM), 144, 180
audio-enabled drives, 35
audio files, 3
Audio Fingerprinting, 91
AudioNet, xvif, 178
audio quality, 53–54
Audiostocker, 53
audiotape, 21
aura, 215n3
AutoRun, 217n4

Bandcamp, 209
Barnes, Kevin, 192–93, 205–6
Barry, Hank, 108–9, 129
Bauhaus artists, 216n1
Beam-It, 178
Beats, 174
Berliner records, 21
Berry, David, 19
Bertelsmann (BMG), 97, 107, 109–10, 137–38, 167, 219n1
Best Buy, xviif, 7, 97
beta testers, 111
BigChampagne, 96, 120–23, 125, 128, 195, 202
Big Culture, 203
Big Data, 203
Billboard, 37, 43, 120, 161
Billboard Radio Monitor, 122
BitTorrent, 122, 125–26, 129, 198
Bjork, 201
"black hat" hackers, 102
black market, 169–70
Blockbuster, 7
BMG (Bertelsmann), 97, 107, 109–10, 137–38, 167, 219n1
Boldyrev, Dmitry, 216n3
the Born Ruffians, 152

Bose, 53
Boston, 53
Bourdieu, Pierre, 78
Bowie, David, 75
Bowie at the Beeb, 90
Bragg, Billy, 183–84
Braman, Sandra, 138
branding, 94–95
Brazil, 98
BroadcastDataSystem, 120
burning, 36–37
business method patents, 219n2
business models, 209–10
buycott, 109

California, 26–27
Canada, 200–201
capitalism, digital, 153
Capitol Records, 122, 137
Casady & Greene, 220n7
cataloguing, 78
CBS, 221n2
CD Baby, 155
CD burners, 36–37
cdda2wav, xvif, 36–37
CDDB (Compact Disc Database), 8, 22–24, 27, 67–73, 77, 90–91, 194–95, 202, 217n1; CDDB2, 84–85; Classical Music Initiative, 80; fields, 78–79; founding, 217n3; user contributions, 83–89
CDDB Online, xviif, xvif
CD-I, 217n6
CD-Key, 90
CDNow, 132, 136, 219n1
CD players, 35, 74
CD-ROM discs or CD-ROMs, xvif, 36, 42
CD-ROM drives, 35–38
CD-ROM Professional, 37
CDs (compact discs), 2–3, 13–14, 21, 35, 47–48; burning, 36–37; buycott of, 109; CD-ROM discs or CD-ROMs, xvif, 36, 42; counterfeit, 169–70; enhanced, 77; mega-CD changers, 66; metadata for, 74; mixed CDs, 64, 91; packaging, 74; Red Book Standard

for, 70–71; as storage devices, 170; Super Audio CDs (SACD), 76

CD-Text, 75–76

celebrity mixes, 220n11

celebrity playlists, 159, 220n11

Cerberus, xvif, 137, 139–40, 145

Cercure, 137

Cerf, Vint, 172

the Charlatans, 208

Chion, Michel, 55–56

chronology, xvif–xviif

Chun, Wendy, 118

classical music, 79–80

Classical Music Initiative (CDDB), 80

Clear Channel, 122

ClickReward, 135

cloud computing, 22, 25–26, 166–91; music services, 8, 167–68, 177–85; storage formations, 169–77; time line, xviif

Cloud Drive (Amazon), 172–74, 188

code, 197–98

codejects, 88

coders, 102

collections of music, 187–90, 215n5

Columbia House, 167

commodities: algorithmic, 203–4; cultural, 10; cybernetic, 201–3; digital, 29, 205–13; digital music, 1–29; music, 9–11; reaggregated, 158–63

commodity communities, 105–12, 128

commodity fetishism, 9–10

communities: of circulation, 112–19; commodity, 105–12, 128; virtual, 108–9

community building, 159

Compact Disc Database (CDDB), 8, 22–24, 27, 67–73, 77, 90–91, 194–95, 202, 217n1; CDDB2, 84–85; Classical Music Initiative, 80; fields, 78–79; founding, 217n3; user contributions, 83–89

compact discs (CDs), 2–3, 13–14, 21, 35, 47–48; burning, 36–37; buycott of, 109; CD players, 35, 74; CD-ROM discs or CD-ROMs, xvif, 36, 42; counterfeit, 169–70; enhanced, 77; mega-CD changers, 66; metadata for, 74; mixed CDs, 64, 91; packaging, 74; Red Book Standard for, 70–71; as storage devices, 170; Super Audio CDs (SACD), 76

Compaq, 42

CompuServe, 131

computer art, 54–55

computer industry, 33–34

computer music, 35–36

computers, 203–4; human-computer interaction (HCI), 17, 219n9; personal computers, 35; romantic framing of, 44–45

consciousness, false, 9

contingency, 181–83

contracts, "360 deals," 164

cookies, 220n8

copyright infringement, 123–24, 216n3; Digital Millennium Copyright Act (DMCA), xvif, 27–28; intellectual property, 220n7; rights of musicians, 183–84; rights of users, 184

copyright policy, 109–10

costs, 206–7

cracked software, 54–55

Creative Commons, 104

CreativeWave Studio, 30–31

CRM (customer-relations management), 144, 180

crowd-sourcing, 208–9

Crystal Ball (Prince), 6–8, 132, 193, 199

cultural commodities, 10

cultural entrepreneurs, 205

cultural ownership, 157

culture, 198–205

curation, 186–87, 203–4. *See also* metadata

customer-relations management (CRM), 144, 180

cybernetic commodities, 201–3

Cydia, 205

dance music, 204

data. *See* metadata

databases, 203–4

data-mining, 126

Dee, 53
definition, 216n5
"Definitive 80s" playlist (Apple), 160
demoparties, 54–55
demoscene, 54–55
Denmark, 98
descriptive metadata, 77–83
The Desktop Multimedia Bible (Angell and Heslop), 38
Diamond MX-300, 53
digital capitalism, 153
digital commodities, 29, 205–13
digital distribution, 131
digital downloads, 132
digital enclosures, 119–20
digital file(s), 14–15, 120
digital metadata, 69–70, 77, 88. *See also* metadata
Digital Millennium Copyright Act (DMCA), xvi*f*, 27–28
digital music, 14, 30–65, 195–96; interface for, 16–22, 46–61, 197–98, 212; market for, 132–33; metadata for. *See* metadata; promise of, 205–13; time line, xvi*f*–xvii*f*
digital music commodity, 1–29, 192–98; as local, 168; re-tuning, 60–65; usability of, 140–41
digital retail, 131–65
digital revolution, 64
digital rights management (DRM), 138–45, 158, 180, 195–96, 219n3
digital signatures, 142–43
digitization, 1–2, 12–14, 19, 22–29, 199, 220n10
Dion, Celine, 152
disaggregation, 158–59
distribution, 131, 140–41; cloud-based services, 177–85; digital, 131, 179; release strategies, 6–8, 132, 186–87, 192–93, 201; streaming services, 27, 154, 177, 179, 207
DMCA (Digital Millennium Copyright Act), xvi*f*, 27–28
Doe, Jane (nycfashiongirl), 123–24
Dolby, 40
Do Make Say Think, 80

Dr. Dre, 94
Dreamworks Records, 166
Drew, Rob, 159–60
DRM (digital rights management), 138–45, 158, 180, 195–96, 219n3
drums, Roland TR-808, 204
Dublin Core Metadata Initiative, 70
Duran Duran, 137
DVD-Audio (DVD-A) standard, 76
DVD Group, 76
Dylan, Bob, 152

The EchoNest, 202
ECM, 137
economies: gift, 20, 119; long-tail, 153–54; pay-what-you-want, 161, 208–9; platform, 84; shadow, 126
Eddie Bauer, 42
Edelstein, Neal, 201
Edison cylinders, 21
egalitarianism, 152–53, 155
Elberse, Anita, 153
"Electric Barbarella" (Duran Duran), 137
Ellipse (Heap), 208
Ellison, Larry, 172
EMI, 137–38
eMusic, 92, 136, 174
Enhancer, 53
Eno, Brian, 75
EQ Sliders, 54–55
equalizers, 194
Escient, xvi*f*, 84–85, 89–90
Essential Bob Dylan playlist, 159
Europe, 160
Evens, Adan, 15
exceptional objects, 192–214
exchange value, 9
Explosions in the Sky, 80

Facebook, 83, 99–100, 111, 163–64, 189–90; as infomediary, 202; "like" button, 185
Fairfax, 125–26
FairPlay (Apple), 141–45, 164
false consciousness, 9
fan fiction, 205

fan-funding, 208
Fanning, John, 97, 106–7, 219n6
Fanning, Shawn, 45, 96–98, 102–3,
    108–9, 112–13, 127, 219n6
feature artists, 220n9
Federal Trade Commission (FTC), 219n7
fetishism, 9, 118; commodity, 10
fidelity, 54, 216n5
file sharing, 8, 20–25, 72, 103–4,
    125–29, 140–41, 216n4
"Final Countdown" (Europe), 160
FixTunes, 81
Flickr, 70, 217n2
FMC (Future of Music Coalition), 153,
    155, 206–7
folksonomies, 70
4Shared, 198
Frankel, Justin, 42, 44–46, 48, 62,
    216n6
fraud, 216n3
Fraunhofer Institute, 39, 43, 48, 71–72
Freedb, 84
freemium model, 156
free music, 5, 20, 140–41, 158, 195,
    208, 210; on Napster, 96–98, 111–12,
    119, 129; problem of, 151
FreeNet, 104
Frere-Jones, Sasha, 204
Friday Night Lights, 80
Fry, Christine, 105
Future of Music Coalition (FMC), 153,
    155, 206–7

Gabrels, Reeves, 90
Gabriel, Peter, 75
Galloway, Alexander, 41
game studies, 17
gaming, 35–36
Garland, Eric, 121
The Gathering Field, xvif, 131
Geffen records, 37
"Genius" mix function (Apple), 162,
    184–85, 189–90
gift economies, 20, 119
Girl Talk, 208
Gitelman, Lisa, 40
Gmail, 173

Gnutella, 45–46, 111, 216n4, 216n6
GoodNoise, 132, 139–40
Google, 163–64, 172–73, 188
Google+, 173, 185
Google Docs, 173
Google Music, 174, 179
Gopinath, Sumanth, 168
Gracenote, xviif, 88–90
Grady, Steve, 139
Graphical User Interface (GUI), 48–49
Graphical User Interface (GUI) gallery,
    215n6
Griffin, Jim, 37
GrooveShark, 174, 177, 220n1
Guberman, Daniel, 54
GUI (Graphical User Interface), 48–49
GUI (Graphical User Interface) gallery,
    215n6

hackers, 102, 182
Hair, Arthur R., 132
hardware studies, 17
hashes or hash tags, 124
Hayles, N. Katherine, 50
HCI (human-computer interaction),
    17, 219n9
Headcandy (Eno), 75
"Head First" (Aerosmith), 131
headphones, 53
Heap, Imogen, 208–9
Hesmondhalgh, David, 85
hip-hop, 204
history: digital music time line,
    xvif–xviif; digitization of music,
    22–29
Hotmail, 42
Hulu, 202
human-computer interaction (HCI),
    17, 219n9
Hummer Winblad, 107

IBM, 42, 137–40; cloud computing,
    172; Project Madison
    (AlbumDirect), xviif, 137–38
iCloud, 174, 188
ID3 tags, 22–24, 27, 67–68, 71–73, 77,
    194, 217n1; user contributions,

ID3 tags *(continued)*
83–89; version 1 (ID3v1), xvif,
78, 217n7; version 2 (ID3v2), 72,
78–79
IFPI (International Federation of the
Phonographic Institute), 34
iMixes, 159–60, 162, 197
immaterial labor, 84–86
India, 98
infomediaries, 201–4
info-mining, 126
information access, 154–55, 174–75
innovation, 21, 205
In Rainbows (Radiohead), 161–62,
208, 210, 212
instant messages, 122
intellectual property, 220n7
Interactive *(Prince)*, 75
interface: de-tuned, 4, 16–17; digital
media, 16–22, 46–61, 197–98, 212;
integrated interfaces, 145–51;
iTunes, 146–47, 147f, 148–50, 149f;
iTunes Store, 145–50, 148f, 149f,
154; Napster, 112–14, 114f, 115–16,
115f, 128, 197–98; recorded music,
47–48; re-tuning, 46–61; Winamp,
47–50, 54–61, 64, 212
International Federation of the
Phonographic Institute (IFPI), 34
International Organization for
Standardization (ISO), 69
International Standard Book Number
(ISBN), 74–75
international standard recording code
(ISRC), 74–75
Internet Archive, 23, 100
Internet Movie Database, 70
Internet Underground Music Archive
(IUMA), xvif, 39, 42–43, 102, 136
iPads, 164
iPhones, 9, 164, 181–82
iPod, xviif, 129, 142, 146, 163–64, 184,
187
iPod Touch, 164, 181–82
IRC (Internet Relay Chat), 102
ISBN (International Standard Book
Number), 74–75

ISO (International Organization for
Standardization), 69
ISRC (international standard
recording code), 74–75
iTunes, 33, 63, 68, 129, 142–50, 153, 207,
220n10; AAC (Advanced Audio
Coding) format, 3, 40, 141–42, 144,
186; "Genius" mix function, 162,
184–85, 189–90; as infomediary, 202;
media interface, 146–47, 147f, 148–50,
149f; metadata, 80; partnerships, 186–
87; time line, xviif; version 3.0, 147
iTunes 360, 155
iTunes Essential Halloween Mix
playlist, 159
iTunes Essentials playlist, 159
iTunes Match, 174, 186
iTunes Radio, 80, 162–63
iTunes Store, 8, 22–25, 132–34, 143–
50, 158–65, 174, 186, 196, 216n7;
access to, 154–55; founding
principle, 165; launch event, 141,
152; limitations, 154–55; media
interface, 145–50, 148f, 149f, 154;
partner playlists, 159; playlists,
159–60; pricing policy, 151–56;
purchasing process, 163–65; terms of
use, 183; time line, xviif; user
contributions, 197; user-created
playlists, 159
IUMA. *See* Internet Underground
Music Archive

Jaguar (Atari), 55
jailbreaking, 181–82
Jannink, Jan, 111
Japan, 98
JBL, 53
Jesus, 9
Jive Records, 166
Jobs, Steve, 141, 152
Johnson, B., 172
Jones, Scott, 66, 89–90
Jstalilwyrd, 30
jukeboxes, celestial. *See* cloud
computing
jukebox players, 23, 64, 168

Jump (Bowie), 75T
Justine, 4, 6

Kan, Ti, 72–73, 79
Karaganis, Joe, 27
Kassabian, Anahid, 175
Katz, Mark, 203–4
KaZaa, 111, 120–21, 123–24, 133
Keating, Zoe, 207
Kemp, Erik, 71–72
Kickstarter, 209
Kindle, 144, 181, 221n4
Kois, Dan, 220n11
Kubrick, Stanley, 131

L3enc, 30–31
labor, 84–86, 204–5; immaterial,
    84–86; user contributions, 83–89,
    100, 123, 159–60, 197
Last.Fm, 174, 184, 221n2
The Late Age of Print (Striphas), 6
Lazzarato, Maurizio, 84
Led Zeppelin, 122
Lee, Geddy, 90
Lessig, Lawrence, 104
Library of Congress Subject Headings,
    70
Licklider, J.C.R., 171–72
LimeWire, 111, 120–21, 133, 216n4
liner notes, 91
Liquid Audio, 40–41, 43, 137, 139–40
listening, ubiquitous, 175, 191
Live Nation, 121–22, 126–27
Lobato, Ramon, 126
locker services, 166, 174, 179, 188,
    198
logjects, 88
long-tail economy, 153–54
Love, Courtney, 109
Lucas, 6, 20
Lycos, 116
Lymbyc System, 80

Machine Readable Cataloguing
    (MARC), 69, 217n2
Macworld, 37
mailing lists, 121

Mann, Aimee, 121
MARC (Machine Readable
    Cataloguing), 69, 217n2
marketing, 132–33, 145, 218n5;
    branding, 94–95; promotional
    campaigns, 121–22; release
    strategies, 6–8, 186–87, 192–93, 201;
    sustainable, 132–33; viral, 218n5
Marx, Karl, 9
Marzorati, Gerald, 64
McCarthy, John, 171–72
Media Defender, 125–26
media interface, 16–22, 46–61, 197–98,
    212; integrated interfaces, 145–51;
    iTunes, 146–47, 147f, 148–50, 149f;
    iTunes Store, 145–50, 148f, 149f,
    154; Napster, 112–14, 114f, 115–16,
    115f, 128, 197–98; recorded music,
    47–48; re-tuning, 60–61; Winamp,
    47–50, 54–61, 64, 212
Media Monkey, 81
media player software, 8, 22
media storage services, 179
Meehan, Eileen, 99
mega-CD changers, 66
MegaUpload, 174, 179, 186
metacommodities, 162
metadata, 8, 19, 24, 64, 66–77, 194;
    advanced, 82–83; for classical music,
    80; descriptive, 77–83; digital, 69–70,
    77, 83–89; function of, 91–92;
    inconsistent, 81, 89; incorrect, 81;
    key functions, 68; linking user
    names via, 124; for mix tapes and
    CDs, 74; for MP3s, 72, 78; for music,
    70–71, 80, 92; paratextual
    information, 73; prescriptive, 77–83;
    proprietary, 80; rise of, 22; standards
    for, 27; technical forms, 75; user, 80,
    83–89, 217n2. *See also* tags
metadata services, 83
Metallica, 94, 107
"Method for Transmitting a Desired
    Digital Video or Audio Signal"
    (Hair), 132
micromaterials, 19
Microsoft, 40, 172–73

Middle Ages, 10–11
MIDI (Musical Instrument Digital Interface) standard, 36
Mini Disc (MD), 75–76
Minimum Advertised Price programs, 109, 219n7
Minter, Jeff, 55
mixed CDs, 64, 91
mixes: celebrity, 220n11; iMixes, 159–60, 162; iTunes "Genius" (Apple), 162, 184–85, 189–90; user-created, 159–60
mix tapes, 64, 74
mobile music, 21
morselization, 160
Motion Picture Experts Group (MPEG), 39, 71–72
MP3: The Meaning of a Format (Sterne), 6
MP3.com, 116, 132, 140; Beam-It, 178; time line, xvi*f*
MP3 format, 3, 39–41, 43–44, 53–54, 137, 216n2; metadata, 72, 78; time line, xvi*f*
MP3 generation, 32
MP3 players, xvi*f*
MP3 Power! With Winamp (Frankel), 44
MP3 Tunes, 174, 179
MPEG (Motion Picture Experts Group), 39, 71–72
MPEG format, xvi*f*, 39
MSN, 142–43, 181
multimedia, 216n1
Multimedia Madness, 38
multimedia revolution, 23, 37–39
MuseArc, 48
music: "anytime, anywhere," 167; classical, 79–80; cloud-based, 22, 166–91; as code, 197–98; as commodity, 9–11, 31; computer, 35–36; contingent, 181–83; delivery of, 140–41; digital, 14, 16–22, 30–65, 195–96, 205–13; digital music commodity, 1–29; in digital stores, 131–65; digitization of, 1–2, 12–14, 22–29; disaggregation of, 158–59;

distribution of, 131; free, 5, 20, 111–12, 129, 140–41, 151, 158, 195, 210; interface, 16–22, 46–61; metadata for, 70–71, 80; micromaterials of, 19; mobile, 21; as omnipresent, 175; online sales, 131–34; ownership of, 151–58; popular, 18; promise of, 205–13; recorded, 34, 47–48; re-tuning of, 16–22; ripping, 36–37, 47–48; social life of, 212–13; time line, xvi*f*–xvii*f*; value of, 210; without metadata, 68, 69*f*
Musical Instrument Digital Interface (MIDI) standard, 36
Music Boulevard (N2K), 136
Music Box (Trantor), xvi*f*, 35
Music Brainz, 84
music collections, 187–90, 215n5
musicians: as cultural entrepreneurs, 205; feature artists, 220n9; rights of, 183–84; royalties to, 207–8. *See also specific musicians*
music industry, 33–34
MusicLand, 7
MusicMatch Jukebox, 73, 147
MusicNet, xvii*f*
music products, 75. *See also* CDs (compact discs)
Music Xray, 202
My Chemical Romance, 122
Myles, David, 152
My.Myp3.com, 178
MyPlay.com, xvii*f*, 166–68, 173, 178
Myspace, xvii*f*, 27, 100, 174, 183–84
MZ1, 76

N2K, 132, 136–37, 219n1
Napoli, Philip, 100
Napster, 8, 22–27, 34, 45, 89, 92, 189–90, 194–95; appeal of, 140–41; audience measurement, 120–21, 125–26; as business, 94–130, 217–18n1; challenges posed by, 128–29; Chat feature, 116–18, 117*f*; community-oriented features of, 116; company goals, 106; copyright policy, 109–10; as digital

enclosure, 120; Frequently Asked Questions, 110; functional aspects, 116; growth of, 96–98, 106–8; Hot List feature, 116, 117f, 118; key features of, 129; marketing strategies, 218n5; media interface, 112–14, 114f, 115–16, 115f, 128, 197–98; as revolutionary, 103, 107–9; search window, 113, 114f; Terms of Use, 109–10; time line, xviif; transfer window, 115–16, 115f; user base, 97–99, 101–6, 109–11, 118, 128, 130, 218n2; user contributions, 106, 111, 197; user participation, 123

Napster 2.0, 174
Napster Action Network, 109
Napster Inc., 94–97, 105
Nasal-Mist Flu Shot, 165
Netflix, 153–54, 199, 202
New Communalists, 38–39
new media, 201
new media research, 17, 100, 119–28
News Corp., 183
new technologies, 135–36
New York Times, 207
Nexxus, 30
Nielsen Ratings, 120
Nike, 159
Nilsson, Martin, 72
Nine Inch Nails, 208
"99¢ solution" (Apple), 151–52, 155–56, 164
No World Order (Rundgren), 75, 217n6
"Nude" (Radiohead), 161–62
Nullsoft, 42–43, 45–46, 50, 216n6; CD/Line Input Player v0.100, 59. *See also* Winamp
nycfashiongirl (Jane Doe), 123–24

the Offspring, 94, 107
Offspring.com, 94–95
Of Montreal, 192–93, 196–98, 205–6
Ogg Vorbis, 40–41
"Old Timers" discussion (Winamp), 30–31

OneJ1Way, 30, 110
online music, 8, 166; music in the cloud, 22, 25–26, 166–91; music in digital stores, 131–65
online retail stores, 8, 22, 195–96
Open Market, 135
open source, 40, 72
Option A drives, 35
the Orchard, 155
Orwell, George, 181
ownership, 20, 168, 215n5; copyright infringement, 109–10, 123–24, 216n3; cultural, 157; Digital Millennium Copyright Act (DMCA), xvif, 27–28; digital rights management (DRM), 138–45, 158, 180, 195–96, 219n3; intellectual property, 220n7; of music, 151–58; of patents, 132, 219n2; subscription services, 151–52, 158, 167, 179

packaging, 20, 74, 197–98
Pakman, David, 166
Palmer, Amanda, 208–9
Pandora Radio, xviif, 80, 174, 177–78, 207
paratexts, 18–19, 73
Parker, Sean, 97, 111
patents, 132, 219n2
Pavarotti, Luciano, 152
pay-what-you-want, 161, 208–9
PC Magazine, 37
peer-to-peer file sharing, 8, 20–25, 72, 103–4, 125–29, 140–41, 216n4
personal computers, 35
Phenner, Chris, 94–95
Philips, Glen, 121
Philips audiotape, 21, 75
phonographic effects, 203–4
Pioneer, 76
piracy, 5, 72, 102
Pirate Bay, 27, 129, 198, 209
platform economics, 84
playback, 36–37
playlists, 62–64, 74, 159–60, 194; celebrity, 159, 220n11; "Definitive 80s" playlist (Apple), 160; iMixes,

playlists *(continued)*
159–60, 162; as metacommodities, 162; seasonal, 159; user-created, 159–60
popular music, 18
post-fidelity era, 54
pranks, 94
prescriptive metadata, 77–83
PressPlay, xviif, 151–52
Priceline.com, 135
pricing, 151–58; free, 219n10; minimum advertised price, 109, 219n7; "99¢ solution," 151–52, 155–56, 164; pay-what-you-want, 161, 208–9
Prince: *Crystal Ball*, 6–8, 132, 193, 199; *Interactive*, 75
production credits, 91
profit, 221n3
Progressive Networks (RealNetworks), 40
Project Madison (AlbumDirect) (IBM), xviif, 137–38
promotional campaigns, 121–22
property rights, 220n7. *See also* copyright
proprietary metadata, 80
prosumers, 100
purchasing, 163–65

quality, 53–54
Quickflix, 153

Rachel, 4, 6
Radian 6, 125–26
radio, 177–78
Radiohead, 122, 161–62, 208, 210, 212
Radionomy, 32
RapidShare, 179
Rdio, 119, 174
reaggregated commodities, 158–63
Real Audio, 40–41, 174
Really Rare Wares, 215n6
RealNetworks, 140
Real Player, xvif, 27
recorded music: interface, 47–48; value, 34

recording industry, 33–34
Recording Industry Association of America (RIAA), 34, 43, 97, 106, 123–25, 128, 139
Red Book Standard, 70–71, 75–76
release strategies, 6–8, 132, 186–87, 192–93, 201; promotional campaigns, 121–22; viral marketing, 218n5
retailing: digital, 131–65; online stores, 8, 22, 195–96
re-tuning, 4, 16–22, 32, 46, 58, 60–67, 87, 113, 163, 168, 186, 192
Reznor, Trent, 208
Rhapsody, 97, 151–53, 174, 178
RIAA (Recording Industry Association of America), 34, 43, 97, 106, 123–25, 128, 139
Richardson, Eileen, 108
rights: digital rights management (DRM), 138–45, 158, 180, 195–96, 219n3; intellectual property, 220n7; of musicians, 183–84; of users, 184. *See also* copyright
Right to First Sale, 143
The Ring, 201
"Rip, Mix, Burn" campaign (Apple), 141
ripping, 36–37, 47–48, 123–24
Roberts, Ty, 90
Robertson, Michael, 178–79
Robo-lobster (US Navy), 165
Roland TR-808 drum machine, 204
Rolling Stone, 37, 166
Rolling Stones, 152
Rosen, Hilary, 127
Roxio, xviif, 97
royalties, 207–8
Rundgren, Todd, 75, 217n6

s1138, 30
SaaS (software as a service), 172
SACD (Super Audio CDs), 76
scalping, 126–27
Scherf, Steve, 72–73, 79
Schwartz, Hillel, 179–80
Scour.net, 116

SDMI (Secure Digital Music
Initiative), xvi*f*, 27, 139
SDMI (Some Dubious Motive or
Initiative), 139
Secure Digital Music Initiative
(SDMI), xvi*f*, 27, 139
Sennheiser HD 280 Pro, 53
sentiment analysis, 125–26
shadow economies, 126
shareware, 42
SHOUTcast, xvii*f*, 43–44
Shuggles, 164
SightSound Technologies, 131–33, 135,
145, 219n1
signatures, 54–55
single-copy concept, 1
Skeletal Lamping (Of Montreal),
192–93, 196–98, 208, 212
skeuomorphs, 49–50, 58–59, 194
skins, 56–58, 57*f*, 190, 194
Smythe, Dallas, 99
software, cracked, 54–55
software as a service (SaaS), 172
software media players, 8, 22
software studies, 17
Some Dubious Motive or Initiative
(SDMI), 139
Songs of Innocence (U2), 186–87
Songza, 80
Sony, xvii*f*, 36, 40, 73, 75–76, 137–38,
167
Sony Betamax, 116
Sony MDR-V600, 53
Sony Music Entertainment, 34, 167
Sony/Philips, 21, 70–71
Sony Walkman, 146
SoulSeek, 111, 216n4
Soundblaster live platinum 5.1, 53
soundcards, 53
Soundcloud, 174
SoundJam, xvii*f*
SoundJam MP, 220n7
SoundScan, 101, 120, 122, 202
sourcery, 118
space shifting, 178
spam, 122
speakers, 53

Spectrum Analyzer, 54–55
Spinner, 166
Spotify Music, 11, 33, 63, 80, 119, 174,
177, 182–85, 189–90, 207; as
infomediary, 202; subscribers, 129;
success of, 200–201; time line, xvii*f*;
user base, 129
spyware, 180
standards, 27
Stanyek, Jason, 168
Starbuck's Playing for Change: Songs
from around the World playlist, 159
Sterne, Jonathan, 6, 40, 216n5. *See
also* lo-boy
Sting, 201
storage, 166; CDs (compact discs), 170;
cloud-based, 22, 25–26, 166–91;
locker services, 179
stores: digital, 131–65; online, 8, 22,
195–96
Straw, Will, 169–70
streaming services, 27, 154, 177, 179,
207
Streeter, Thomas, 44
Striphas, Ted, 6
Studio 3, 71
subscription services, 151–52, 158, 167,
179
Super Audio CDs (SACD), 76
Sweden, 200–201
Swift, Taylor, 207
Sysomos, 125–26

table of contents (TOC) (CD), 74–76
tags: hashes or hash tags, 124; ID3
tags, 22–24, 27, 67–68, 71–73, 77,
83–89, 194, 217n1; user, 217n2. *See
also* metadata
Target, 220n10
Target Music Marketing programs
(MyPlay), 166
Taylor, Bob, 172
Taylor, Timothy, 11, 194
technology, 66–93
technology of the self, 21, 191
terms of service, 183
terms of use, 183–84

"Terms of Use" Myspace, 183
Théberge, Paul, 33
3D technology, 136
"360 deals," 164
TicketMaster, 126–27
Time magazine, 165
Time Warner, 45
TiVo, 88
Toad the Wet Sprocket, 121
Toal, Graham, 217n3
TOC (table of contents) (CD), 74
Todd Rundgren-Interactive (TR-I),
  217n6
Toshiba, 76
Tower Records, 21, 136–37
Toyota, 42
Toyota Prius, 165
track names, 91
transectorial commodities, 31
transectorial innovation, 21, 33
Trantor, xvi*f*, 35, 37
TR-I (Todd Rundgren-Interactive),
  217n6
TuneBase, xvi*f*
TuneBase 2000, 66, 89–90
TuneUp, 81
Twitter, 83, 99
2001: A Space Odyssey, 131

U2, 186–87
ubiquitous listening, 175, 191
Ulrich, Lars, 107
"Ultimate Chart" (BigChampagne),
  121
United Kingdom, 200–201
United States, 26–27, 98, 200–201
United States Navy, 165
Universal Music Group, 34, 107,
  137–38
Universal Product Code (UPC), 74–75
user contributions, 83–89, 100, 106,
  111, 197, 217n2
user-created mixes, 159–60
user-created playlists, 159
user experience design, 17
user-generated content, 100
user metadata, 80, 83–89, 217n2

user participation, 100, 123
user rights, 184
user table of contents (UTOC), 75–76
use value, 9–10
UTOC (user table of contents), 75–76
Uzelac, Tomislav, 216n3

value, 151–58, 209–10; of cultural
  commodities, 10; exchange, 9;
  perceptions of, 209; use, 9–10
Vanuatu, 98
vaporware, 139
Verizon, 123
video games, 208
viral marketing, 218n5
virtual albums, 156
virtual communities, 102, 218n3
virtual light machine (VLM), 55
virtual music stores, 132
VisiCalc, 35
visualizations, 54–56, 55*f*, 197–98
visualizers, 194

Walkman (Sony), 146
Wal-Mart, 220n10
Warner Music, 34, 137–38
WAV files, 3, 30–31
Wayback Machine (Internet Archive),
  23, 215n7
Web 2.0, 84, 100, 111
Webspins, 125–26
Western Union, 172
"white hat" hackers, 102
Whitehead, Jonathan, 123
Wikipedia, 70
Wikström, Patrik, 210
Winamp, 8, 22–24, 30–32, 41, 60–61,
  194–95; development of, 42–46,
  216n6; equalizer and playlist
  window, 51–52, 52*f*; hi-fi features of,
  52–53; key features of, 56, 59–60;
  lite version, 62; main window,
  50–51, 51*f*; marketing strategies,
  218n5; media interface, 47–50,
  54–61, 64, 212; minibrowser
  window, 62, 63*f*; "Old Timers"
  discussion, 30–31; origins, 216n3;

plug-ins, 53; pro version, 62; skins, 56–58, 57*f*, 190; slogan, 43; system requirements, 32–42; time line, xvi*f*; visualizations, 54–56, 55*f*, 197–98
Winamp.com, 42
Windham Hill, 137
Windows Media Audio, 40
Windows Media Player, 33, 68
WinPlay3, 48
Wired, 153
woowoo, 102
The Wu—Once upon a Time in Shaolin (Wu-Tang Clan), 1
Wu-Tang Clan, 1

Xbox 360, 55
X-Gamer 5.1, 53
XingSound, 36–37
XMCD Player, xvi*f*, 72, 74
Xplora1 (Gabriel), 75

Yahoo!, 142–43, 173, 181
Yamaha, 36
Yorke, Thom, 207, 209
YouTube, 70, 83, 100, 200, 217n2

ZDNet, 42
Zoho, 173